Blogging to Drive Business

Create and Maintain Valuable
Customer Connections

Second Edition

ERIC BUTOW
REBECCA BOLLWITT

800 East 96th Street,
Indianapolis, Indiana 46240 USA

Blogging to Drive Business, Second Edition

ISBN-13: 978-0-7897-4994-9

ISBN-10: 0-7897-4994-7

Library of Congress Cataloging-in-Publication data is on file.

Printed in the United States of America

Second Printing: January 2013

Trademarks

Warning and Disclaimer

Bulk Sales

Que Publishing offers excellent discounts on this book when ordered in quantity for bulk purchases or special sales. For more information, please contact

U.S. Corporate and Government Sales
1-800-382-3419
corpsales@pearsontechgroup.com

For sales outside of the U.S., please contact

International Sales
international@pearsoned.com

Editor-in-Chief
Greg Wiegand

Acquisitions Editor
Michelle Newcomb

Development Editor
Ginny Bess Munroe

Managing Editor
Sandra Schroeder

Project Editor
Seth Kerney

Copy Editor
Chuck Hutchinson

Indexer
Tim Wright

Proofreader
Paula Lowell

Technical Editor
Morten Rand-Hendriksen

Publishing Coordinator
Cindy Teeters

Book Designer
Anne Jones

Compositor
Mark Shirar

CONTENTS AT A GLANCE

TABLE OF CONTENTS

7 Who Will Write the Blog?   121

8 Getting Eyeballs to Your Blog   141

About the Authors

Eric Butow is CEO of Butow Communications Group (BCG), web design and online marketing ROI firm in Jackson, California. Eric has written a wide variety of computing books since 2000, and his latest titles include *How to Succeed in Business Using LinkedIn*, *Droid Companion*, and *My Samsung Galaxy Tab*. When he's not working in (and on) his business or writing books, you can find Eric enjoying time with friends, walking around the historic Gold Rush town of Jackson, and helping his parents manage their infant and toddler daycare business.

Rebecca Bollwitt is the co-founder of sixty4media in Vancouver, British Columbia, which specializes in WordPress development, and she has been blogging on Miss604.com about West Coast life since 2004. Miss604 is Vancouver's most award-winning blog and was voted "Best Local Blog" in 2009, 2010, and 2011. Rebecca was also named one of the *Vancouver Sun's* Top 100 Women of Influence in British Columbia. She is the local Twestival organizer and a member of the Canadian Red Cross Twitter Team, and spends her spare time at baseball and hockey games with her husband, or researching local history.

Dedications

Eric: To my friends, who always believe in me even when I doubt myself. You amaze me.

Rebecca: To my father, for his wisdom and contagious thirst for knowledge.

Acknowledgments

From Eric: Thanks to my coauthor, Rebecca Bollwitt, for being such a pleasure to work with. Michelle Newcomb at Que made the editing and authoring process easy. And I want to give a big shout out to the best literary agent in the world—my literary agent, Carole Jelen of Waterside Productions. To all of you and to everyone at Que responsible for making this book a reality, thank you.

From Rebecca: Thank you to Eric Butow for being an inspirational coauthor and to Carole Jelen at Waterside for her support. Thanks to Michelle Newcomb and everyone at Que for making this book possible.

We Want to Hear from You!

As the reader of this book, *you* are our most important critic and commentator. We value your opinion and want to know what we're doing right, what we could do better, what areas you'd like to see us publish in, and any other words of wisdom you're willing to pass our way.

We welcome your comments. You can email or write us directly to let us know what you did or didn't like about this book—as well as what we can do to make our books better.

Please note that we cannot help you with technical problems related to the topic of this book.

When you write, please be sure to include this book's title and author, as well as your name, email address, and phone number. I will carefully review your comments and share them with the author and editors who worked on the book.

Email: feedback@quepublishing.com

Mail: Que Publishing
           ATTN: Reader Feedback
           800 East 96th Street
           Indianapolis, IN 46240 USA

Reader Services

Visit our website and register this book at informit.com/register for convenient access to any updates, downloads, or errata that might be available for this book.

Introduction

Blogs represent a great opportunity for businesses to get their names out into cyberspace as experts in their line of work. Often, however, businesses don't know where to start or about potential pitfalls (for example, how to attract the most people to their blog, what to say, and perhaps more important, what not to say).

Blogging to Drive Business will help businesses of any size learn more about blogging, from both the technical and strategic perspectives. After all, you need the specific technical instructions to set up your blog and add information to it, and you need to know how to get eyeballs looking at your blogs and how to leverage your blog with your other online (and offline) marketing efforts.

How This Book Is Organized

There's a lot of material to cover, but we cover it step by step through 11 chapters:

- **Chapter 1, "Why Are Blogs So Important?"** covers blog basics, how blogs can help you serve customers better, and how to use blogs to get more information about your customers.

- **Chapter 2, "Making the Most of Your Blog with Marketing Tools,"** shows you how to build an integrated online and offline marketing toolbox that includes blogs. You also learn how to push your blog information to your customers, pull customers to your blog, and take care of your readers.

- **Chapter 3, "Creating a Blogging Strategy,"** gets into the nuts and bolts of blogging. You learn about popular blogging platforms, how to find the blogs that are best for your business, and how to combine blogs with other networking sites such as Facebook, LinkedIn, and Twitter.

- **Chapter 4, "Blogging Responsibly,"** explains how you need to listen to your audience to be an effective blogger and how to respond professionally to comments made to your blog posts.

- **Chapter 5, "Choosing a Blog Topic,"** answers the question about how to write topics on a regular basis to keep your audience engaged and coming back for more. You also learn about how to create one or more internal blogs for your company.

- **Chapter 6, "Designing Your Blog,"** helps you understand the function of your blog and your blog audience. Then the chapter shows you how to find popular blog themes and design your blog so it's easy for your audience to read and find information.

- **Chapter 7, "Who Will Write the Blog?"** identifies ways to find one or more people within your company to write a blog. Your writer can be someone who is already on your staff, such as the marketing manager (perhaps with a message from the CEO on a regular basis), or you can hire a professional blogger. This chapter also explains how to write effective blog posts.

- **Chapter 8, "Getting Eyeballs to Your Blog,"** tells you how to get your blog noticed. Start by reading blogs so that you can see how other companies in your industry blog successfully. The chapter then examines how to link your blog and make it searchable, how to get crowd-powered content, and how to promote your blog using other marketing techniques such as press releases and your company website.

- **Chapter 9, "Getting Interactive with Multimedia Blogging,"** shows how to create podcasts and screencasts, post them on a blog, and create multimedia blogs for different audiences.

- **Chapter 10, "Taking Advantage of Web 3.0 Blogs,"** provides an overview of Web 3.0 technologies so that you can be ahead of the curve as we navigate the second decade of the twenty-first century. This chapter also explains how to integrate Web 3.0 technologies such as the Semantic Web into your blog.

- **Chapter 11, "Maximizing Your Blog's ROI,"** explains how your blog affects your online influence. Then we discuss how to create a blogging strategy and present your recommendations, track your blog performance, and spot trends from what you measure.

- **Appendix A, "Important Blogging Sites,"** is a good place to start if you want to see where people go when they want blogging platforms or want their blogs to get noticed. Many of the sites in this appendix are also discussed in this book.

- **Appendix B, "Moblogging Apps,"** gives you a convenient list of moblogging apps all in one place.

In every chapter of this book, we've included at least one example of how companies use blogs effectively (or, in some cases, ineffectively). Our examples give you a good idea of what you can do (and what you shouldn't do) for your business blogs. At the very least, these examples will get your creative juices flowing.

Conventions Used in This Book

We hope that this book is easy enough to follow intuitively. As you read through the pages, however, it helps to know precisely how we've presented specific types of information.

Web Pages

Obviously, this book contains a lot of web page addresses, like this one: www.wordpress.com. When you see one of these addresses (also known as a URL), you can go to that web page by entering the URL into the address box in your web browser. We have made every effort to ensure the accuracy of the web addresses presented here. Given the ever-changing nature of the Web, however, don't be surprised if you run across an address or two that have changed since this book was published.

Special Elements

As you read through this book you'll note special elements, presented in what people in the publishing business call *margin notes*. There are different types of margin notes for different types of information, as you see here.

 Note

This is a note that presents some interesting information, even if it isn't wholly relevant to the discussion in the main text.

 Tip

This is a tip that might prove useful for whatever it is you're in the process of doing.

There's More Online

To provide you the most up-to-date information about blogging to supplement (and sometimes correct) what you find in this book, we've set up a website at www.bloggingtodrivebusiness.com. This site is... a blog! It's also a great place to get more information from Eric and Rebecca about what's going on in the blogosphere.

You can also visit Eric's business website (www.butow.net) and Rebecca's personal site (miss604.com) to learn more about books we've written, upcoming speaking engagements, and yes, to read our blogs.

Now that you know how to use this book, it's time to learn why blogs are so important to your business marketing strategy, a subject we cover in the opening chapter.

1

Why Are Blogs So Important?

You might have picked up this book because you have seen a blog on a website you frequent. Or maybe you've heard about the term blog used by the media; after all, it's a huge buzzword, and some people believe that it is important for a business to have one. In any case, you might not know what a blog is exactly and why it's so important for your business to have one. So, this chapter explains what a blog is and how you can use blogs to promote your business and gather more information about your customers.

Media Growth Is in One Area: Online

With all the attention paid to the Web since the mid-1990s, you know that it has become, for many people, a preferred way to get information. This preference comes at the expense of more "traditional" media such as radio, television, and newspapers. For instance, at the time of this writing, the newspaper industry is contracting, and those in the newspaper/media business are openly wondering whether printed newspapers will even exist in 2020.

Improvements in computing technology and connection speeds have made traditional media content accessible on the Web as never before, and at prices that are reasonable or even free. What's more, the explosion in the tablet market, which didn't exist when the first edition of this book was published, has pushed online content to the market-leading Apple iPad and Android tablets. New smartphones with bigger screens and better video resolution have also made mobile options for viewing media more popular.

Many people are bypassing traditional media entirely and are reading content on the Web, and some are even creating content of their own. One popular way users create content is via a blog, which is short for *Web log*. You can integrate other technologies into a blog—for example, social networking functionality, your website, a hosted blogging website, such as WordPress, or a combination of these. (The next section considers these combos in more detail.)

And here's the kicker: Online media is the only area of media currently growing. As that growth accelerates, people are finding more and more different kinds of information online. Blogs are increasingly popular, too. Although it's hard to get up-to-date and consistent information about how many people use blogs, there are strong signs that blogging continues to grow. As of May 2011, the eMarketer website forecast that there would be 122.6 million blog readers in the United States, which made up 53.5 percent of U.S. Internet users, and that number would rise to 150.4 million readers (60 percent of U.S. Internet users) by 2014 (www.emarketer. com/blog/index.php/tag/number-of-people-who-read-blogs/).

Technorati (www.technorati.com), which tracks blogs, noted in its 2008 "State of the Blogosphere" report (the last we could find with specific numbers) that 346 million people worldwide read blogs, and that number is likely far higher now considering that NM Incite (www.nmincite.com) tracked more than 181 million blogs around the world. The Technorati 2011 "State of the Blogosphere" report stated that more than 20 percent of bloggers are people who blog for the companies they work for or companies they own (see Figure 1.1).

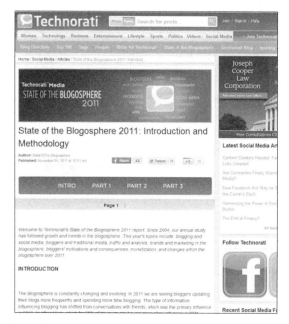

Figure 1.1   *The Technorati 2011 "State of the Blogosphere" report.*

Even so, these factoids don't tell you why people, especially businesspeople, create blogs. So let's start at the beginning: What is a blog good for, anyway?

Get the Message Out

A blog is an online journal that you can keep on your own website, house on a site specifically designed to host blogs (see Appendix A, "Important Blogging Sites," for a list of the important ones), or produce on social networking websites such as MySpace that offer blog functionality. Like many computing technologies before it, blogging enables people to communicate with large numbers of people quickly and publicly. Bloggers may also produce and publish content anonymously (in case they want to write about hot-button issues, such as politics, without people learning their true identities). For example, one of Eric's favorite blogs is the Halfway There blog shown in Figure 1.2; a friend of Eric's, who uses the pseudonym Zeno Ferox, writes it.

Figure 1.2 *The Halfway There blog, written by Zeno Ferox.*

Blog Popularity

People have been blogging since web browsers became widely available in the mid-1990s, and blogs have steadily become more popular since then. The NM Incite website illustrates the rapid growth in the number of blogs. In 2006, NM Incite tracked about 36 million blogs worldwide. By the end of 2011, that number had increased five-fold to more than 181 million blogs.

So, which blogs are the most popular? The answer depends on what source you use to measure blog popularity. Technorati lists its up-to-date top 100 blogs on its website by authority (that is, the number of comments posted on the blog, which notes the level of user activity) or by the number of fans who have bothered to vote for their favorite blog on the Technorati site. When we checked Technorati in March 2012, the most popular blog site was the Huffington Post, shown in Figure 1.3 (www.huffingtonpost.com), a news and opinion website owned by Internet portal AOL.

Figure 1.3 *The Huffington Post site.*

According to the eBizMBA website, which tracks the most popular blogs (www.ebizmba.com/articles/blogs), the Huffington Post surpassed 54 million unique visitors as of March 2012, which is nearly three times as many visitors as the second place finisher, TMZ. Different sites have different criteria for ranking blogs. For example, Technorati considers the Boing Boing blog (www.boingboing.net) to be the most popular blog because it has the most fans—that is, the number of Technorati readers who read it—even though eBizMBA ranks Boing Boing only as the fifteenth most popular blog.

Hello, World!

So, how did businesses learn about the blog phenomenon? In many cases, employees talked about their own blogs. Employees kept track of what was going on with marketing and customers learned about blogging. And the mainstream media picked up on blogging, especially as people started turning to blogs such as Ars Technica (www.arstechnica.com) for technical news, as shown in Figure 1.4. All this information was passed along to C-level executives in the business, which in turn got businesses thinking about how they could make their businesses known in the blogosphere.

Figure 1.4   *The Ars Technica website.*

The Technorati 2011 report noted that the majority of bloggers—60 percent—are hobbyists. Although that's still a lot, that's a drop from 64 percent in 2010 and 72 percent in 2009. Corporate bloggers accounted for 8 percent of the total, and self-employed bloggers accounted for 13 percent. The rest were professional bloggers who used their blogs as their sole or supplemental source of income.

Bloggers who write for money do so on blogging sites such as Ars Technica and may also perform other duties for a company—for example, an engineer or a marketing person, such as for the Intel Inside Scoop blog that we describe in this chapter's case study.

The professionalization of blogging has attracted advertisers who pay a price to have their banner ad on the blog. For example, Eric's company blog might have a banner ad from the photographer he works with to help drive business to her company, and the photographer can also have a link on her website to Eric's blog so that it benefits both companies. The 2011 Technorati blogging report noted that ads are the second highest means of generating revenue, with a mean annual revenue of $3,400. The highest revenue generator is paid speeches about topics bloggers write about, with a mean annual revenue of $3,500.

You learn more about writing your blogs in Chapter 5, "Finding Topics to Write About," and Chapter 7, "Who Will Write the Blog?"

Promote Products and Services

Blogging can be an additional income source, and perhaps even lucrative if you dedicate the resources necessary to build it up. But after you create your blog, what then? The most immediate use of a blog is to talk about your products and services. The conversation benefits not just your existing customers but also potential customers who might have questions about your company and its products/services.

If you offer general information and commentary about the state of your industry or profession, your blog can also highlight your expertise to the community at large. For example, suppose you use Rubbermaid products and want to get additional information about how to use them to organize your life more effectively. You can just go to the Adventures in Organization blog, shown in Figure 1.5. This blog discusses general organizational issues and problems and tips about how you can use Rubbermaid products to solve them from Rubbermaid personnel, guest columnists, and blog visitors who comment on blog posts.

Figure 1.5 *The Adventures in Organization blog, produced by Rubbermaid.*

If you're looking for a good example of a blog that talks about a company's services, visit the LinkedIn blog at http://blog.linkedin.com. It's a great place to find information about what's happening with the LinkedIn social networking service for business professionals. That information comes from both LinkedIn customers and from guest authors. Figure 1.6 shows the LinkedIn blog page.

Figure 1.6   *The LinkedIn blog site.*

Reach People

Your business might have many audiences in addition to customers, such as suppliers, vendors, colleagues, and employees. Therefore, before you start writing your blog, identify whom you want to reach with it. You may find that a one-size-fits-all blog that tries to reach all potential audiences is a bad idea. If that's the case, consider maintaining multiple blogs, each dedicated to a specifically identified audience.

For example, you can have a blog on your website that's written for your customers. You can have another that lives on your intranet and is for the benefit of your employees. Chapter 3, "Creating a Blogging Strategy," discusses blogging strategies in greater detail, and Chapter 8, "Getting Eyeballs to Your Blog," explains how you get people to read your blog.

The type of blog you create also determines the level of personalization in the blog. For instance, you might want to make your customer blog more personal. After all, you want your customers to "connect" with your products and services, and you certainly want to make people feel that they can trust you. If you have a blog for your internal suppliers, however, you might not want it to be so personal.

You must also decide whether to allow comments on your blog (and if you do allow them, how to manage them). By default, blog sites let readers comment on blog posts, but the blog site owner can turn off this feature. For instance, you might want to have customers comment on your blog posts. In contrast, however, an internal supplier blog might be informational only, with no commenting functionality.

Suppose a blog reader has a question or comment. Most blogging platforms allow you to respond to that question or comment in a message thread that other readers can view. Sometimes people leave inappropriate comments, so you must moderate them. We consider the moderation issue and responsible blogging in Chapter 4, "Blogging Responsibly."

✉ *Note*

What is a *message thread*, anyway? This term refers to a sequence of responses to an initial message posted by someone about a specific topic or discussion. In the case of a blog, when someone comments on an original blog posting, that's the first message in the thread. As you'll learn about later in this book, you can not only comment about an original post but also comment about comments you read in a message thread.

Keep Pushing Content

Your faithful blog readers no longer have to go to your blog site to get your latest post (or to see whether you've posted recently). Instead, they can easily set up and use feed readers. Many blogging platforms allow people to receive your new blog posts automatically via the Really Simple Syndication (RSS) method. If you have a program with an RSS reader such as Microsoft Outlook, or if you go on the Web to view RSS feeds such as Google Reader, you can subscribe to your favorite blogs and be alerted when new posts are available. Chapter 2, "Leveraging Your Blog with Marketing Tools," tells you more about subscribing to blogs and getting others to subscribe to yours.

✉ *Note*

Web designers and marketing people will tell you that you should update your website frequently. Their reasoning is that regular updates keep people coming back and search engines are always on the lookout for new content on sites. (If your web designer or marketing people haven't told you this, perhaps it's time for you to look for new ones.)

Drive People to the Blog

Just because you build it, you can't expect people will come to and comment on your blog. You've got to "say" something. If you can't even think of something to say, what makes you think that others will have anything to add? Therefore, update your blog content at least every few days with new and interesting information about your company specifically or the industry in general. Search engines, especially Google, take particular interest in blog posts because they're updated often and they usually include a lot of the key phrases that you want Google to notice in your website. If one of your competitors is continually blogging about your industry and you aren't, search engines will find your competitor's blog and place it, not yours, high on the list of search results when someone searches for one or more terms in your industry.

You can also take advantage of other online and offline marketing tools that we discuss in Chapter 2.

Crowdsourcing

Blogs are helpful for keeping in touch with your customers and for finding out who your customers are and what they're thinking about. For example, you can write a post that asks readers where they live, how they use your product, and what improvements they want in your product. They can then answer these questions in the comments.

You can even create a *crowdsourcing* blog. This term refers to asking readers of the blog for feedback so that the business can meet those customers' needs as directly and immediately as possible. The optimal result is that customers will be happier and the business will see greater profit.

Some businesses have been built around crowdsourcing. One example is InnoCentive (www.innocentive.com), shown in Figure 1.7. InnoCentive is a company that posts "challenge problems" in a number of areas, from engineering to math to life sciences to business. The site opens with problems for anyone in the crowd to solve and promises cash prizes to solvers who meet the solution criteria. You can view the various challenges, solutions, and the latest news on the InnoCentive blog.

Figure 1.7   *The InnoCentive blog.*

The challenge with crowdsourcing is critical mass. You need to get enough people to both respond to you and give you enough feedback that you can act upon. To help meet that challenge, we discuss in Chapter 2 other online and offline marketing tools that you can leverage with your blog.

Case Studies

Like all marketing efforts, there are right ways and wrong ways to do things, and the same is true of blogging. In this section, we look at a more traditional blog from Intel that keeps you posted on the goings-on at the chip maker. We also look at Starbucks Coffee's My Starbucks Idea blog, which does an effective job with crowdsourcing.

Intel Inside Scoop Blog

The Intel Inside Scoop blog (http://scoop.intel.com), shown in Figure 1.8, is a good example of a blog that gives you everything you're looking for near the top of the blog (and the first few scroll downs). Having information at or near the top of the blog is important for usability's sake because if your readers don't have to scroll down to find information, they will be happier with your blog and more inclined to come back.

Figure 1.8 *The Intel Inside Scoop blog.*

So, why might you want to emulate this blog when you create your own? It has a number of useful features, including the following:

- A menu at the top of the page takes you to specific sections (for example, a list of tech tips such as a roundup of Intel's activities at the latest Consumer Electronics Show).

- The most recent blog post appears near the top of the page.

- You can readily see where you can subscribe to the blog feed.

- A Recent Posts area links to all the recent posts on the blog home page.

- A list of bloggers and their photos appears in the Meet the Bloggers area. You can read more about the blogger by clicking on the blogger's name or picture.

- In the Blog Poll area you can give Intel your opinion or feedback to their question of the day.

- Connections link you to other social networking sites. This blog has links to Intel's Twitter, YouTube, and Facebook sites in the Subscribe to Daily Updates and Feeds section, the latest Twitter posts in the Latest Tweets section, and links to pictures on the Flickr photo-sharing site within the Inside Scoop Flickr section.

Notice that the blog posts on the home page have embedded a variety of information in each one, including text, photos, and videos. For example, when we visited the site we found a link to the Intel LANFest at Intel's Folsom facility, shown in Figure 1.9, which is near where Eric lives.

Figure 1.9   *The Sacramento LANFest 2010 video embedded in a blog post.*

You can also post blogs on social networking sites to help reach your target audience more directly, but the rules of blogging still apply, such as updating your blog every few days (as the Intel Inside Blog scoop does), so that you don't lose momentum, as we discuss in the next section.

My Starbucks Idea Blog

Starbucks serves as our second case study. If you're one of the few people on Earth who hasn't heard of Starbucks, it's a multinational coffee company based in Seattle, Washington, that has multitudes of coffee shops around the world and also sells its coffee products in grocery stores. Starbucks is a good example of how to use a customer-to-customer model for creating brand value by using a crowdsourcing blog. This blog, called My Starbucks Idea, is also a good example of how to use a customer-to-customer model to create a "momentum effect."

The Momentum Effect

One great online resource for social media marketing examples is the Being Peter Kim website (www.beingpeterkim.com/2008/09/ive-been-thinki.html). Peter Kim has compiled a number of social media marketing examples and resources.

One of those resources is a presentation that was made in 2007 by Rex Briggs, the CEO of Marketing Evolution. The presentation talks about what Rex calls "the momentum effect" (http://s3.amazonaws.com/thearf-org-aux-assets/downloads/cnc/online-media/2007-10-23_ARF_OM_Briggs_Nagy.pdf).

The Briggs presentation discusses the old versus new model of creating value for a brand. You probably know about the business-to-customer (B2C) model of reaching consumers, such as paying for an advertisement in the local paper that will reach only a certain number of people (and hoping it will elicit some business). This is what Briggs calls the old model.

The new model is the customer-to-customer (C2C) model. In this model, each interaction is an impression. People are influenced to visit your community for one or more reasons. For example, a customer may have visited your Facebook page because she saw the link in your email newsletter.

With each potential customer interaction on the Facebook page as an impression, some of those potential customers pass along what they find to other users. Some of those users will visit your Facebook page and perhaps more of what your company has to offer, and others won't visit the page but will be positively influenced anyway and pass along the information about your business to others.

If you want to get the most bang for your buck, the Briggs presentation recommends maximizing both B2C and C2C models. The B2C model requires advertising (such as an advertisement on Facebook) and integration with other offline marketing tools such as magazine advertising. The C2C model brings people to your profile through links (such as from the Starbucks website to its My Starbucks Idea blog), referrals from one person to another, or someone who is self-directed.

So how do you take advantage of the momentum effect? It's all about engaging the customer, and Briggs lists three tips for doing just that:

1. Recognize your brand is a persona so people can identify with you.

2. Make your site (or blog) personal to give people a reason to talk about it.

3. Give the consumers a chance to realize a dream or fantasy.

You need to use all three tips to realize the momentum you seek.

The My Starbucks Idea Blog Sustaining Momentum

Based on the Briggs report, we decided to visit the My Starbucks Idea blog to see what it offers (see Figure 1.10).

Figure 1.10   *The My Starbucks Idea crowdsourcing blog.*

Starbucks already has a strong brand persona because many people visit it often. (For the record, Eric has a Starbucks gold card for regular visitors.) Starbucks puts out the call to its customers both in its stores and to online visitors to its website to visit the blog and provide suggestions for making Starbucks better.

This approach makes the blog personal and also gives visitors the chance to realize a dream—to directly influence how Starbucks does business. Visitors can also comment on others' ideas and rate the popularity of the ideas. Starbucks lists not only the most recent ideas but also ideas implemented in its stores that come directly from visitors offering ideas.

This tactic has resulted in sustained momentum for the blog as evidenced by the number of ideas posted on the blog. As of mid-March 2012, there were more than 127,400 ideas spread across 15 different categories. The result is that Starbucks gets new sources of inspiration from its customers at little to no cost and the blog invites a more engaged customer base.

Summary

Blogs have been rapidly growing in popularity to the point where they are no longer written just by home computer users; now they also are written by professional bloggers (those who do so for money) and by businesses that want to get out their message. Businesses use blogs to market their products, keep driving messages to their customers, and get customer feedback.

So how do you leverage your blog to ensure that it's a valuable part of your overall marketing strategy? Let's continue on to Chapter 2.

2

Making the Most of Your Blog with Marketing Tools

Blogs are not a panacea for your business challenges. You can't just post a message saying "Hello, world!" or something to that effect on your blog and expect people to come beating down your door. Your blog should complement your other marketing tools to help drive business. For example, if you have a storefront and you want to announce a special sale, you can use the blog to offer a discount to blog readers only (who give the sales clerk a special coupon code found on your blog, for example).

Before you start creating a blog for your business, think about two things: creating an integrated marketing toolbox that includes your blog and creating a plan to leverage your blog with those tools to get more business (or at least keep your income at a level that keeps the bills paid).

Today, to have any chance of success, an integrated marketing toolbox must include both "online" and "offline" components. You must have an online presence (one that you're actually proud of) to come across as credible, even when you attend a networking event sponsored by your local chamber of commerce or give a potential client your business card. You also can't have all your marketing efforts online and expect people to automatically find you that way. On a regular basis, you need to get out of your office and talk to your existing and potential customers. Online marketing, even video-based marketing, is somewhat impersonal and is no substitute for face-to-face conversations. Customers look for a personal connection with a business owner, and if they can't get it from you, they'll look to your competition.

Online Marketing

Blogs can mesh with your other online marketing efforts (for example, your website, email marketing, and your efforts to promote your business on social networking sites). These efforts must be as consistent as possible to ensure that you constantly reinforce your brand. In this section, we describe the various online marketing tools and how you can use them in tandem with blogs.

Website

Your online marketing efforts start with your website. Around 2000, having a website was seen as a luxury. Today, it's a necessity if you're going to be taken seriously by potential customers, competitors, and your industry. And if you expect your website to actually bring you business, it can't just be a placeholder or a brochure. Your site must actively engage visitors by including interesting content, and you must update the site regularly with new information to keep people coming back (as shown by the case study later in this chapter).

Email Marketing

Your online marketing efforts have to be part of a system that includes other related marketing efforts, and they require you to have some skin in the game. That is, you need to budget both time and money to your online efforts, and those efforts go beyond setting up a website. After you have a website, you need to initiate a regular email marketing campaign so that you can continue to drive interest to your website, keep in touch with your customers, and give them an incentive to stay involved with you, such as regular coupons or special events.

Plenty of email marketing solutions are available online that don't cost a lot of money. You can view a list of the more popular email marketing services on the

Email Marketing Software Comparison website at www.email-marketing-options. com (see Figure 2.1). Many of them allow you to set the timing of your campaigns, such as when to send them out, and they also let you customize the look of your newsletter.

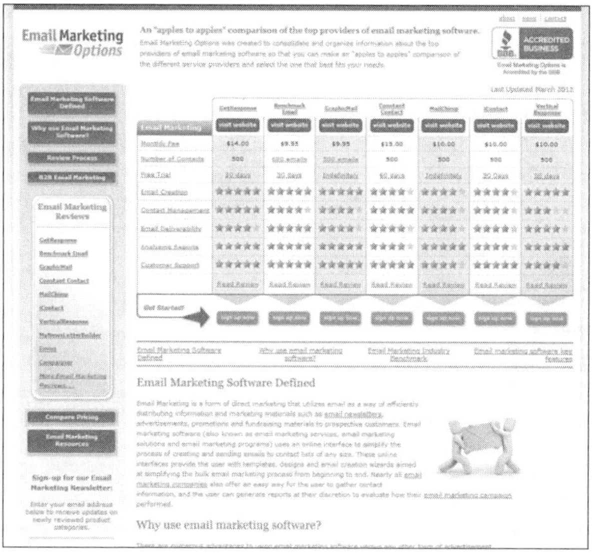

Figure 2.1 *The Email Marketing Software Comparison website.*

Social Networks

Your customers congregate on social networking websites, so you need to have a social networking strategy folded into your marketing strategy. Although there are too many social networking sites to mention, Wikipedia has a list of major social networking sites (excluding dating sites) with their description and/or focus at http://en.wikipedia.org/wiki/List_of_social_networking_websites. You may want to connect with several of the sites in the Wikipedia list that attract audience members in your industry. (If that doesn't work, you can always search for a social networking site for your specific topic or interest using your favorite search engine.)

If you do nothing else, you need to have a presence on the top three social networking websites. According to the eBizMBA website, as of March 2012 the top social networking site with more than 750 million unique visitors every month is Facebook. Twitter comes in second place with 250 million unique visitors per month, and LinkedIn is third with 110 million unique monthly visitors. Though MySpace, the former king of social networking, comes in fourth with more than 70 million monthly visitors, that site may be overtaken by Google+ by the time you read this book.

LinkedIn is the leading site designed for use by business and professionals. Although Facebook is designed for a general audience, the Facebook BranchOut app shown in Figure 2.2 is a "network within a network" for maintaining business relationships. And you can see that Twitter has plenty of current and potential customers who want to get your business updates that have 140 or fewer characters.

Figure 2.2   *The BranchOut app in Facebook.*

If you would rather not update each social networking site individually, you learn about an updating tool that can save you a great deal of time later in this chapter.

Of course, you can't just put your Facebook fan page or LinkedIn profile online and expect things to work right away. You should follow these tips for starters:

- Know your audience and your brand before you set up your social networking profiles so that you can appeal to your audience right away and communicate in a way that's real and honest. Identify your clients and visit their profiles to see what interests them. Also visit profiles from others in your industry (especially your competitors) to see how they approach their customers.

- Set up a schedule for sending information so you can make sure that your readers get timely information about what you're doing. This is especially true for holidays because you don't want to send out a late holiday greeting that makes you and your business look bad.

- Participate in online groups as much as you can. One of LinkedIn's strengths is groups, so be sure to join groups that have topics that relate to your business. When you participate, don't plug your business. Instead, provide free answers. If people like your answers and see that you're an expert, they will find your profile and learn more about your business.

You may also want to consider other marketing options such as Facebook Ads. You may want to contact other advertisers, even those in your same industry, to get their feedback about how advertising on social networking websites has (and hasn't) worked for them.

Search Engine Optimization and Marketing

Search engines such as Google love blogs because they're filled with keywords and they're updated often. So if someone is looking for work you do, such as setting up blogs, it's more likely that the searcher will find your blog high up in the search results (that is, as high up on the first page of the results as possible). Of course, you can't do this if you don't do two important things: update your blog often, and include key phrases not only when you set up your blog but also in your blog posts.

Because Google is by far the most popular search engine—900 million unique monthly visitors as of March 2012, according to eBizMBA—it makes sense to take advantage of Google's free tools to make your blog as visible as possible. When you click on the Business Solutions link at the bottom right of the Google home page, the Google Business Solutions page, shown in Figure 2.3, appears, containing a lot of different options for you to promote your business.

Figure 2.3   *The Google Business Solutions page.*

The links you'll be interested in are located near the bottom center of the page under the Enhance Your Website heading. The Website Optimizer and Webmaster Central tools help you optimize your blog site so it can reach the most visitors and fix problems with the site, respectively.

You may also want to consider paid search engine marketing solutions such as Google AdWords. With AdWords, your text advertisement is displayed next to or above Google search results that are relevant to your business. For example, if Eric wants to promote websites for his business, he can create an AdWords account, set up the ad, and specify how much he can afford each month. Then Google maximizes the number of clicks to fit within Eric's budget. Eric can log in to his AdWords account, as shown in Figure 2.4, to see how people are finding his ad.

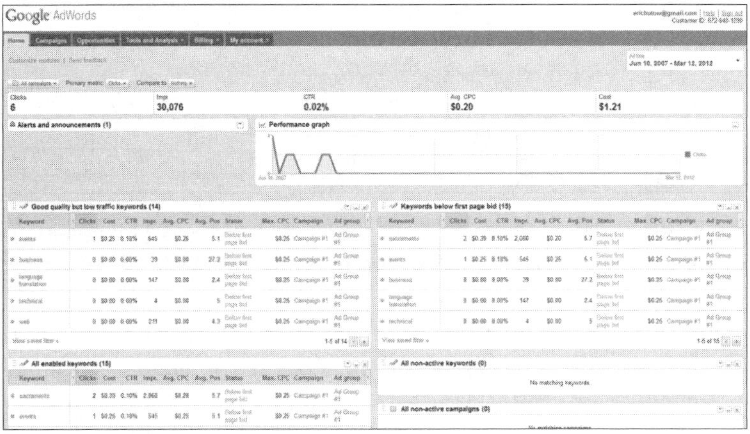

Figure 2.4   *Eric's Google AdWords home page.*

There are some drawbacks to solutions such as AdWords. If a lot of businesses or people do the same work as you do and they've paid more than you have, your ad may be pushed down lower on the first search results page or on a lower page. Any visitors who prefer just to see the top of the first results page may not see your ad at all.

Another major drawback is the problem of "click fraud." In this case, people who want to damage your business for fun or profit click on the ad repeatedly until you reach your maximum number of clicks. After that, your ad will disappear for the rest of the month. Consequently, the ad brings you less business.

Google realized a while ago that click fraud could damage its business, so it has a very vigorous system in place to cut down on this type of fraud, including giving credits to advertisers when one or more invalid clicks get through its system. Even with this system in place, click fraud is an issue you should be aware of as you monitor your ad results.

▶ *Caution*

Another caveat to note is that when you sign up for Google AdWords you agree not to artificially inflate the number of clicks your ad receives by clicking on your ad yourself. Google monitors your ad very closely and can tell when you are clicking on your own ad. If you click on your own ad, or violate any other part of the Terms and Conditions, Google will ban you from AdWords...for life. Be sure to read the Terms and Conditions in their entirety before you sign up for AdWords.

More Work... and Potential Solutions

In today's Web 2.0 world, you also need to

- Have a blog so that you can continue to drive people to your online presence. You also need to moderate and respond to comments made to your blog posts (if you allow comments on your blog).

- Devise a strategy for reaching your audience on mobile devices, including smartphones and tablets. You learn more about blogging on mobile devices in Chapter 10, "Taking Advantage of Web 3.0 Blogs."

- Go to related sites, including those belonging to your industry and your competitors, so that you can stay current with what's going on.

- Create a strategy for maximizing your online marketing efforts so you can maximize your *ROI*, which is a business-buzz acronym for *return on investment*. You learn more about maximizing ROI with your blog in Chapter 11, "Maximizing Your Blog's ROI."

When you add it all up, you have to do a lot of work to keep your online marketing system running, and some businesses cringe when they learn they must budget for their online marketing initiatives just as they budget their time, money, and personnel for other marketing programs. Businesses often want to know how much time it takes. But, of course, that depends on what you want to do.

Larger businesses often hire someone full time to manage their online marketing efforts. (Sites such as Dice.com have job postings for occupations with titles such as "online marketing specialist.") Smaller businesses and nonprofits have other possibilities: They can hire a part-time assistant to handle the tasks discussed in the next section, or they can pick and choose what tools to use.

Hire a Part-Time Assistant

You can offload a number of tasks onto a part-time assistant tasked with updating your current status on blogs and social networking sites. You might have to spend only 10 minutes or so talking with your assistant about what's happening. The assistant can then do the work from a home computer at a minimal charge.

Tip

Contacting local chambers of commerce is a great way to find virtual assistant companies that offer small business owners flexible options for helping them take care of daily tasks for a small fee (including updating social networking sites). Through your networking, you may learn about freelancers who are interested in working from home part time on a flexible schedule. You may also want to check out your local colleges to see whether they offer internships. If so, you can provide students with the valuable experience of learning social marketing aspects of a business at little to no charge.

You may want to write a rough draft or an outline for your assistant to follow (and you may want to do the same for blog entries you write). Although you may task your assistant with writing the final copy, only you can tell your customers what you think they need to know. (This doesn't apply, of course, if your assistant can read your mind.)

The one thing that your assistant may not be able to do (or not be able to do without significant training) is respond to comments made to your blog posts. You might need to do most of the replying yourself, at least at first. You can help steer your respondents and make your life (and your assistant's) easier by giving them clear guidelines for leaving comments and encouraging your blogging community to police themselves.

Pick and Choose the Tools to Use

Fortunately, you don't have to use every tool in the toolbox we've mentioned in this chapter if you don't have the manpower or cash to get everything you want right away. Here are some tips to help you get the most out of your time and money when it comes to online marketing:

- Use the Ping.fm web service (www.seesmic.com), shown in Figure 2.5, to quickly update your status on social networking sites and blogs. After you set up the blogs and social networking sites, you need to update in Ping.fm. To update all of them, you just log in to Ping.fm, type your updated status, and submit it. Then Ping.fm forwards your updated status to those sites and saves you quite a bit of time.

Figure 2.5   *The Ping.fm website.*

- If you can't afford to have someone create a website for you (and you don't have the personnel to do this yourself), you can create a blog and have that act as your website. If you want to have your own URL, talk with your Internet service provider about having your website index page point directly to the blog home page. To view an example of a blog as a website, visit the Waterside Productions website, which is our literary agency, at www.waterside.com (see Figure 2.6).

Figure 2.6   *The Waterside Productions website.*

- Take advantage of free email marketing trials. Many email marketing firms offer free trials so that you can see how their systems work before you decide whether you want to pay for them. For example, Constant Contact and MailChimp are two of the more popular email marketing solutions available. Constant Contact offers a 60-day free trial for new members, as shown in Figure 2.7.

Figure 2.7   *The Constant Contact free 60-day trial offer button.*

- Add Google Alerts so that you can get email updates in the topics of interest to you. If you were to try to go through all the websites to glean information from the Web, you'd never do anything productive. Google Alerts checks the Web for you based on the topics you select and then sends a digest email to you with links to the full articles. When you visit Google Alerts at www.google.com/alerts (see Figure 2.8), you can select your search terms, how to search, and where to send the results. If you already have a Google account, you can sign in to manage your alerts.

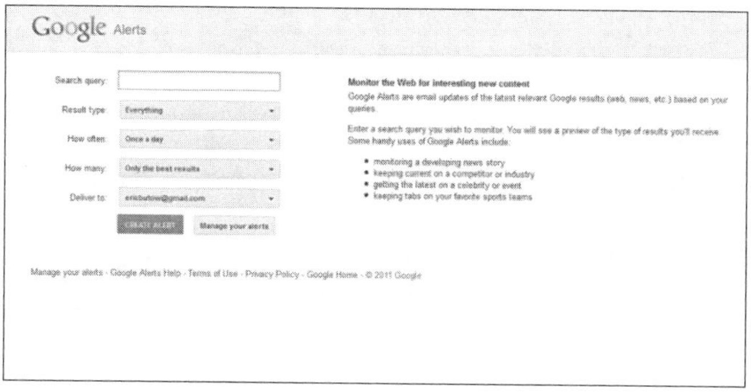

Figure 2.8   *The Google Alerts website.*

Offline Marketing

Offline marketing is the traditional marketing that your customers may still expect you to engage in to get their business. *Traditional marketing* refers to getting out and networking in person; perhaps advertising in print, radio, or television; or perhaps going out to a local or area trade show to promote your business.

Although you might need to leverage some types of traditional advertising because your market research has determined that your customer base is more receptive to such, you may still want to be on the cutting edge when it comes to marketing to bring in other types of clients. For example, your older clients may prefer printed materials, such as direct mail delivered directly to their offices. Younger recipients may view such direct mail not only as ineffective but also wasteful. Or you might decide to network at chamber of commerce luncheons rather than young professionals' organizations because you have a better chance of finding solid leads at those events.

So how can your blog help you determine whether any offline marketing strategies are right for your business? The blog can both inform customers about what you're doing to gain their business and ask for feedback. One 2009 blog we viewed when we wrote the first edition of this book was on Frogloop (www.frogloop.com), shown in Figure 2.9. That blog sparked a debate about whether direct mail was dying or already dead in light of the popularity of blogs and social media sites.

Figure 2.9   *The Frogloop blog post about the future of direct mail (www.frogloop.com/ care2blog/2009/5/29/is-direct-mail-really-headed-for-the-exit.html).*

Various conversations like the one on Frogloop are taking place on the Web. (Just search for "direct mail advertising blog" using your favorite search engine.) If you start a conversation about your marketing practices and ideas on your blog with your customers, you'll most likely get some valuable information that will help you determine which offline marketing strategies you should employ, if any. You may also get some ideas for new blog posts and new conversations.

▶ *Caution*

Timing is also important when you write blog posts about something you find interesting. For example, in 2009 I attended a chamber of commerce presentation by a fellow chamber member. The following day, I produced my biweekly newsletter and included a critique of the member's presentation. She immediately emailed me when she received my email newsletter, and expressed her embarrassment at my critique because several people on my mailing list were also chamber members and knew her (and could recognize I was referring to her in my critique).

Another problem can be that search engines can pick up text in a blog that the writer doesn't want people to see. Such an unfortunate occurrence happened to the Poor Richard's Almanac blog in 2008. Google decided not to use the first sentence of the blog post in the search results, but instead used a sentence that the author carefully buried so as to turn the search result from a PG rating to an NC-17. You can read more about the episode on the Poor Richard's Almanac blog at http://ourfriendben.wordpress.com/2008/05/02/how-humiliating.

Pushing Information via RSS

Okay, so is there anything about online marketing that actually makes things easier for you? Well, perhaps not for you, but certainly for your readers. You can set up your blog so that your customers can subscribe to your blog feed using RSS technology. RSS is an acronym for Really Simple Syndication, and there are many different applications for reading RSS feeds, from software applications like Microsoft Outlook to Web apps such as Bloglines (see Figure 2.10). These sites not only let people subscribe to blogs but also categorize them (and in the case of Bloglines, it allows you to search for blogs in one or more of your favorite cities).

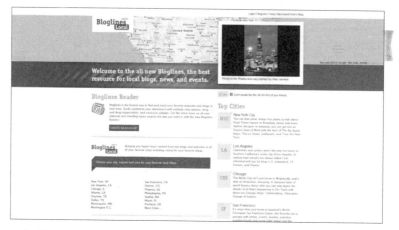

Figure 2.10   *The Bloglines website.*

You create your own Bloglines account with a unique username and password, and then you can search for blogs that you want to add in one or more local areas. As you read the blogs, you can click the Discuss link underneath the post if comments are accepted for that post, and Bloglines takes you directly to the blog so that you can read other comments and add a comment of your own.

Many blogging platforms that we discuss in Chapter 3, "Creating a Blogging Strategy," enable you to add RSS subscriptions for your readers. RSS subscriptions let users receive your new blog posts automatically either within a newsreader program (like Microsoft Outlook) or within an online newsreader (like Google Reader). The first time the user reads the blog, she can click the orange RSS icon either on the blog page or in the browser address bar to subscribe to that blog feed.

The orange RSS icon is the easy way to add an RSS feed to your preferred news-reader program. Just click the icon, and your browser asks you where you want to read the feed. For example, the Being Peter Kim site, shown in Figure 2.11, discusses social networking, Web 2.0 technologies, and more. The RSS icon appears in the top center of the page.

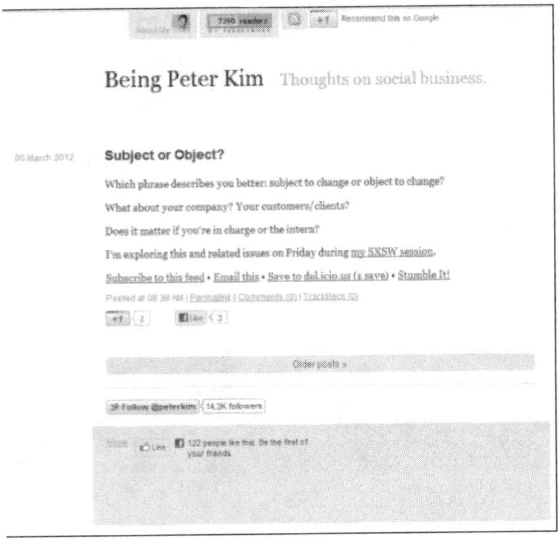

Figure 2.11   *The RSS icon on the Being Peter Kim website.*

The benefit of an RSS feed is that you can push information to your clients repeatedly, which gives you an opportunity to keep them coming back to your business. For example, you could give subscribers to your blog special offers that no one else can get.

Getting Customers to Subscribe

So how do you get your customers to subscribe to your blog after they've discovered it? You can employ a number of simple strategies to encourage customers to read your blog:

- Put an invitation to read your blog (and a link to the blog site) in a conspicuous location on every page of your website.

- Put a link to your blog and an invitation in your email newsletter.

- Share the blog entry on other social networking sites such as Digg, LinkedIn, and Facebook. Most social networking sites, including the ones listed here, connect directly to blogs, and you learn more about that in Chapter 3.

- If you have an audio/video podcast as well as a blog, be sure to mention your blog in each broadcast.

- If you have several different blogs, ensure that each blog links to the other.

Taking Care of Your Readers

After you get a list of your readers, it's important to keep them interested by sharing quality information often. Here are some pointers for taking care of your blog readership:

- As mentioned earlier in this chapter, it's always good to keep on top of what's going on both online and offline to try to find recent topics to write about and share with your audience.

- Readers expect to read information written in your voice, not someone else's. So if you're going to lift quotes from another blog or another source, be sure that it's properly quoted and referenced.

- Your blog is a reflection on you and your company.

- Your blog is going to stick around in the Internet ether for a long time. Be sure that what you say has value.

- If you're not sure about any of the previous points after you finish writing a blog entry, run it by a trusted friend, colleague, or business mentor. A fresh set of eyes can give you the insight you lack because you're too close to the material.

- Consider enabling your readers to leave comments about your entries. The more involved your readers are, the more likely they will be to come back to your blog and to your site. However, there are some caveats that are discussed in the next section and in Chapter 4, "Blogging Responsibly."

- Consider sending a survey to your readers through a survey website such as Constant Contact or SurveyMonkey.com to find out what they think about your blog and your other marketing efforts so that you can make it better.

We go into more detail about these tips in later chapters.

Case Studies

Having plenty of information in your blogs is a great way to keep your readers interested and coming back for more, although doing so presents its own set of challenges. In these case studies, we look at blog management from two perspectives: from a small business called JumpStart Your Marketing and the Northern Voice conference.

Katrina Sawa, JumpStart Your Marketing

Katrina Sawa is a business and marketing consultant who offers one-on-one coaching, online classes, speeches, and products to make small businesses more successful. Katrina and her business, JumpStart Your Marketing, are based in the Sacramento area. Because Eric has known her for years, he contacted Katrina to learn more about her blog, shown in Figure 2.12.

Figure 2.12   *The JumpStart Your Marketing blog (http://www.katrinasawa.com).*

Katrina maintains her business blog at www.katrinasawa.com. When you scroll down the blog, you see that it includes plenty of information. Not only does Katrina update her blog regularly with new posts, but she also has videos, podcasts through the Blog Talk Radio platform, links to related sites including her online magazine (called an e-zine), and widgets that let readers view Katrina's latest posts on Twitter and Facebook. Katrina says the blog is "meant to be informative, interactive, and educational for the small business owner."

Katrina has an assistant who takes care of nearly all the posting of information on the blog, and although that relieves Katrina of a time-consuming task, she said it does come with a downside: "I'm not entirely sure all that is being done for SEO on the blog." (SEO is an acronym for Search Engine Optimization, and you'll learn more about SEO in Chapter 8, "Getting Eyeballs to Your Blog.")

The blog also links to the JumpStart Your Marketing website (www.jumpstartyour-marketing.com), shown in Figure 2.13. The previous version of Katrina's website wasn't capable of including a blog, so she developed the blog separately. When her current site was developed, the blog had so much information that Katrina decided the integration of the blog and website was unfeasible.

Figure 2.13   *The JumpStart Your Marketing website.*

Even so, Katrina worked on integrating the website and blog as much as possible: "The opt-in box on my blog links to the freebies on my website, and the website is also linked to the blog in many places, including inside most posts one way or another. The blog is also listed on my website as a page. Whenever possible, we link back and forth to both for maximum traffic on both."

A subscribe link on the blog entices readers to receive Katrina's blog posts via RSS. She isn't sure how many blog subscribers she has, but she does get feedback that she says usually includes "'great info, keep it up' types of things."

Katrina posts as much information on the blog as often as possible, and does swap blog posts with other professionals "if it's a good fit for cross-promotion." She doesn't use her blog as her primary means of communication. Instead, she uses the blog to get readers to subscribe to her e-zine and get free information from her website. Katrina isn't concerned about sending too much information on her blog; she reserves that worry for her e-zine.

As of this writing, Katrina says she's working to create a new website on a blog platform. She's undecided about what to do about the old blog site that will contain her archives: "I may leave the archives where they are [on the old blog] and repurpose information occasionally and/or relink to it."

When the new site is done, Katrina says she'll take the opportunity to "have my web developer and/or specific SEO expert take a look at what could be enhanced, then train my team on how and what to do moving forward."

In sum, Katrina says the purpose of her blog is to "inform, educate, and inspire small business owners to do more, be more, and go after what they want." When her business blog and website are combined into her new blog, that purpose will remain.

Northern Voice Conference

Northern Voice launched in 2005 and was Canada's first blogging conference. Once a year bloggers from all walks of life and backgrounds gather to share stories, ideas, and talk about what works for them and what doesn't.

One of the original members of the organizing team, Travis Smith, says, "Blogging conferences give bloggers a valuable touchstone, where they can check in with other bloggers about urgent practices and futures trends."

Over the years speakers at Northern Voice have included Flickr cofounder Stuart Butterfield, Sun Microsystems' Tim Bray, Open Web advocate Chris Messina, and information-technology researcher Bryan Alexander, among many others. Anyone can apply to lead a session on anything from dealing with negative comments, to knitting blogs, and how to use social media and social tools in conjunction with the local transit system.

"When Northern Voice started, there weren't blogging conferences at all. Now, there are many, and most are focused on blogging to make money: business and corporate blogging, SEO, and monetization and ads," Smith adds.

A benefit of this "mixed bag" of bloggers is that beginners can learn from seasoned veterans, and those who have been blogging for years can be exposed to the latest trends and tools.

"As for types of bloggers, that does vary year to year. Photo bloggers are well represented, as well as author blogs, cooking blogs, and generally eclectic blogs. There are a lot of environmental and activist bloggers, too, and yes, plenty of mommy bloggers."

Attendance at Northern Voice has grown from a hundred to hundreds over the years, with some of the most interesting conversations and valuable networking taking place in social spaces, outside the workshops, and keynotes. Being able to gather in person, sharing the common thread of blogging, can help you hone your online publishing skills but also get the word out about who you are and what you do.

Most blogging conferences, like any other conference, also have sponsorship spaces available and would provide instant exposure for your brand to a large group of influencers from various industries. Companies can potentially sponsor a Twitter wall (a wall on which all conference Tweets are posted, scrolling live in real-time), they can get a logo on conference t-shirts, and set up a table and offer gift items (stickers, keychains, water bottles, and the like). Sometimes the most creative gift items, or "swag," garner more attention and online buzz than the talks at events like these.

Unique sponsorship items or freebies can get people talking, both online and off. A t-shirt with a Twitter hashtag or a QR code printed on it can become regular wear for conference goers—getting you exposure beyond the walls of the event. A useful item like a pen with a scroll-out map or terminology cheat sheet can become a keepsake; just keep in mind what might be useful to bloggers, what they might want to scoop up at the event, and what they would want to keep around.

Even a mascot like HootSuite's "Owly" can grab attention. HootSuite's owl mascot appears at events to pose for photos (which are then posted online) making bigger fans out of current users of the social media management service. Play up a logo, character, or brand ambassador that you have for your company or product and make them assessable at conference and events. Photos and interactions with them can build a buzz as well.

Whether it's getting out to learn more about blogging and network with other bloggers to build your own presence online, or if you would like to reach the blogging audience and spread the word about your brand, blogging conferences are ripe with opportunities.

Northern Voice takes place in Vancouver, British Columbia, each spring, and BlogWorld—the world's largest blogging conference—happens in Las Vegas and also in New York. BlogHer is a conference for women (men are also welcome) that takes place annually, and Mashable.com (the web's most influential social media account) posts a list of upcoming social media and blogging events around North America each year.

Summary

Although blogs aren't the solution to your business challenges, they can mesh with your other marketing efforts. However, you must plan ahead for the additional workload that a blog brings and also ensure that all your marketing efforts are consistent so you constantly reinforce your brand. Let's move on to Chapter 3 to learn more about creating a blogging strategy.

3

Creating a Blogging Strategy

When you decide to create a blog for your business, finding out where to start can be a bit overwhelming. There are plenty of blogging platforms for you to choose from that are hosted by companies on websites or are available for you to download, customize, and host on your own website.

Discovering the right blogging platform for you has to be the first part of a holistic blogging strategy. In this instance, holistic means that you consider the entire strategy and not just the individual parts. For example, you can have people subscribe to your blog and send updates automatically and in real time through a Really Simple Syndication (RSS) feed. You'll also want to connect your blog to your website so that people who visit your blog will be compelled to visit your website to learn more about you (and vice versa). These are all parts in a larger, holistic strategy of driving readers to your blog and making it as easy as possible for your readers to find and read your blog.

You should also have a profile on social networking sites and a link to your blog on that profile. In these ways, you can establish *thought leadership* or *mind share*. You might have heard these terms in reference to companies such as Apple and Sony, who don't have a lot of market share, but the media is always talking about these companies anyway. Blogs help you gain mind share, and because of that mind share, others will recognize you and your company as an expert in your field. This eventually leads to more interest and more business for your company.

This chapter begins with a review of blogging platforms. If you already know what platform to use, you can skip the next section and move ahead to "Finding the Best Blog for Your Business."

Blogging Platforms

You can produce your blog in one of two ways. You can host your blog free on a site that lets anyone create a blog using a set of stock templates (or an HTML template if you want to have your own look). These sites include the name of the blogging site in the URL, such as http://zenoferox.blogspot.com, which is the website for the Zeno Ferox blog site on Blogger that we referenced in Chapter 1, "Why Are Blogs So Important?" If you want a blog to be on your own site, you can download software that you can install on your web server and configure it. Some download options are free, but others are not, depending on the features you want on your blog.

If you want to start blogging quickly and get your name out there right away, hosting your blog on a blogging site is the best way to go. The following sections discuss some of the more popular blogging sites.

WordPress.com

In 2003 WordPress started as open source software for people to publish blogs on their own websites, but in 2005, WordPress decided to host its own blogs for the web public at www.wordpress.com, which is shown in Figure 3.1 (http://en.wikipedia.org/wiki/Wordpress.com).

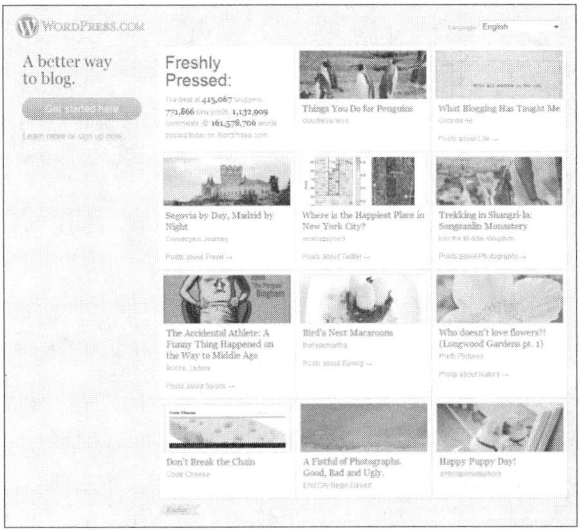

Figure 3.1   *The WordPress.com website.*

You might notice that we used WordPress.com instead of WordPress. The reason is that there are two separate WordPress sites: one with the address www.wordpress.com and another with the address www.wordpress.org. The difference between the two is that the WordPress.com site hosts blogs on its site; all you have to do is go through a few steps to create your blog.

WordPress.org, on the other hand, is a site shown in Figure 3.2 that lets you download the WordPress web publishing application so that you can install it on your server, configure it, and then post blog entries.

Figure 3.2 *The WordPress.org website.*

The difference is that on WordPress.com you create your blog from a set of stock templates, as discussed earlier in this chapter, and the URL has *wordpress.com* in it. With WordPress.org, you download and configure the WordPress system so that you can have greater control over how the blog looks and have a custom URL.

Is WordPress the best option for your blog? And if it is, should you use WordPress.com or WordPress.org?

To answer the first question, WordPress is a popular web publishing system that creates both websites and blogs, and WordPress blogs are rated highly by Google and other major search engines. The downside to using WordPress.com is that you have the Wordpress.com site name in the URL, so your blog doesn't look as though it comes from your business. In addition, unless you pay for WordPress premium features, your readers will occasionally see Google text ads on your blog (these ads help fund the free accounts from WordPress).

You can download the WordPress system free from WordPress.org. You just need the open source web language PHP and open source database MySQL installed to install it. WordPress is customizable, and despite the fact that WordPress provides excellent instructions for setting up a system (and even suggests offering hosting services if you need them), it takes time for your team to get a blog up and running.

If you have the manpower to create a blog, and branding its URL under your own name is important to you, consider downloading and using WordPress to power your blog.

TypePad

SAY Media's TypePad sprouted from Movable Type, a blog platform that was developed by Six Apart. Since the first edition of this book was published, the company VideoEgg purchased Six Apart, renamed the company SAY Media, and sold both Movable Type and the Six Apart name to the Japanese company Infocom. SAY Media still operates TypePad as of this writing.

Like WordPress.com, TypePad is a blog that is hosted on the SAY Media site.

TypePad, shown in Figure 3.3, has become a popular paid service that many mainstream media companies use, including ABC, MSNBC, the BBC, and Sky News (http://en.wikipedia.org/wiki/TypePad). TypePad prides itself on being a full-service blogging site that's also reasonably priced; as of this writing, the Plus plan costs $8.95 per month, and TypePad offers two other plans up to Premium at $29.95 per month.

Figure 3.3   *The TypePad website at www.typepad.com.*

So why do businesses use TypePad? According to the TypePad site, you can do a lot of things in TypePad that you either can't do in Blogger or WordPress.com or that cost extra in WordPress.com. For example, you can password protect your blog, which costs extra in WordPress.com. However, the blog platforms are constantly improving. So what some sites tell you is an advantage really isn't. For example, the TypePad site's comparison page states that TypePad easily connects to your social networking profiles, but recently WordPress.com and LinkedIn (as well as other sites) have become much more proficient at connecting with each other. So do your research.

Speaking of research, TypePad does give you a free 14-day trial so that you can learn whether it is right for you. If you like it, you can view the TypePad pricing page to determine what features you need in your blog that correspond to the plan TypePad offers.

In the first edition of this book, Six Apart offered the free Vox blogging service for people who didn't want to pay for TypePad. Because VideoEgg acquired Six Apart, the Vox service was permanently closed at the end of September 2010, and Vox users were given the ability to export their blogs to TypePad.

Blogger

Blogger, shown in Figure 3.4, was created in 1999 by Pyra Labs, and was one of the earliest blog publishing systems available on the Web (http://en.wikipedia.org/wiki/Blogger_(service)). Blogger's popularity got the attention of Google, which bought Pyra Labs in 2003, and Google's increased popularity over the years has resulted in more popularity for Blogger.

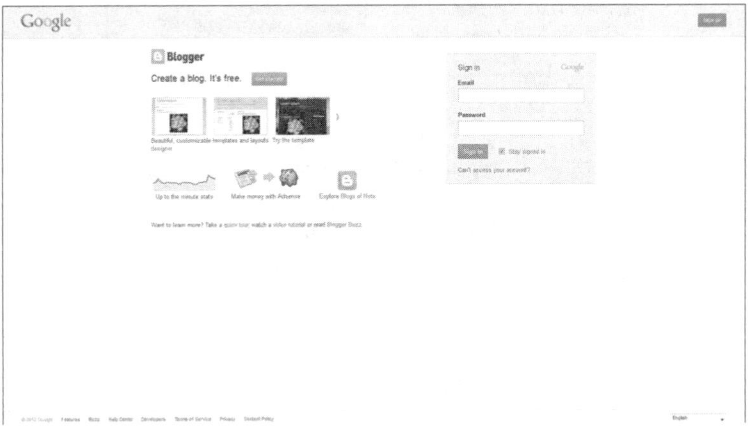

Figure 3.4   *The Blogger website.*

LiveJournal

LiveJournal, shown in Figure 3.5, claims on its website that it is a "community publishing platform" that combines blogging and a social network. As with Facebook and some other social networking sites, you can add and connect to other "friends" in the system. Only people who can view your blog post can comment on it. So if your post is visible only to your friends, only your friends can comment.

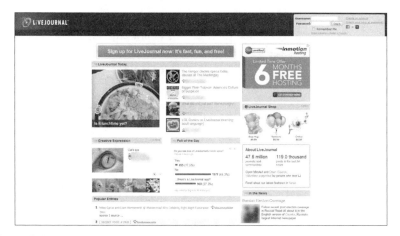

Figure 3.5   *The LiveJournal website.*

Posterous Spaces

The Posterous Spaces blog, which is owned by Twitter, is much like WordPress and Blogger in that when you create a name for your blog, the URL (that is, your website address) contains the name followed by posterous.com. As with WordPress and Blogger, you can also update your blogs from your Posterous Spaces account from the website or on your iPhone or Android smartphone. Figure 3.6 shows examples of blogs that Posterous Spaces thinks exemplifies the best of what its service offers.

Figure 3.6   *Examples of blogs created using Posterous Spaces at http://examples. posterous.com/.*

You can also post to your blog in an email message. You send a message to your blog name at posterous.com. The subject line becomes the subject of your blog and the text of your email is the text of your blog. When you attach a file to your email message such as a photo or video, Posterous Spaces places the attached file within your blog so others can view it. You should check your blog post after you send the email to ensure that it looks the way you want. If you want to tweak the post, you can edit it in the Posterous Spaces website.

Blog Software

You might decide that you want your own web server to host your blog, to keep all your pages under the same URL. For example, if you have a website called www.nancysnursery.com, you might want the blog to have the URL blog.nancysnursery.com rather than something like nancysnursery.wordpress.com. You might also want to have a blog development platform so that you can customize it to your needs. A number of free and commercial blog packages are available, some of which are offered by companies that also host their own web-based blogs for others to use. We take a brief tour of some of these sites, starting with the free blogging systems.

TypePad, WordPress, and LiveJournal all have their own server software that you can download free from their sites, but the LiveJournal and WordPress blog systems have different names. LiveJournal lets you download its server code free from its website. If you want to download the WordPress platform, you have to visit www.wordpress.org and download the application from the download page, as shown in Figure 3.7.

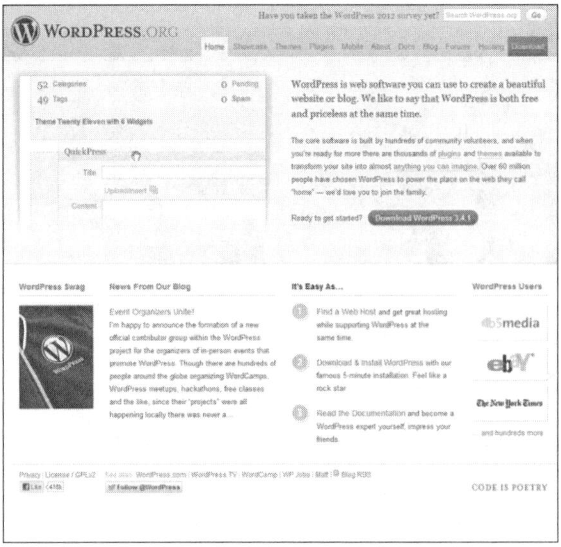

Figure 3.7   *The WordPress.org website download page.*

The downloadable version of TypePad is called Movable Type. You can download the Movable Type Developer or Moveable Type Blogger versions of Movable Type free, as shown in Figure 3.8. However, if you want even more functionality, you must download the Business or Enterprise versions and pay for those services.

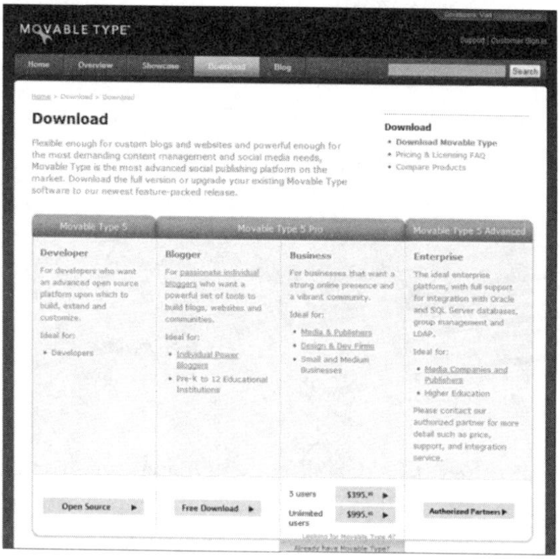

Figure 3.8 *The Movable Type website's Download page.*

A couple of other interesting free blogging applications take a somewhat different approach. Thingamablog, with the website shown in Figure 3.9, doesn't require a third-party host, and it doesn't require you to configure any programming languages or a database to get your blog up and running. You need the Java programming language installed on your computer (available free from Oracle), and all you have to do is install the Thingamablog application to your computer and go through the installation procedure.

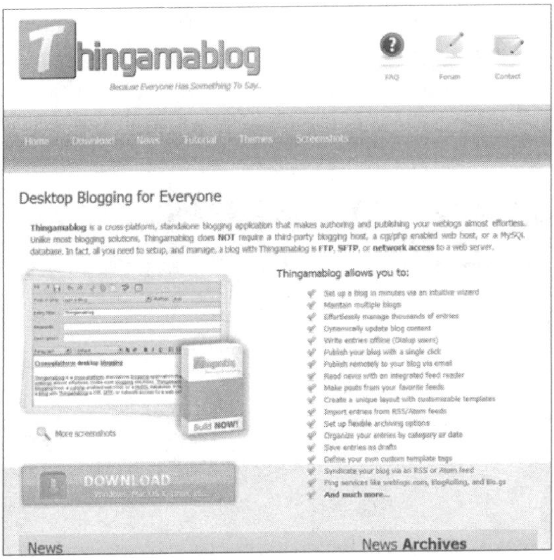

Figure 3.9   *The Thingamablog website.*

Drupal goes even further: It's a flexible content management system that can be modified for a number of requirements. As the Drupal website's About page explains, there are a number of applications for the free Drupal system, from discussion websites to e-commerce applications to social networking websites (see Figure 3.10).

Figure 3.10   *The Drupal website at www.drupal.org.*

Finding the Best Blog for Your Business

In the beginning, there was the text blog, and it was good. As blogging became more popular and multimedia objects exploded on the Web, blogging sites and software kept up and eventually created different types of blogging that fall into many different categories.

Vlogs

Vlogs, which is a portmanteau from the words *video blogs*, include video clips that you can view in the blog. Some sites, such as YouTube, let you post videos on their site for others to view. Blogging sites also let you import video objects into blog posts. Some blogs, such as Adverblog shown in Figure 3.11, also let you embed the video on your website or in your email as well as share the video through Facebook, Twitter, and/or Google+.

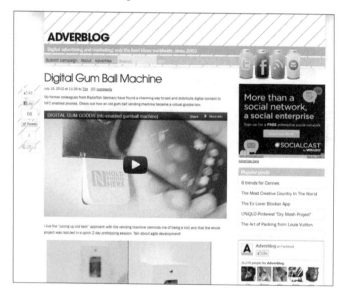

Figure 3.11   *The Adverblog vlog.*

For example, Nancy's Lullaby Nursery (mentioned earlier in this chapter) started off with a text blog about infant and toddler care. But Nancy, the owner, decided that she wanted to put together a video showing some care techniques. Her husband recorded the video for the blog, edited the blog on his computer, saved the file in the appropriate format for the blog, and posted the video along with a little text in a new blog post. To avoid any permission issues with putting photos and videos of babies on their blog, Nancy uses several different-sized dummies in her examples.

Photoblogs

Photoblogs are self-explanatory: They are blogs that use photos as their primary means of communication. Kathleen Connally's photoblog of Durham Township, Pennsylvania, shown in Figure 3.12, was a finalist in the 2010 Best American Photoblog (www.photoblogawards.com).

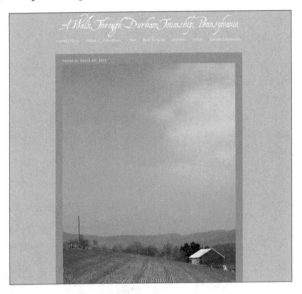

Figure 3.12   *The Kathleen Connally photoblog.*

In the case of Nancy's Lullaby Nursery, Nancy decided she wanted to take pictures of babies who had "graduated" from her program. (Nancy cares for babies and toddlers up to three years of age.) So, Nancy put her husband to work again and had him take pictures of her with happy toddlers upon their "graduation." She then added them to the latest blog post.

Podcast Blogs

Soon after Apple's iPod became a sensation, people learned how to record audio files and have them download onto iPods for listening. Thus, the term *podcasting* was coined. Today, the *New Oxford American Dictionary* defines podcasting as "a digital recording of a radio broadcast or similar program, made available on the Internet for downloading to a personal audio player." As newer iPod models became able to display videos, and blogs were able to do that, the definition of a podcast expanded to include video as well. The This Week in Tech blog produced by Leo Laporte shows the list of podcasts in the Latest Posts section, as shown in Figure 3.13. This is an example of a blog that lets you play streaming audio by clicking the Play button underneath the TWiT logo or download the audio podcast in MP3 format.

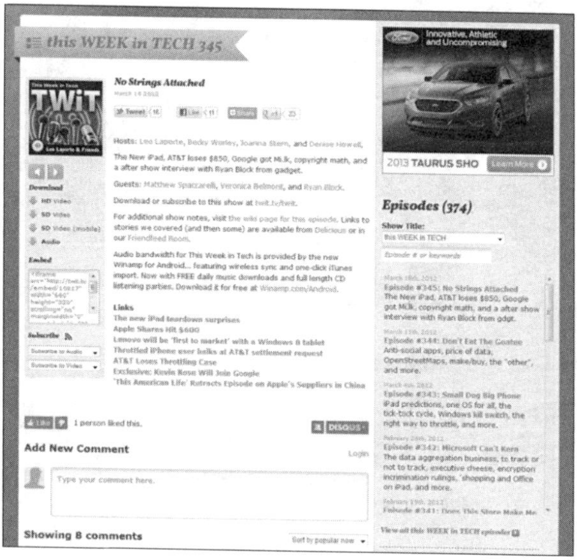

Figure 3.13   *The This Week in Tech blog with a streaming and downloadable podcast.*

For Nancy's Lullaby Nursery, she found that she was starting to become a trusted resource and people began asking her for more information. She decided to entice people to receive an email newsletter by offering access to a members' area of her website that included free podcasts that she recorded using her husband's computer, headset, and the free, open source Audacity sound recorder. Podcast topics Nancy has talked about include how to calm a teething baby, when to feed your baby different types of foods, and how to select the right daycare provider. Nancy also made the latter podcast available to the public on her website so interested customers could hear Nancy talk about finding the right provider.

Tumblelogs

The term *tumblelog* describes a blog that includes a wide variety of blogging types, such as videos, audio, and photos along with text. The popular Tumblr blog, shown in Figure 3.14, is a good example of a tumblelog.

Figure 3.14   *The Tumblr tumblelog.*

As you can tell from the figure, tumblelogs are primarily lighter on text and heavier on multimedia elements such as photos and video. Usually, the text describes the photo or video shown in the tumblelog. The text doesn't have to be brief, and you can post more than one photo and/or video in your Tumblr tumblelog. For example, we found a tumblelog on Tumblr that had four photos and a long post with not only a makeup tutorial but also notes about the model and lipstick featured in the photos.

In the case of Nancy's Lullaby Nursery, the addition of videos and photos has turned her blog into a tumblelog, and as her blog has become more popular with the addition of multimedia elements, she's focused on that more than writing text.

Microblogs and Sideblogs

A fairly recent trend in blogging is called *microblogging,* where people don't have to type much to communicate. Indeed, microblogging sites such as Twitter let you post only 140 characters in each blog post, so you must be brief. Eric's Twitter site, shown in Figure 3.15, has a lot of updates from people and services he follows on Twitter.

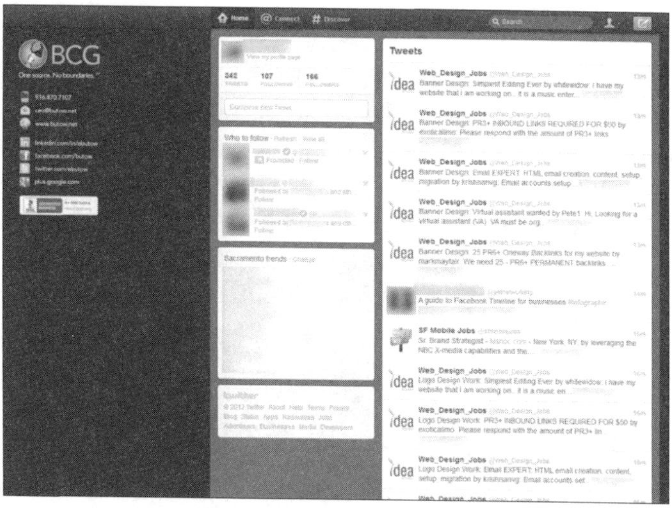

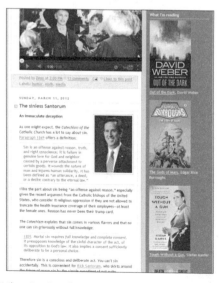

Figure 3.15 *Eric Butow's Twitter page.*

A related feature of microblogging is *sideblogging*, where you can post little snippets of information that don't require a lot of thought. For example, in the Halfway There blog shown in Figure 3.16, the What I'm Reading section that shows readers the books Zeno Ferox is currently reading is considered a sideblog because it contains snippets of information with graphics of book covers as well as the book titles and authors. Sideblogs have become so popular on blog sites that you can add your own sideblog widgets on blogging platform sites such as WordPress.

Figure 3.16 *The What I'm Reading sideblog on the Halfway There blog.*

Moblogs

As cell phones and personal digital assistants (PDAs) started merging into complete communications devices with which you can talk to people, get your email, listen to music, and surf the Web, blogging sites such as Moblog (mobile log = moblog) made it easy for people to upload text and photos to their blog. People can then log on to the Moblog website, as shown in Figure 3.17, and view your latest photos.

Figure 3.17   *The Moblog website.*

 Tip

If you're not sure where to start, the plethora of blogging options to choose from can seem rather daunting. The best thing to do in this case is to just go back to the basics and listen to your customers. If you ask them where they congregate online, how they do so, and what information they'd like from you, you'll have a better idea of how to build your blog. For example, if your clients tell you they primarily use their smartphones to travel and share information, you might want to create a moblog to invite your customers to upload their photos and videos from their smartphones to share with other blog readers. You may also want to include videos in your blog, such as showing people how a new product works. It's all part of responsible blogging that you learn about in Chapter 4, "Blogging Responsibly."

Combining Blogs with Other Networking Sites

Your business might want to participate in a number of other social networking sites. For example, if you market one or more products to people in the 18-to-29 age range, you might be interested in marketing on social networking sites such as Facebook, Google+, and Twitter. If you market products or services to the business community, LinkedIn may be the site you target instead.

Social networking and blogging sites have become much tighter in the past few years, and now it's easy for you to post a new blog entry and have it post on all your social networking sites so that viewers can read it and also link back to your blog and website. Facebook, LinkedIn, Twitter, and Google+ are the big-four social networking sites when it comes to businesses trying to get in front of their customers, so we focus on how to combine blogs with those sites in this section.

Facebook

Facebook was originally popular with college students who didn't want to deal with the younger crowd on MySpace and preferred Facebook's cleaner interface. Eventually, more users of all ages and from many countries worldwide came to Facebook to make it the largest social networking site in the world as of this writing.

Both Facebook and LinkedIn have built-in applications for you to link your blog, which is either hosted on a website or hosted on your own server, to your Facebook or LinkedIn profiles so that you can update simultaneously to all your blogging sites.

You can easily get to the list of Facebook blog applications to review. In the Search box near the top of the page, type **blog** and then click See More Results for Blog at the bottom of the list. In the Search Filters list at the left side of the page, click Apps. You see the first 10 search results with blog applications you can use (see Figure 3.18). Click See More Results at the bottom of the list to view the next 10 results.

Figure 3.18   *Page 1 of the list of blog applications on Facebook.*

When you find an app, click Go to App. What happens next depends on the app you choose. For example, when you click on Go to App, you might see the app developer's website in the Facebook window.

LinkedIn

LinkedIn launched in 2003 as a social networking site designed solely for business professionals. The site has continued to grow in popularity because it's a place not only for business people to connect, but also for people to search for jobs and for recruiters to find potential job candidates.

LinkedIn introduced its suite of applications in 2008, and one of them is a direct link between your WordPress blog and LinkedIn. Open the Applications in the LinkedIn home page by clicking More in the menu bar at the top of the screen and then clicking Get More Applications. You see two blog applications, as shown in Figure 3.19.

Figure 3.19   *The LinkedIn Applications page with the Blog Link and WordPress applications.*

One is for linking your blog on the WordPress.com site, and the other, Blog Link, connects not only your WordPress and WordPress.com blogs but also any blogging platform produced by Six Apart (TypePad and Movable Type) and to other blogging platforms such as Blogger and LiveJournal.

Twitter

The Twitter website is the most popular website in the microblogging category. Twitter lets you send microblogs, or *tweets,* of 140 or fewer characters to your Twitter friends. You can also add cross-reference tags to a specific topic so that you can see all tweets from all Twitter users that are related to that topic.

You can also view popular Twitter applications developed by third-party companies. Open the Applications list by clicking the Profile icon to the right of the search box at the top of the screen and then click Settings in the menu. Next, click Apps in the menu that appears below your user name.

The list of applications appears in the list. The problem with this list is that it's too long and it's very hard to find blogging applications short of searching for the word *blog* in your browser.

To avoid undue hassle, head to the twitterfeed site shown in Figure 3.20 (www.twitterfeed.com). This site checks your blog for new feeds at an interval you specify and then posts the information to your Twitter feed so that your followers can click the blog link and read your latest posts.

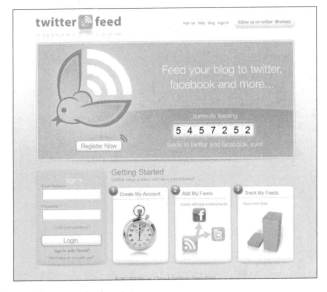

Figure 3.20   *The twitterfeed website.*

Google+

Google's own social network features individual profile pages and business pages for professional accounts. Sign up through a Gmail or Google account and add contacts to *circles,* which are collections or albums of contacts such as Family, Work Colleagues, and Friends. Edit privacy settings to share updates with the world or just with people in one of your circles.

To promote your team, you can set up a circle including all members on Google+ and make that circle shareable. Users can then follow that entire circle at once.

You can share blog posts by adding a link to a Google+ update and filling out the description. Share images and link them back to your blog posts or share videos straight from YouTube. Completing descriptions on these items helps them get picked up in the Google search engine, ultimately allowing more people to find and access your content through web searches. Using the Google+ Direct Connect feature, anyone can put a plus (+) sign in front of a Google search and look for content specifically found within Google+.

Upload photos to Google+ to showcase your products and services, as Zen Bikes has done in Figure 3.21.

Businesses can also allow users and connections to add their own images, posts, and video to their Google+ business page, as they can do with a Facebook fan page.

Figure 3.21   *The Zen Bikes Google+ business page.*

Google+ also features *Hangouts,* which are live video chats that are either public or viewable by contacts in your circles. In early 2012, U.S. President Barack Obama hosted his first Google+ Hangout.

YouTube

According to ComScore, YouTube surpassed Yahoo! as the world's second largest search engine in 2008, a position it still holds in 2012. It would make sense for businesses to tap into this massive network to not only reach its audience, but to bring traffic back to their blogs.

When creating a YouTube account or channel, be sure to fill in all profile information and include links back to your blog whenever possible, such as in the video's description. This gives YouTube users a leash back to your blog where they can read expanded articles, see photos, and get more information on a topic that perhaps a video briefly introduced.

On a business blog, YouTube videos can be embedded, breaking up text and complementing a story. The embed code for a video can be found under its sharing options on YouTube.

YouTube also keeps statistics on how many views your video received and which websites referred users to your content. These analytic features, combined with analytics tools you might already have in place on your blog, allow you to track both incoming and outgoing clicks for your blog and your YouTube account.

Vimeo

Vimeo is another video-sharing site that is free but also offers a paid PRO version. Although it's not the world's second-largest search engine, it does have a strong community of users. You can use tags to describe and categorize your videos, making them visible to searches, and play with the customization settings, which include a logo or watermark overlay for your videos.

You can embed Vimeo videos on your blog and link to your blog from the descriptions on your Vimeo video's page, as you can with YouTube. However, when your video finishes playing, related video thumbnails appear, and they are always other videos from your account and not from other users (as is the case with YouTube).

Vimeo is also seen as a more professional video service, often featuring video art, high-caliber music videos, digital design features, and documentaries. It's seen as a creative network for serious video users and developers as opposed to YouTube's looser audience and producer network with a wide variety of content—from silly cat videos to dancing babies. From scientific slow-motion captures to impressive sound and video quality, the Vimeo user base takes video quality seriously.

Vimeo's policies prohibit posting content strictly for promotional value so videos that you consider posting yourself should adhere to this standard.

Instagram

Instagram (http://instagr.am/) is a minimalist social network for photos that can share content with Twitter, Flickr, Facebook, and via email. Available for iPhone and Android in 2012, this mobile-only platform allows users to take photos, apply artistic filters, and share in a network of contacts. Contacts can then leave a comment, share the photo, or "Like" the image. The result is a steady stream of images that you can scroll through. Businesses are using Instagram to share mobile photos of products, employees, their neighborhood, and more.

Although the interface is primarily the photo stream, users can still fill out a biography in the User Profile area and include a link to their website. Users can also "check in" to locations, using a geolocation service powered by Foursquare (http://foursquare.com). All photos associated with a place can then be searched and referenced. This can create buzz for restaurants, eateries, cafes, and more as users publish their images and announce where they were taken.

Sign up for Followgram to see a web-page version of your Instagram photos (http://followgram.me/miss604), as shown in Figure 3.22.

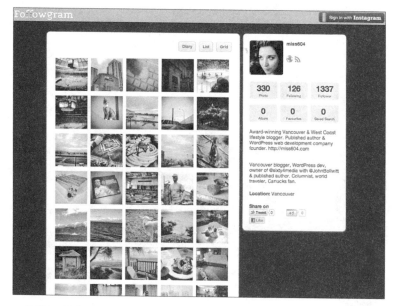

Figure 3.22 *Followgram.me page.*

Pinterest

Pinterest can be equated to a digital bulletin board or cork board on which users *pin* photos they have taken, items they like, recipe cards, and more. It's another purely visual social network that allows for sharing or *repinning* to your board from another's.

You can pin items from blogs and websites by adding a bookmarklet to your browser. A bookmarklet is a saved bookmark that shows up in your browser and when clicked, it performs an action. In this case the "Pin It" bookmarklet will pop open a window so that you can "Pin" content from a page you're currently viewing. Each pinned item contains an image, the name of the original user who pinned it, and a link to the website or blog from where it came.

Pinned items can be sorted into *boards*—for example, a board for "Food," another for "Black & White Photography," or "My Favorite Cars." Businesses are classifying their products by pinning images to specific boards, such as Ben and Jerry's "Our Mission," "Our People," "Flavor Graveyard," or "Vermont" boards, as shown in Figure 3.23. You can also allow your Pinterest followers to add their own images to a board. Users can follow single boards or all boards created by another user.

There are outstanding issues with Pinterest with regards to the copyright of images that are shared so it would be prudent to limit your own pinning—the selection of the photo you chose to represent the pin—to an image that you have the right to share.

Figure 3.23 *Ben & Jerry's "Scoop Shops" Pinterest board.*

Case Studies

You can easily integrate blogs and social networking sites because the various sites make it easy. However, social networks are not the only way to push people to read your blog. Your website also needs to integrate your different blogs and social networking sites. This isn't only important, it's vital.

Okay, so how do you go about it? Let's look at a couple of examples from the real world and see what a small insurance company in northern California and Vancouver Film School are doing to stay connected online with their readership.

InsuranceMommy.com

Maureen Mulheren and Jenifer (Jen) Bazzani have been friends since sixth grade and have stayed in Ukiah, California, where they both grew up. So it's probably no surprise that Maureen and Jen went into business together in 2010. Jen has more than 15 years of experience in the insurance industry (the last 12 years as an agent), and Maureen brought her marketing experience and became an insurance agent soon after she and Jen founded their insurance business. Two years later, InsuranceMommy.com is a small but fast-growing insurance agency that serves three counties in northwest California.

One goal of InsuranceMommy.com is to bring a more personal approach to the fairly dry subject of insurance. The name of the business appeals to women because, Maureen says, there is online research (see www.yoursmartmoneymoves. com/2010/07/08/who-pay-the-bills-men-or-women/) that says in Generation X households—those with members born between 1965 and 1979—more women than men pay the bills. And, says Maureen, "we notice that the majority of our clients are women."

Therefore, Maureen and Jen strive to provide the personal touch not only because of their clientele but also because of their philosophy. "When you sell a service you are selling yourself," Maureen explains, "and when it's something like insurance that you have to buy, why wouldn't you want to go to someone who you know?" Living in a small city of about 15,000 people also requires a more personal touch. "We see our clients at sporting events and at grocery stores," Maureen says, "and they know as much about us as we know about them."

So early in the life of their business, Maureen and Jen decided to communicate with their current and potential clients through Facebook and a weekly vlog on YouTube. Figure 3.24 shows the InsuranceMommy.com YouTube channel at www.youtube.com/user/insurancemommydotcom.

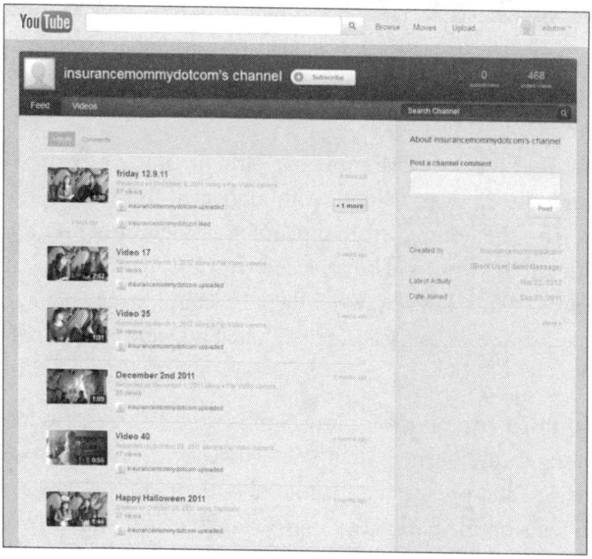

Figure 3.24   *The InsuranceMommy.com YouTube channel.*

All the vlogs feature Maureen and Jen talking about insurance or whatever they feel like talking about that day. Some of the videos feature their outtakes…and that's by design. "That's what makes us unique," Maureen says. "We aren't stuffy or boring or perfect. We're relatable and that's what sells us." Maureen adds that their clients notice their vlogs: "People say 'you girls are too funny' and if we don't get the video done every week, they say 'where's this week's video?'"

About 80 percent of business that comes to InsuranceMommy.com comes from the Facebook site. However, InsuranceMommy.com launched its new website in February 2012, as shown in Figure 3.25, and Maureen says she and Jen already receive 10 percent of their business from the site.

Figure 3.25   *The InsuranceMommy.com website with Maureen on the left and Jen on the right.*

Maureen notes that InsuranceMommy.com still has a ways to go to get its online marketing where she and Jen want it. Although as of this writing the website has one recent vlog on the home page that people can view either on the site or on the YouTube channel, this vlog will be replaced with a welcome video and a link to the YouTube channel. More links between their Facebook page and YouTube channel are also planned so the website, Facebook, and YouTube assets are tightly connected.

The fast growth that InsuranceMommy.com is experiencing also makes Maureen excited about the future of their vlog. "We would love to have a regular 'show' on the local television station and have it filmed in their studio," she says. At the rate Maureen and Jen's online popularity is growing, it's likely that dream will be fulfilled sooner rather than later.

Vancouver Film School (VFS)

The Vancouver Film School began blogging in 2006 at http://blog.vfs.com (see the VFS Blog in Figure 3.26) and has been using YouTube, Vimeo, Twitter, Facebook, and Flickr to spread the word about its programs ever since.

Stephen Webster, Director of Marketing for VFS, says the school's staff spent a lot of time deliberating what the blog was going to be because they knew there were many different processes that could be used in its development. Factors such as maintenance and consistency were key for VFS as well as the type of blog the school was going to create. The staff discussed a gossip blog, industry-focused blog, or a recruitment blog.

"We decided it was going to be a window into which somebody could look at VFS from any specific angle," says Webster. "You could be from the industry, a prospective student, a parent of a student—you could be anybody that's interested in exploring any facet of programming at VFS."

For VFS, the blog is just one facet of the school's overall marketing or "social" strategy. It combines the use of Twitter, a Facebook page, a Vimeo profile, and a YouTube channel. Webster states that the student portfolio channel on YouTube has grown into the largest of any academic institution in the world with close to 53,000 subscribers to date.

"We don't put up sales or marketing pitches, or collateral," Webster adds. "What we're saying is if you're considering another educational institution, and they say they're as good as they are, our question is then 'where are they and where are the results those programs are creating?'"

This "pull" strategy doesn't push a sales pitch on the viewer. Webster says it's his personal mission to debunk the myth that student work is amateurish and not of a high level of quality. The YouTube channel allows people to see for themselves what VFS students are capable of. "First and foremost we wanted to entertain people with our work. Then, create a sense of curiosity in them of 'where did they do that, I'd like to do that, I'd like to go there.'"

Webster does admit that VFS did make mistakes early on. "I think it's a classic trap for someone to fall into. We were treating all social media channels in the same way, just to push a message." The staff then finely tuned the blog and social media plan with an understanding as to which tools are the best tools for specific opportunities. The interconnectivity of the blog and social networks since 2006 has led VFS to a 200 percent increase in prospective student inquiries, and the school noticed a 10 percent increase in market share. The key to the social strategy is being committed and focused on creating brand awareness, without a sales pitch. The staff upload a new video to YouTube every day of the week and post two to five blog posts each week while the school's blogger nurtures the VFS conversation online.

Figure 3.26 *The Vancouver Film School blog.*

Summary

You have many different options when it comes to the types of blogs you can create and the blog platforms you can choose from. This chapter gave you an overview of several different types of popular blog platforms and also discussed how to use different types of blog platforms. The case studies in this chapter could get your own creative juices flowing and provide inspiration about how to create blogs, what type of blogs to create, and how to integrate them with your other online offerings.

Before you do that, however, it's important to know how to blog responsibly, so let's continue on to Chapter 4.

4

Blogging Responsibly

In the online and offline worlds, people chat and share opinions about businesses, products, and services. Whether it is through a word of mouth endorsement, a post written on a Facebook wall, or a quick chat with a colleague over lunch, chances are that the public is already discussing your company in some form or another.

By learning how to engage people through open, online channels, you can truly connect with your customers. With a business blog, you not only get your messaging out to your audience but also bring your audience's comments in, making your blog the home base for these online conversations.

Listen to Your Audience

Listening to your audience and enabling it to speak builds a trust that can motivate your readers to help you spread the word. When your audience members are ambassadors for your blog (and as a result, your brand), the impact of what you write can extend far beyond your own existing reach. Audience members will carry a message about your blog or brand.

The following sections discuss the importance of "listening," covering topics such as two-way discussions, listening by sharing, tools to help you listen, and listening to what is being said.

Two-Way Discussions

Often, news blasts and company updates are one-way transmissions from a business to a recipient list or client base. With blogging, everything becomes more personal, creating more intimate and specialized discussions through content sharing. Opening up your blog to facilitate two-way discussion can help build and maintain your audience through acknowledgment of and encouragement of their input.

A comment form lets your readers know that you value their input, feedback, and commentary. These audiences of readers, clients, and potential customers want to be engaged in discussions and know that their opinions matter to your business.

According to Technorati's State of the Blogosphere 2011 (see Figure 4.1), bloggers are using social media more and more to spread their message and bring conversations from those networks back into their blog. Seventy-seven percent of bloggers who use Twitter do so to promote their blog. The same goes for Facebook where 61% use it to promote their blogs. The conversation used to take place solely in a blog's comment section but now, linking in social media allows for the discussion to reach further, pulling in a larger audience for your posts.

Bloggers have also begun to integrate social media as the method of commenting on a post. With services such as Disqus (http://disqus.com/) or embeddable Facebook commenting (https://developers.facebook.com/docs/reference/plugins/comments/) blog publishers can allow readers to comment by logging into their Facebook, Twitter, WordPress, or Tumblr accounts (among others) to post their comment and display their identity. The benefit for the blog owner is that anonymous comments may be cut down (they can still be allowed on services such as Disqus) and when users post a comment as their Facebook identity, their followers can see that they've added to your discussion because a notification can appear right on their Facebook account.

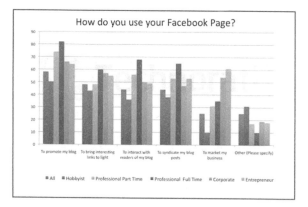

Figure 4.1 *Technorati's State of the Blogosphere 2008.*

A blog with a conversational tone, while still being professional, welcomes the audience to become a part of what you are creating and broadcasting. Through comments and feedback, you can get a feel for what makes your audience and customers tick, and you can tailor your posts to meet their needs. By requesting feedback, polling your audience, or asking a question at the end of your blog post, you put out the welcome mat for readers to add their two cents to the discussion you started. By responding to these comments, or even updating your post if readers provided new information for your topic, you are able to engage in a blog-hosted conversation with your readers.

In the professional blogging realm, comments are highly regarded. When a reader feels moved enough by your content to write a message, you can use this to measure your blog's success. Comments show that your blog has achieved a valuable bidirectional communications platform.

The purpose of a business blog is to connect with existing or potential clients or customers, so it's important to make sure your blog achieves this open, two-way discussion. Without a two-way communications platform, readers aren't free to elaborate and share information, which is a key element to growing your site's visibility and audience. Two-way discussion lets readers know you are open to hearing their thoughts and opinions, and it lets them know your business values information sharing.

The information you share is not the final word. Instead, it should encourage comments and conversation from your readers. This "dialogue" creates a community feeling that makes readers comfortable with your online space.

Listen by Sharing

You can also reach your audience through listening by "sharing." Sharing has replaced one-way transmissions that can be seen as advertisements or billboard-type postings and gives the reader an inside look at what your company is interested in promoting, aside from just yourself. It can also tell the reader that you're interested in what they have to say. The following subsections tell you how to spread your content outward using others as examples and showcasing the fact that you care about your users', readers', and customers' opinions.

Gather Feedback Through Polls and Contests

One way to encourage discussion and feedback is through polls that enable readers to vote for their favorite options or picks. In a web poll, you can give your audience multiple choices or a chance to select their favorite options. Polls could be used for the blog itself, such as "Would you like to see more photos on this blog? Yes, No, Other (please leave a comment)." They can also be used to get product feedback; for example, "Do you like our company's new logo?" or "What color should the logo be?" Because polls are limited to preset responses, you'll often find even more feedback or expanded answers in the comments section of your post.

Contests are also a great crowd pleaser. When readers' opinions are considered with regard to a new ad campaign or perhaps a logo for a business, those readers feel a sense of ownership, knowing their opinions truly matter to the company. People enjoy seeing something they've created being used online (when credited appropriately), so hosting a contest is a great way to show your readers that you appreciate their input while showcasing their talents.

For Super Bowl XLIII, Doritos sponsored a contest that solicited audience-submitted commercials that were then added to the company's website (crashthe-superbowl.com). Those ads then went through several rounds of voting before a winner was selected. The ad that ended up running during the Super Bowl, created by ad-making amateur readers of the Doritos site, was hailed by many as the best Super Bowl commercial of 2009. The ad was also the TiVO "stop watch" winner for the first half of the game, meaning more people went back on their TiVOs to view this ad than any other during the broadcast. Doritos was grateful to the two unemployed brothers from Batesville, Indiana, who created the popular commercial.

In 2009, in preparation for Super Bowl XLIV in 2010, Doritos used the public video-sharing website Vimeo (http://vimeo.com/crashthesuperbowl) to promote the contest using the previous year's winners in the videos. These videos were embedded and shared on other blogs so that viewers could spread the message or enter the contest for 2010.

Use Images or Photos

To complement the text on your blog, you should also use images. Many bloggers use popular photo-sharing sites such as Flickr.com to showcase their images or host the photos they then add to their blogs.

With Flickr.com, you can create public groups, through which readers can share photos with the group. Companies can create Flickr accounts and start groups (composed of their prospective audiences) to encourage photo sharing.

If your company sells blue jeans, you could set up a group so that any viewers with photos of themselves or others in blue jeans can add their images. Your audience is then showcased in your group. Flickr group images can be made into slideshows that can be embedded into your blog. Suddenly, your blog content is populated by readers' submitted images. You aren't simply putting your images and your message out, but you're showcasing your audience.

You may also want to consider using submitted photos on your own blog (only with permission, of course). If you do so, remember to link to the original bloggers' websites. Doing so showcases their images and reminds them that you value how your customers use your products. Flickr.com also enables you to create slideshows of images currently submitted to the group.

Consider the example of Libre Tea, makers of loose-leaf tea containers (http://libretea.com). Libre Tea's Flickr group allows anyone to share what the company calls "tea moments." The company encourages you to take a photo when you are enjoying a cup of tea, whether on the go or at home. It then highlights these photos on its website. These pictures show how versatile the Libre Tea containers are, and they also inspire ideas about how to unwind and enjoy the product.

Pinterest is also a great tool for showcasing your readers and customers while getting feedback all at the same time. Using the previous blue jeans example, you can create a public Pinterest Board to which anyone can post their favorite jeans photo. Pay attention to which styles appear the most, post comments, "like" images, and "re-pin" your readers' submissions. You can also create your own board with various styles and ask readers to "like" their favorites. Pinterest images are also embeddable so you can feature the most-liked pins on your blog.

In Figure 4.2, an image from the City of Surrey's 2012 Fusion Festival is being pinned to tourism Surrey's public board on Pinterest. The image links back to the blog post, is sourced from Flickr, and will get exposure on the public board.

Figure 4.2 *A photo that has been pinned on Pinterest.*

As you can understand from these example, two-way blogging discussions occur not only with text but also with other forms of content. When you encourage readers to share their content with you (instead of just you sharing your information with them), you create a different level of interaction and engagement for the audience, making your blog a two-way street of information.

Tools to Help You Listen

On most platforms, when you open your site to comments, you can request a commenter's URL (for a blog or website, for example). This is another way to gauge your audience members, such as whether they work in a similar business, write similar blogs, or do not have websites of their own. For example, if you discover your readers are predominantly other bloggers or they are more Internet-savvy, you can formulate specific ways to interact with them on your blog.

Publishers can use standard blog comment forms that come with their platforms, or they can use tools to follow conversations about their site across the Web. The following subsections discuss various tools that enable you to listen to what people are saying about your blog.

Track Mentions

Google Alerts is the most basic way to find mentions of your site online. You can
create custom alerts so that every time your brand, product, service, or company
name is mentioned on the Internet, Google sends you an email alert. Figure 4.3
shows the Google Alerts Setup page.

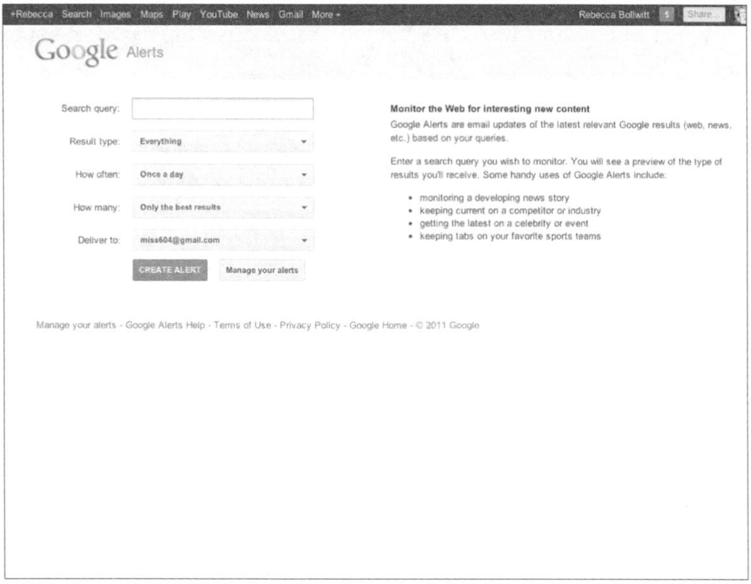

Figure 4.3 *Google Alerts Setup page.*

Visit http://twitter.com/search to search the Twitter service for instant mentions.
The popular microblogging service is used by millions worldwide, and it enables
140-character updates that can include anything from links to favorite sites to
comments about what the user had for lunch that afternoon. Twitter's brief character limit enables short conversations to lead to expanded discussions online and
offline.

Because the Twitter service is fully searchable, you can use the search function to
find any users in the world who are including any word in their updates at any
time. All words posted in updates on Twitter are searchable, and the Twitter search
archive keeps them documented for several weeks.

Often, popular words and phrases are tracked using hash tags (pound signs). This
hash tag feature comes in handy when you want to track specific events, such as
a conference. For example, if you are an attendee at the 123 Conference, you can
include #123Conference in a Twitter update and encourage other attendees to

do the same. You can then track all #123Conference updates with ease using the http://twitter.com/search page and typing in the keywords in the search box. The search results then display all mentions of #123Conference, from all Twitter users.

Twitter also lists its top 10 trending topics on the sidebar of all profile pages. These are words or hashtagged topics that have been posted in Twitter updates the most frequently. Using this intuitive search feature, you can enter your search terms and find those on Twitter who are currently discussing a topic pertaining to your business.

When Rebecca was traveling and looking for a hotel, she wrote the following Twitter update: "Looking for hotel recommendations for San Francisco #WordCamp in the Union Square Area." Another Twitter user replied with the following: "@Miss604 Check out the Kimpton Hotels www.kimptonhotels.com." Within a few hours, Kimpton found the Twitter conversation and replied, "@Miss604 we hope you'll let us take care of u in SF. We have 9 hotels here. DM if you would like insider info on any." As you can guess, Rebecca ended up staying at a Kimpton hotel (and paying for a stay) because of this attention to her conversation. The person running the company's Twitter account was searching Twitter for specific keywords, perhaps *hotels* or the company name *Kimpton*, and her conversations appeared.

Site Statistics

The same type of tracking can be used to find mentions of your specific blog posts. By locating these links, you can get an idea of your reach and your audience. You can see who is listening, who is responding, and who thought your content valuable enough to expand upon or link in their own post. This also creates the opportunity for you to leave comments on other sites. You can thank the author for linking your site or comment on the content she wrote in the post. The simplest way to find incoming links is to use a statistics tracking program. These tools, mostly online, enable you to set up an account after which you can paste specifically generated code into your website so that it can begin tracking your statistics.

Google offers Google Analytics, which produces detailed statistical data after 23 hours, or you can use instant trackers such at SiteMeter (http://sitemeter.com) or StatCounter (http://statcounter.com). Platform-specific tracking systems also are available, such as Mint (http://haveamint.com); see Figure 4.4.

Figure 4.4   *Mint: Statistics for your website or blog.*

Most statistics-tracking systems show you who is coming to your site and their origin online, such as a link from another site or a search engine result. You can also see the readers' IP addresses and which browser they are using to view your blog. By using these statistics-tracking applications on your site, you can see data such as the geographical location of your audience and what type of computer they are using to access your content.

Using this statistical data, you can determine whether your audience is using outdated browsers (an understanding that will come in handy in terms of your blog's design specs), whether they are on a Mac or PC, and whether they are mostly mobile readers.

Your Mobile Audience

You want to make sure that your blog is viewable across any platform (browser or computer type). The popularity of mobile devices is growing, so including tests to make sure your blog is compatible with these tools is beneficial. To test, simply access your blog from a mobile device and see whether it displays the same way as when you look at it from a web browser on your computer. Sometimes blogs optimized for larger viewing might not be able to fit all information onto a tiny mobile screen. To help with this, you can use applications or services that will display your blog's post and/or pages in a way that is optimized for mobile viewing.

Some applications such as Mobify.me (http://mobify.me) and plug-ins for blogging platforms such as WordPress directly target mobile audiences. WordPress users can download the WPtouch plug-in to convert their blog for reading in mobile devices (see Figure 4.5). After the plug-in is activated on the blog, it requires a few tweaks to the settings before your site is ready to go mobile.

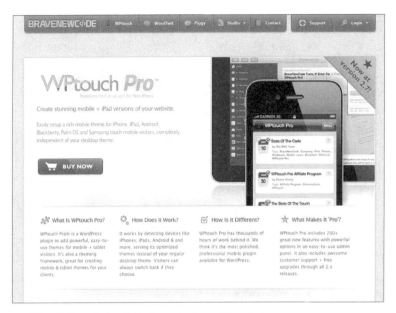

Figure 4.5 *WPtouch for WordPress by BraveNewCode.*

By knowing how your audience is accessing your content and by listening from behind the scenes to their viewing needs, you can optimize their reading experience on your site.

Listen to Readers

Although your goal is not purely to encourage comments, it's definitely a factor in the success of your blog. You need to post something that readers find worth expanding on, or better yet, that they reference in their own blog posts.

When your work is referenced (with a link) in another's post, that reference is called a *trackback*. A trackback shows up as a comment; however, it's simply a message notifying the author that someone has linked to his blog post. Your commenting system should be set up to allow trackbacks. After all, trackbacks notify you when someone has expanded on your thoughts or deemed them worthy of reference, and it enables the conversation you started to be expanded on in other blogs, ultimately expanding your reach. Others will see your openness to the conversation, and organically, through mentions on blogs or sharing on social bookmarking sites, your work will be passed along.

People are talking about your company, its services, and its products, and you can't stop that. However, you can make yourself aware of these conversations. By using tools to track links and mentions, you can then engage in these outside discussions to record new feedback, clarify data, or just to show appreciation for the writer's interest in your business. Suppose, for instance, that you run an amusement park and find a blog post online about someone's experience on your roller coaster. That is a prime opportunity to show you are listening. If the roller coaster ride was a positive experience, you can leave a comment and thank the author for her patronage or perhaps encourage her to stop by again in the future. You could even link her post on your own blog, either in a blog post or on your blogroll or link list. In a blog post, you could showcase the positive experience the author had at your establishment and let others know that you truly value the patronage. Suddenly, a blog post becomes a fantastic marketing tool to highlight your business. Should the post have a negative tone, use your discretion to escalate the feedback to client services or drop a comment to let the author know you are looking into the matter (and be sure to follow up).

With negative feedback published online, your goal should not be to control the message by demanding the author remove the content (unless it is defamatory and in need of escalation). Your mission should be to embrace the feedback and handle it with care and tact. Letting authors know you are listening, that you value their opinion, can go a long way in terms of a customer's impression of your company.

Comments and Responses

Having a comments section on your site lets your readers know that their input is just as valued as the information you are presenting. However, you will receive several types of comments. You need to be prepared for whatever might be submitted.

Comment Forms

Most standard comment forms request the user's name, email, and website for authentication, which is a good idea if you want to know about the person leaving the message. If your blogging platform contains these options, you can activate or deactivate them at any time. For an extra measure of protection against spam, you can request that commenters complete a captcha form (either an image or text) before their comment can be submitted. Captcha generators can be found online and pasted into your platform's settings. These scrambled images feature letters and numbers that need to be typed before the message can be sent. This level of authentication ensures that human beings and not spam-generating computer programs are leaving the comment messages. Captcha authentication might seem like overkill, but if you are having problems with spam comments, it's an option you should consider.

WordPress also packages up its default spam comment blocker plugin, Akismet, with your WordPress.org installation. The plugin is automatically installed but will need to be activated and a license is required. Follow the step-by-step instructions to purchase and apply a license and save time stopping potentially thousands of spam comments from appearing on your blog.

With all these fields in place, you can determine who is visiting your site and how best to reply to comments or follow up on an issue. When you are replying to comments in your own thread, it is courteous to direct your response to the message's original author. Some blog sites use the Twitter @ reply method to target their replies (for example, "@John Smith, thank you for the feedback!")

When to Moderate Comments

Comments are an option on most blog platforms, and the commenting tool usually includes the option to moderate. Moderation is when a completed comment form does not get published automatically but sits in a queue awaiting your approval. Learning when and how to moderate enables you to maintain control of all content that is published to your blog. The following subsections describe some of the types of comments you'll receive.

Levels of Moderation

Various levels of moderation are available on most blogging platforms. The first, and the simplest, is to allow all comments that are submitted to be published. The next would be to allow all comments from previously approved authors. So, for example, if a reader has previously left a comment on your blog, you can automatically approve the rest of his comments going forward. The next few levels of moderation depend on the author's preference and the settings she would like to put in place.

Anonymous Comments

Anonymous comments can come from anywhere (for example, from someone who was unable to properly complete a form, a malicious spam attack, or simply someone who does not want to be identified). Having required fields helps to prevent anonymous comments, but you can also set up your blog so that anonymous comments are held for moderation. This means you need to approve them before they go public.

Spam

When it comes to spam, most blogging platforms have ways to prevent these comments from being published automatically (especially if you have moderation settings in place). These comments can include multiple links or simply unpleasant content you don't want to share with the public on your site, so it is recommended you monitor your comments to find them. After you identify comments such as these, you can moderate them (not approve them for publishing) or delete them entirely.

Overloading sites with links to spam sites is one of the goals of spam marketers. Having more links on your site boosts the spam site's ranking, and you don't want your site to be a vessel for this type of behavior. When moderating comments, use your best judgment to determine whether the comments should be held for approval. Comments can be set up so that any new message is moderated, or you can leave them open to be posted automatically (see Figure 4.6). Moderation settings vary based on the platform you're using, but common features include indicators such as IP address tracking, holding a comment if there are links in the body of the text, or giving approval if the author is a returning user.

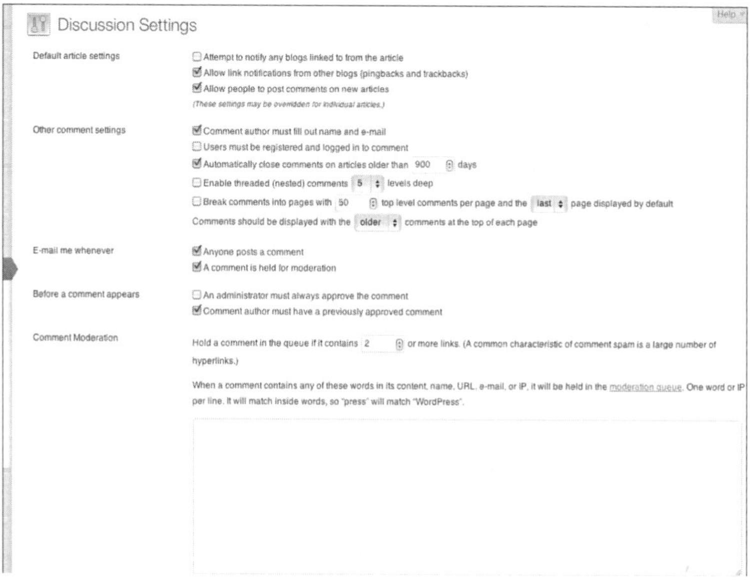

Figure 4.6 *Comment moderation on WordPress.*

If you receive a comment that is hateful or simply not possible to publish because of questionable content, you can use your statistics-tracking program to log the IP address of the user. An IP address is a unique location marker for the user's access point to the Internet. You can then flag this IP address or set up features to automatically hold future comments from this user in the moderation queue. When a comment thread ceases to set a professional and respectful tone, negative messages can be deleted or held in moderation.

In some circumstances, you can contact the author if he has left an email address. In this contact, you can let him know why you have held his comment (for example, foul language or defamatory content). Doing so lets the author know you are paying attention, and it enables the author to write something more concise and tactful. Commenters might not enjoy seeing their comment being held for moderation; however, this is a way to maintain control of the content on your site while still being approachable and reasonable.

Negative Feedback Can Help You Grow

If you receive a comment on a blog post that is less than complimentary, the manner in which you respond to the post reflects on your company. Participating in a flame war, or back-and-forth battles with an aggravated commenter, is not the most productive way to address an issue. Negative comments might not necessarily need to be deleted unless they are defamatory, libelous, or anything similarly malicious. However, if comments contain negative but productive feedback, you should respond in a courteous manner.

For example, suppose you are a clothing distributor and you have just published a blog post about a new pair of pants. A complaint is then received in the comments section from a customer who says she recently bought a pair and they already have a tear in them. You can approve the comment and reply directly, saying that it's unfortunate and you will be happy to have customer service follow up. You can then send the commenter's information to your customer service department; you'll have the customer's name and email from the comment form. You can also link to the appropriate section of your site where customer concerns can be submitted. By dealing with this matter publicly, your audience will know you are attentive and you truly care about your customers.

Deal with Negative Feedback

The saying "no news is good news" applies to the blogging world, too. When posts are positive and your readers are pleased and informed, they might not always leave a comment. However, when readers write something congratulatory, be sure to respond promptly and thank them for their participation on the blog.

A large part of blogging for your business is being personal and approachable (for your customers and readers) in your posts and within your comments section. Responses should be professional and respectful. (So you should adhere to proper grammar and punctuation, as well as common conversational courtesy.) You want to be informative and transparent and never immature in your replies, even if the original comment has set that tone.

Dealing with negative comments is a bit trickier, however, so here are some tips:

- Address negative comments on your own site as soon as possible so that they do not fester in the mind of the author and cause any adverse effects if they do not receive some type of response.

- If the comment is negative yet constructive or is conducive to a productive discussion, by all means feel free to approve it. Publishing negative feedback, and the way a company deals with it, can truly reflect on your brand in a positive way. Your readers come to your site for information and valuable content.

- Should the comment be destructive and critical of the blog post itself, your options are to hold it for moderation, delete it, or take things offline.

- When a comment is libelous, allowing it to be published and then responding publicly are not the best course of action. You can email the commenters privately about sincere concerns (if they provided a valid email address). Although the subject of being responsible for allowing libelous comments made by others to be published on your blog is technically a legal "gray area," it may still be deemed as slander. In severe cases, threats may need to be dealt with on a private/personal level. In most instances, however, the Delete key is all you need.

- When a comment contains expletives you reserve the right to edit the comment and still let it be published. Make your edit obvious to the reader (for transparency purposes). For example: "I love the loose-leaf tea containers, they are [removed] great!"

It is also important to protect other members of the community. Therefore, you should also monitor the discussions in your comments section for attacks between commenters.

In October 2009, a ruling was made to settle a lawsuit between 2 plaintiffs and 30 people who posted anonymous and derogatory comments about them on an online message board called AutoAdmit. "According to the plaintiffs, the suit was necessary because the discussion board, a site designed for law school graduates, was often monitored by firms looking to hire. Because the comments were associated with their names, the women claimed that it would hurt their chances of being offered a job." (Source: ReadWriteWeb, www.readwriteweb.com/archives/watch_ out_trolls_your_menacing_comments_could_lead_to_fines.php.)

Avoid Slip-Ups

An English proverb advises one to "hope for the best, but prepare for the worst." You should keep this quote in mind as you prepare your blog and any other related online marketing endeavors, such as a presence on one or more social networking sites, because there are things that are out of your control. For example, you can't control what comments people will leave on your blog or social networking site. If you plan ahead, you won't eliminate any potential issues, but you will be able to control and resolve them more quickly.

Form a Game Plan

You're already reading this book, so you know that you need to have a game plan ready to go before you blog. However, just reading this book isn't enough; you have a lot of homework to do before you start building your blog. You might want to consider doing one or more of the following:

- Determine what you want to include on your blog and perform a *SWOT analysis* of each blog feature. You may be familiar with this business acronym that stands for *Strengths, Weaknesses, Opportunities, and Threats.* You should write down all the thoughts you have in each of the four SWOT categories and study them to determine whether your planned blog feature is right or wrong for your blog—or if the feature might be right in the future. You learn more about features you can include in your blog in Chapter 6, "Designing Your Blog."

- Research other blogs both inside and outside your industry or business area. Look for those that have done things on their blogs and other social networking sites that you're thinking about. You might find good and bad things going on with the blogs that you can prepare for with your own blog. Consider talking with the companies that sponsor these blogs to get feedback and ideas. You might not get the response you want, or get a response at all, but you won't know unless you ask.

- Start a discussion on a blogging group within one or more social networking sites to get insight from other group members. For example, you can join The Blog Zone group on LinkedIn, shown in Figure 4.7; search for the information you're looking for in past discussions; and/or start a discussion yourself.

- Find a company that's experienced in social networking to help you create your social networking presence and/or consult with as you go along so you can set up your blog and other social networking sites to maximize your return on investment (ROI) and minimize headaches.

Figure 4.7 *The Blog Zone group on LinkedIn.*

Combine Blogging and Social Networking

It's natural to combine your blog with social networking websites and your website (and your website may not even be in the picture if your blog is your website). Before you combine your blog and social networking sites, you should determine what social networking sites you'll use and how you'll use your blog in conjunction with those sites.

If your business already has a presence on one or more social networking sites, you need to do some research and see how your company uses those sites to promote the business. Be sure to talk with the person or persons who manage those social networking sites to get some tips and ideas from them about what to include in the blog and how to promote your blog on the sites.

When your business doesn't have a presence on any social networking sites, you need to do even more research. For example, you need to find out where your customers congregate online, and one way to do this is to ask your existing clients about the social networking sites they visit.

You may also want to find out what social networking sites your competitors use and establish a presence on or more of those networking sites, find others that your competitors aren't using, or use some combination of these two strategies. Even if you have a presence on social networking sites, you may decide to promote your business on other social networking sites either now or in the future.

As discussed previously, you should also track how people on social networks are interacting with your blog so you can determine whether you need to change your strategy, which can include changing your message, adding new features such as a contest to push people to your blog, or even adding and dropping profiles on one or more social networking sites.

Focus on What Matters

For example, you might decide that you want to have a presence on some of the largest social networking sites such as Facebook and LinkedIn—or even YouTube if you have vlogs. Then you can focus on connecting those sites together with your blog (and your website if you have one) and refining your message to attract customers.

As with any business strategy, a social networking strategy that includes blogs requires you to plan for the medium to long term as well as the short term. You might want to set milestones to see where you are as you get more comfortable (or not) with blogging and social networking sites. As you reach each milestone, you might find that you need to change your strategy or even the plan itself.

Think About Fixes Before Slip-Ups Happen

In late 2011, the *Sacramento Business Journal* featured an article about how a dental group that runs social media contests every month decided to promote a video contest to find the child who could dance best (www.bizjournals.com/sacramento/print-edition/2011/12/16/social-media-slip-ups.html). Parents had problems submitting videos, comments about the kids' abilities turned nasty, and there were allegations of cheating.

This dental group didn't think of all the things that could go wrong until everything did. Although the success of social networking promotions on your blog, social networking websites, or both can be a matter of trial and error, you can mitigate errors by thinking about how you'll fix problems before they happen.

For example, if you're involved in a contest on your blog, you should think about everything that could go wrong, such as if people think that someone is breaking the rules. In that case, you need to clearly define what those rules are and communicate them on your blog, put together a checklist as you review each video, and communicate with those who don't follow the rules clearly and immediately.

If you're going to hand off management of the blog or a feature on the blog, such as a contest, to one or more people, you need to be clear with them about the rules, what to do if there is a problem, and when the situation needs to be escalated to you or someone else with the authority to fix the problem. When you talk with others about rules and handling problems on your blog, you'll undoubtedly start a discussion that could lead you to add to or change part of your original plan.

You should also consider getting some of your best customers involved in planning and producing any promotional events on your blog. Your customers can help you test any features such as submitting a video or other file to your blog, and also provide you with valuable ideas and concerns that you can address before you "go live."

Implement Fixes Quickly

So what if something does go wrong even after you've planned everything? If you've planned correctly, you have a list of contingencies at the ready. Some of those contingencies may come in the form of communication on the blog, such as in a disclaimer that states all comments are subject to review or that all entries for a promotion are subject to review.

You might also consider listing contingencies in a print or online document that describes a number of "if-then" situations; for example, if someone states that she's offended by your blog post, you do three things so you can assuage the offended party.

No matter how you implement fixes, follow the standard rule of customer service by implementing fixes quickly and professionally. If you don't follow this rule, several issues could arise:

- Resentment by the other party goes up.
- Disinterest and distrust by current and potential customers go up. That distrust could come in the form of other people complaining about the same problem.
- The chance of resolving the issue amicably goes down.
- There is a heightened risk that the aggrieved party will communicate his feelings on other online forums and/or to others in person.

Even if things work out, if you don't address a problem right away, you may have to deal with a perception that lingers with your current and potential customers that you're not a responsive company. And working to overcome that will cost more time, effort, and possibly money that you can save if you plan ahead and resolve problems as soon as you possibly can.

Case Studies

Every company wants to ensure that it gets the right message out to the public whether it's through a press release, newsletter, blog post or Twitter update. Providing a genuine voice to go along with your message online goes a long way but that also means that you'll be hearing from a number of other voices—some of which won't always agree with you. Blogging responsibly is about opening up that channel between the company and the customer (reader) and providing accurate information or telling a story in a respectful way. The following case studies address each of these qualities.

Molson Coors Brewing Company

Molson Coors Brewing Company has been brewing since 1786 and produces some of North America's most popular brands of beer, including Molson Canadian, Coors Light, Molson Export, Molson Dry, and Rickard's. The company also is partnered with worldwide labels such as Heineken, Corona, Miller Genuine Draft, Foster's Lager, and Tiger.

After Molson's merger with Coors in 2005, the company went from being purely Canadian to 50% U.S. owned, with headquarters in Montreal and in Denver, Colorado. Being Canada's oldest brewery and using the slogan "I am Canadian," suddenly *Molson Canadian* stopped looking so patriotic in the eyes of the consumers who felt a sense of national pride beaming from each maple-leaf-boasting bottle.

With this new identity crisis, the public and media struggled with their perception of the brand. Molson's chief public affairs officer, Ferg Devins, said that this became the best time to start telling the company's story. In 2007, Molson launched the "Molson in the Community" blog and began covering all aspects relating to the business, the industry, its 3,000 employees, partnerships, and consumers online (see Figure 4.8).

Figure 4.8   *The Molson Coors in the Community blog.*

Hosting a blog for a beer company does have its challenges and requires effort in moderating comments and content in a tactful manner. Devins explained the types of comments the company holds for moderation given the nature of the industry: "We need to make sure that there's no one talking about excessive consumption or under-legal drinking age consumption."

The blog created by Molson made the company approachable to many online, which caused a few problems in terms of customer feedback. Molson saw a trend in which consumers were leaving comments when they had a general company inquiry. In these cases, Molson was able to funnel these messages to the appropriate department in the company.

Tonia Hammer, Molson's community relations coordinator, used Google Alerts along with Truecast and Radian6 to scan the Internet for mentions of its products or brands. Using these tools to monitor incoming links and mentions online, the company came across some backlash online regarding its nationwide blogger outreach campaign, Brew 2.0.

Brew 2.0 was an event held in various cities across the nation where bloggers were invited to a Molson brewery for an evening of beer education. The event received high praise from participants and throughout the online media sphere. The company's intentions, however, were questioned on several blogs, which truly put Molson's social media practices to the test. Having set up alerts so that it could be notified of mentions online, Molson was able to find the discussions and chime in, officially. In particular, one blogger questioned not only the process Molson used to create the invite list for the Brews 2.0 events, but also its commercial motives.

"What it really came down to in the end was the particular people that were criticizing what we had done [with Brew 2.0]," said Devins. "They had this position that we reached out to the wrong people and that it was too strategic."

Adam Moffat, manager, marketing and brand public relations, explained how Molson addressed these concerns in the blogosphere. "We don't want to get pulled into an argument—there's no hope of changing [the author's] opinion; we just wanted to provide clarity on information that they misunderstood, being transparent about what our goal was for this activity." Devins added that public responses should always be deferential. "If it's opinion, we'll counter with our opinion, but we'll also be respectful to people being entitled to their opinion." However when it comes down to the straight facts about the company, "if someone's got information that they're transmitting wrongfully, or they're not on the mark, or it's not fact based—we will definitely come in hard with facts," said Devins.

In this case, Moffat noted that one of the most gratifying parts of being transparent and addressing these concerns online was that Brew 2.0 participants could find these discussions and were able to band together, defending the company simply because they believed in the goals of their online community.

Molson believes that the successful Brew 2.0 event helped the company bridge a gap between consumer and company and connected online entities. Devins described it as going beyond blogging and "into a broader scope of business."

The Molson Coors in the Community blog also became a tool for employee engagement, and as Devins noted, "It's reaching out to our people at the field level. From the ground up, not from the corner suite."

Blog posts nurtured the pride and engagement of the employees, sharing what they do in the field and building the corporate community though this online platform. "Employees across the country are able to tell their story and what they're doing in the community through the blog," said Moffatt. With this outlet, "We're just really doing a better job of publicizing the great work that's being done within our walls, but also out in the community by our employees."

Sample blog posts included "Eric Molson Retires After 50 Years at Canada's Brewery," "The Beer Store Bottle Drive For Leukemia May 23–24," "Calgary Sales Team Plays Their Part at Calgary Inter-Faith Food Bank." They even offered up their blog to guest posts, such as this entry, "A Post by Marcy Robertson, YMCA Relationship Development Manager."

Since hosting Brew 2.0, Molson became involved with the global Twestival event (which raised $250,000 through Twitter in more than 200 cities) and signed on to be a part of a social media strategy for the Vancouver 2010 Olympics.

Sharing stories online with the blog goes beyond the walls of the company, "[The blog] has given us more breadth and depth with respect to our philanthropic effort because we're able to tell and share a story," said Devins. "It's humanizing our company and it's humanizing our brand," added Moffatt.

"No longer do consumers want that faceless monolith preaching at them," said Moffat. They want to feel closer to brands and companies, and certainly given that our company is a social one in its roots and DNA, it certainly just makes a lot of sense that we act in this way."

ING Direct's Direct Talk Blog

As we discuss in Chapter 7, "Who Will Write the Blog?" deciding who will author a blog is an important step to not only putting the blog together but also finding its voice. ING Direct Canada started the "Direct Talk with Peter Aceto" blog (http://blog.ingdirect.ca/) in 2009, providing information, advice, and financial food for thought from CEO Peter Aceto. Because ING Direct Canada is a financial institution, blogging responsibly is also high on its list of priorities. When it comes to money matters, you can never be too careful, but it helps to build trust.

Mark Nicholson, Head of Digital and Interactive for ING Direct Canada, said the blog itself was a part of a larger social platform for social media but sits at its core. In 2007 the company hosted a "Super Star Saver" contest on YouTube that asked people to create a video and share how they save their money. The video campaign served to test the waters and see whether the ING Direct audience was ready for social media and a blog. ING Direct deemed the experiment a success, and the social plan was put into action. In 2010, it introduced a new "THRiVE Chequing" online, no-fee chequing account for Canadians and continued to use social media to get the word out. It posted videos on YouTube such as "INGDirect Canada Makes a Splash" featuring synchronized swimmers. Its 2012 "Save Your Money" campaigns feature more YouTube videos and its iPad application for its customers' banking needs.

"We have a CEO who is very open and transparent, and we think that banking should be the same," said Mark. "We don't feel like Canadians should ever go to a bank and not feel like they're getting the straight goods or able to have an open and honest conversation so the blog was launched exactly for that."

Mark said that the blog is a platform on which Peter can share his view about money and money matters (see Figure 4.9).

Figure 4.9   *ING Direct Talk with Peter Aceto blog.*

Peter also writes posts about corporate culture and leadership. The blog serves to engage Canadians in a dialogue about money, and the corporate culture aspect is outward facing but reflects its employees internally "so that the culture permeates every bit of fabric in this organization." The leadership element of the blog serves employees as much as it does the general public. This public-facing outlet and resource shows that there is great trust between the audience, ING customer or not, and all levels of the company.

Other social networks are managed by the marketing team, but it was important for ING Direct to have the blog as well. Mark said that when ING began the blog, no other financial institutions in the country were running a blog with a core blogger being an officer of Peter's level. "This is Peter's passion and he wants to be out there."

Having the right blogger and knowing the message you want to convey are important, but then comes that next step of wondering whether you can publish what you want to say on your blog. Should it be—or can it be—for the public's eyes?

Mark said that ING Direct has guidelines in place for its entire social strategy. "We are a bank, we are regulated, so there's certain things we can say in social [situations] and certain things we can't say—and certain interactions we can't do." Mark added that when it comes to the blog in particular, there really is no risk to the bank because the CEO, who has good common sense, writes it.

"In terms of divulging secrets. Our whole view is that we shouldn't have secrets. If we're willing to talk about it in a boardroom, we should be willing to talk about it in front of consumers."

Being the outward-facing personality of the company in the online realm, Peter's blog can become the first point of contact when a client has a negative experience. Mark said that concerns and comments do not get ignored and are addressed "head on" by the appropriate team. The blog and the company's social media outlets can also be a platform for customer notices—sending out news and notifications to reach clients quickly. Being accessible in this manner has proven to turn negative experiences into positives. "It pays to be pro-active. It's something that people appreciate and it builds trust."

Summary

Now that you know some best practices, you need to determine your own moderation levels through instant feedback. However, before you can get audience reactions, you need to serve up that great content, worth commenting upon. For inspiration, in the next chapter, you see some innovative writing concepts from companies across many different industries.

5

Choosing a Blog Topic

After you decide to start a blog, you must next find something to write about on a regular basis. When you're passionate about a topic, finding subject matter should be easy enough. However, you likely are always in need of inspiration, especially when it comes to publishing fresh content. Blog posts can include news, insights, information, photos, lists, polls, questions, and almost any other form of content. Finding the content and subject matter that works best for your company can help you establish a strong publishing pace and keep your readers engaged. Being passionate about your subject matter adds value for the readers of your blog and keeps you interested in its maintenance. Because your company is certainly already passionate about its products and industry, your blog will let that passion shine through.

Build Blog Posts

The one thing that might hold up the blogging process from the beginning is that sudden feeling that you have nothing to write about. You may represent a vibrant company ripe with subject matter and industry expertise to share, but this feeling is a problem that even the most seasoned bloggers face. This is where having structure or a theme for your blog posts can come in handy. Creating a writing schedule or outlining a process for formulating your blog posts can save time and energy.

Themed Topics

A simple method for easing your way into blogging is to outline subject themes that you can use every day, once a week, twice a month, or in whatever timeline you prefer. Popular themes that appear once a week on blogs include the following:

- Wordless Wednesday: Publish a post with nothing but photos.
- Wine Wednesday: If you are in the food or beverage industry you can have a theme day on your blog such as Wine Wednesday, Fat-Free Friday, and so on.
- Theatre Thursday: Entertainment-focused blogs could feature a local theatre production.
- Follow Friday: Show your appreciation by highlighing a favorite partner, loyal customer, supplier, partner, or anyone you would like to showcase on your blog, suggesting that others "follow" this person or company on their blog or social networks. The Follow Friday is originally a Twitter theme where users post #FollowFriday or #FF in front of a user name of a company or individual they would recommend others follow.

Each of these themes can also have different authors, making everyone's workload lighter. An example is a real estate blog from a development company. One week's blog posts can be about commercial retail properties, while the next week in the month focuses on condominiums.

You may not even assign themes to specific days of the week or weeks of the month. You can have a general pool of topic ideas that you determine in advance and use as inspiration. General themes include "Top 10" lists or "How To" posts.

For a "Top" post (5, 10, 15), you can create a list in a blog post naming anything from your company's best-selling items that month to the best places to grab a working lunch around your head office (promoting your community or neighborhood). Using lists is a great way to encourage comments because everyone has an opinion about lists. Comments could range from agreeing whole-heartedly to sharing other items that could have been on your list. Either way, you get people engaging in a dialogue. You could have "Top 5 Fridays" or a "Top 20" list that you break up and publish as five items over the course of four weeks. Breaking up the list gives your blog readers a reason to return for the next installment to discover the remaining list items. "How To" posts are a great way to share your company's expertise and passion while offering up valuable tips to your blog audience. These posts could be weekly, monthly, or whenever the mood strikes. A plumbing company could have a "How to unclog a drain using green cleaning solutions" or even a "How to make your own green cleaning solutions for your home" blog post.

THEMES FOR YOUR THEMES

Spruce up theme posts with a logo or graphic portraying the theme name, or with general images, videos, and other multimedia.

Include Photos

Inspiration for a blog post can sometimes come from the most unlikely sources. People say "a picture is worth a thousand words," and in blogging, this can often ring true. An image can be an inspiration for an entire blog post, or it can be the blog post itself.

You might use a photo from a staff event in the community, a new product, an image sent in from a customer or client, or even a historic photo of your business' building. All these images can make for great blog post material. Photos can be placed at the top of a post to attract the readers' eyes, or they can be placed between paragraphs to split up chunks of text. Most blogging platforms include left align, right align, and other options, including fields in which you can provide a caption or photographer credit.

Use Your Own Photos

Upload your own image via your blogging platform or upload it to a photo-sharing site such as Flickr, 500px, or even Pinterest. It's always best to use your own images in a blog post because then you know the exact source and photographer, and you hold any and all licenses. It's also a great way to give readers a look at your company from the inside. Instead of using stock imagery or cartoon icons to illustrate a blog post, snap a photo yourself. Use a company camera, your own, or even your mobile phone.

Use Photos Sourced from Flickr

A benefit of using a photo from Flickr in your blog post is that you get to search Flickr by license, ensuring you are allowed to publish the image on your blog. Another benefit is that you are sourcing the image from a network that has millions of users who could potentially find their way to your blog post.

Flickr enables you to search its entire public database of images, uploaded by millions of users over the years, and using its "advanced search," you can specifically find images that have a Creative Commons License. This means the images that come up in search results have a license that lets you either share, rework, or redistribute the photo. The license also states the terms upon which you can share such as "attribution." This simply means that if you use an image from Flickr on your blog, you must link back to the original source and credit the photographer. On your blog post, you can include the photographer's name within the caption of the photo or somewhere else within the body of your post, as long as it's included.

Some photographers on Flickr also state a preference for attribution on their Flickr profile page. For example, John Smith could ask that you link his Flickr account as well as his website when you credit the image. Should you find an image you would like to use but it is marked as "All Rights Reserved," you can still send a message to the photographer on Flickr and ask permission to use the image. If you choose to use a photo from a Flickr user, you can leave a comment on that user's photo page—including a link back to your blog post—to let her know you have used her image. This comment notifies the owner of the use and shares your link to a wider audience. The other viewers of the image on Flickr can see your link, and the photographer could potentially share your link around, proud that her image was used by someone else.

Create Photo Contests

Contests of any kind can bring in new blog readers and help celebrate the ones you already have by generating buzz online—and offering a great reward. Crowdsourced content encourages participation in your blog and showcases your readers at the same time. For example, Libre Tea, a tea glass company based in British Columbia, combines a theme with a photo contest each month asking readers and customers to share their "tea moments" (http://libretea.com/tea-moments/). The company asks readers to submit a photo of their "tea moment" through Flickr, Facebook, or their blog. Through a random draw of all the entries received, Libre Tea selects prizewinners.

Your company could ask readers to submit a photo of themselves with a product or showing how they use the product or perhaps submit a photo of their neighborhood. You can determine prizes, which can range from company swag (for example, a logo-branded travel coffee mug) to a discount code to a gift card. Contests can be run weekly, monthly, or in other regular intervals. The contest blog posts will break up the text on your site and provide a variety of imagery that you may not normally have access to.

Find out more about Flickr uses, Flickr groups, and how to run contests on your blog in Chapter 9, "Getting Interactive with Multimedia Blogs."

Write Blogs for the Wider World

When you are creating content on a public blog, the goal is to attract readers and appeal to a wider audience. When you make your content interesting and then searchable, readers will not only find your blog but also stick around to see what else you have to share. The following subsections explore how to write your blog to gain exposure and a wider audience.

Create an Industry Resource Blog

Blog topics can cover everything from your own company news to industry updates and information. By supplying a wide scope of reading material and multimedia, your blog can become a one-stop shop for those seeking news and updates for content that pertains to your entire industry. Readers shouldn't need to go anywhere else if they've subscribed to your feed that is complete with a wide range of topics.

An example of an industry resource blog is a winery with a blog that updates its readers about varietals, seasonal offerings, and wine-making processes. By peppering in posts that include tips on wine making, maintaining vineyards, growing grapes, and profiling wine regions, the site becomes much more than a wine blog. Readership expands to those seeking material about wine in general, which you provide, and in turn, readers discover your business and product offerings. This concept can be applied to any business or industry.

By providing industry-wide information, and not just specifics about your own company, you can gain an audience perfectly tailored to your business. With your blog being an online hub, it connects you with current and potential customers by being a true all-in-one resource for your field. The blog also shows that your company is in touch with its industry and is keeping up with the latest news and trends. It fits in with the concept of opening up the floor for discussion with your customers and potential clients while catering to their need for information.

Blogging about the world outside your company (but still within your industry) can turn one-time readers into subscribers. Audiences are repeatedly drawn to blogs if they know they can get regular updates that are not only about a favorite company but also paired with practical tips and industry insights each time they visit.

We're not saying you need to spend exorbitant amounts of time and effort writing in-depth articles about the past, present, and future of your market. However, by providing useful information, data, facts, and links to other articles, you can help build your profile and presence online.

Whole Foods Markets, Natural and Organic Grocery, operates several online and social network presences and maintains a blog called The Whole Story. The blog features in-store events, offerings from the company such as recipes and coupon books, and highlights of partner growers. The blog also talks about food in general (see Figure 5.1).

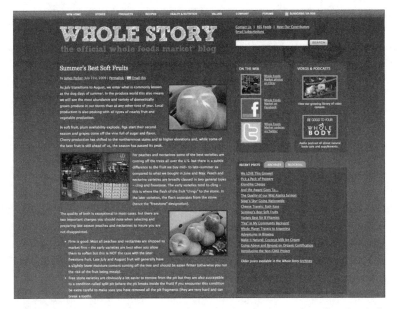

Figure 5.1 *Summer's Best Soft Fruits from The Whole Story, the Official Whole Foods Market blog.*

You can essentially go to any grocery store or market to purchase your ripe summer fruit; however, with an informative blog to remind you of seasonal treats, how to make your selection, and highlights of varieties, you may be more likely to visit the local Whole Foods. Nowhere in the blog post does it mention that Whole Foods has the best fruit. Instead, the site simply features the product (which is available at Whole Foods). Readers may conclude that if a market knows so much about fruit and other foods (enough to write about it and inform the world online), it would be worth a trip to one of the stores to check out these offerings.

By branching out and covering all things pertaining to your industry, your blog can bridge any physical distance between you and your customers and even answer questions before they're asked. For example, if you're in the clothing business and your customer service department receives several calls about how to water treat the jackets you sell, you could write a blog post about the process. In a written post or even a video, you can provide tools and tips for product care. By doing this, you provide interesting content for readers and an added-value service.

Public relations firm Hill & Knowlton operates a group blog with contributions from several staff members (see Figure 5.2). The staff also aggregate or republish content from other blogs that they find informative. Their spin on having a company blog introduces the client base to new elements of public relations. Each author from the company is given a biography page, and the content includes information, links, and interviews about how about to use social media in the public relations industry.

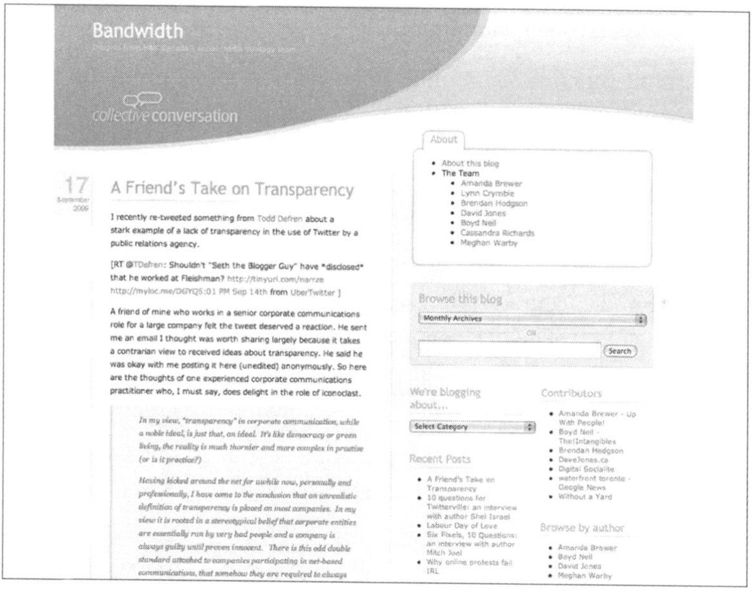

Figure 5.2   *Hill & Knowlton's Collective Conversation Bandwidth blog.*

Helpful and useful information you share in blog posts provides content for a specific audience of customers and clients and an entire world of potential connections who might just stumble across your post online. When you have this content on your blog, it will come up in Internet search results. Perhaps someone will search for "water treating jackets." Chances are, that person may just stumble across the blog post you published. By writing the post, using the proper keywords, and providing this extra content for your readers, you may introduce a whole new audience to your business through searches.

Create an Online Community

Although a blog is a part of your company's home on the Internet, the best way to grow your audience is to give your audience members a sense of ownership of the space. You do this by being open to discussions and hosting interactive content on your blog to create a strong online community.

In some cases, Internet users will create groups, fan pages, or their own blogs dedicated to various products or services they like. Opening up similar access and playgrounds for discussion in your own online space can work to your advantage. By having a community of readers, supporters, and individuals who share your links and content, you can amplify your message. The community might not necessarily be an actual page, forum, or comments section, but you'll find that your readers will become your blog's (and your company's) evangelists. Through that connection, they create a sense of community.

You can help nurture this community by having a blog that promotes conversation with comments, where the author is also engaged. You also need to share what you've posted by allowing readers to copy and paste your latest link to their social networking accounts, by bookmarking it, or by emailing it to their colleagues. If your blog generates its own community, it can also reach out to online spaces or social networks where other communities lie.

To branch out and encourage this cross-pollination of content, you can arm your community with the following blog-sharing tips:

- To ensure that the tools are available, provide links and "submit this" or "share this" buttons on your blog posts (see the AddThis service in Figure 5.3). Encourage readers to pass along your link through social bookmarking sites such as Digg, Delicious, Reddit, Newsvine, and Facebook.

- Twitter also has several plug-ins and widgets (such as Tweetmeme) that cut long blog post URLs into easy-to-share links that are short enough for the service's 140-character limit.

- Readers can also share content through their own blogs, should they also be online content producers. There are no other steps to provide if they want to link back to your post. However, be on the lookout for the trackback so that their link is visible from your site.

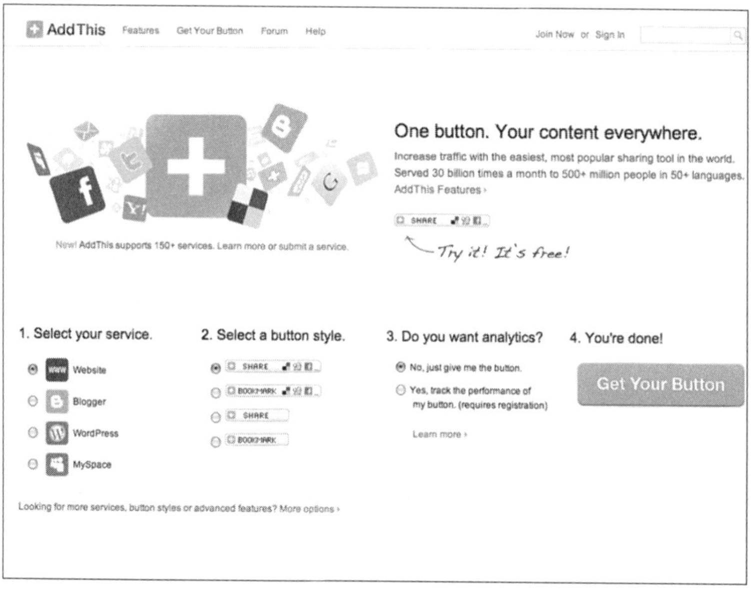

Figure 5.3 *AddThis bookmarking and sharing service for blogs.*

Providing your readers with these online sharing tools so that they can help spread your brand for you is a great way to expand your reach and draw others into your online community.

As evangelists for your blog, through sharing and promoting your content, your readers also become ambassadors of your brand. Arming these loyal followers can involve anything from providing the online space in which they can hold discussions (such as comment forms) to supplying promotional items (perhaps offering them a discount code). Your blog in some ways acts like a loyalty program, rewarding readers and the audience for stopping by through a coupon code or contest giveaways.

You can also give your brand ambassadors tools such as logo badges for their own site so they can indicate that they read or are a fan of your blog. You could also make your content easily shareable (for example, by posting your videos to YouTube or by using the previously mentioned bookmarking tools).

With your blog as the home base of conversations and content for your company, people can find the most accurate information they seek right from the source. As your links and posts are shared, you will draw a bigger and expanded audience to your community. And even though you might not have a profile on other networks where your links, posts, or images are being shared, if a reader submits your story to these services, the audiences there will be drawn back to your site to read the article.

According to a 2009 report by the social bookmarking website AddToAny.com, Facebook has replaced email as the number one way people share links to content online. According to the poll, 24% of the time someone passed along a link it was through Facebook, while 11% of the time it was by email, and Twitter link sharing accounted for 10.8%.

Create an Internal Blog (or Blogs) for Your Company

The ease of publishing content to a blog makes it an attractive platform for information sharing, whether in the public realm or privately on a closed intranet within a company. Users can add content, share links, and provide updates even if they are not shared with the public. Having this outlet can improve communications within a company and perhaps raise morale by promoting a job well done.

There are several ways that an internal or inward-facing company blog can benefit your company, including boosting communications, getting feedback, and helping promote the great work the employees carry out each day.

Keep People Informed

Blogs are public platforms that are highly visible and searchable. However, they can also serve an internal, private purpose. In the same way that business blogs can help share and build a community between the company and its customers, a company blog can also bridge gaps within the organization.

Keeping your employees up-to-date on projects and events helps to promote a healthy team environment. Currently, the standard communication tool for companies is email, along with internal memos, or perhaps proprietary messaging systems. When you take the information that might go into a mass email and publish it for the group in a closed online system, the data is more searchable while still reaching its intended audience.

Allowing employees to showcase their accomplishments, triumphs, and milestones with their peers is also a great morale booster. Promotions in companies are certainly events worth blogging and sharing with other team members. If a salesperson has a client success story to share or receives a recommendation or client testimonial, the blog is a great way to profile these achievements.

You can also use the blog to profile departments by posting company photos and biographies of new hires or long-standing employees. With large corporations, some departments rarely interact. This could leave you wondering what role the dozen other people in the lunchroom with you play in their daily lives with the company. Having an internal blog can put names to faces more effectively than the annual company picnic.

Communications from all branches can include

- Notes from HR about company policies or social events such as birthdays
- A message from the CEO about company changes, updates, or even a holiday greeting
- A posting from the administration about things happening in the company's building such as a monthly fire drill
- Updates on projects to keep everyone in the loop
- Hosting contests for employees or an online poll. For example, "Name the new product" or "Help us choose the new logo."

Departments can also be featured with photo galleries and biographies, if that information is free to share. Those involved with specific projects can also use the blog to not only post updates but also ask questions of their team. The comments section can be used to brainstorm and provide feedback while the blog post-publishing platform can share text, images, and links that may prove useful to the team.

Internal Blogs for Project Management

As with a regular business blog, an internal site must still remain professional and have the main goal of building your business, only from the inside out. It won't replace water-cooler chat, but it can give employees a safe, comfortable, team-oriented environment online where they can keep themselves current on the inner workings of their nine-to-five.

Be sure to create a set of guidelines for the blog (for example, what is acceptable content to share and rules for commenting). Assign a team member to moderate the blog, looking for comments and content to update and making sure the site runs smoothly for all. You will also want the IT department on your side to ensure the internal site is not accessible from outside the company, especially if content pertains to sensitive or private product information.

An internal company blog is not a chat room and should not impede anyone's daily workflow. It is simply a resource on which professional information is shared within a department or companywide.

This blog could also help others collaborate on projects. For example, an image (design spec, potential logo, and so forth) could be shared, and employees could comment and leave constructive feedback. This would be quicker than emailing the image around, and all feedback would be in the same place (in the blog comments). The blog should be open to include all departments, and after it is set up, communications should be sent around as an introduction and encourage others to participate. For example, if Marketing begins an internal blog, this information should be communicated to other departments, and other teams should also feel welcome to contribute.

Internally, a project blog helps track updates, tasks, and progress of a team effort. Various members can post content, comment, and provide input instantly. Issues can be tracked and searched, and the entire project can be documented in a simple, easy-to-read format enabled for multimedia.

Multimedia that can be published on blog posts includes photos and videos, and most video-sharing services offer an embed code. This piece of text can be copied and pasted into a blog post to display a video player. If the video is not to be shared publicly, teams can upload video files through the blogging platform. The subject of these videos could be demonstrations, interviews, or product-related promotional content.

Internal blogs provide communication solutions for developers, sales teams, management, and all other employees of a company. Even though the platform itself is meant to be public and searchable, these same features can benefit your company in terms of productivity.

Departments can publish and track updates on projects and even employee news and announcements. Sharing information in real time and providing updates enables an entire workgroup or company to increase productivity through communication. Feedback can be provided in a secure environment that all can see, without flooding email inboxes, and your company can have fully chronicled project notes.

Internal blogs with multiple authors (perhaps one from each department, with a central moderator) can keep everyone informed, promote projects, feature work, and showcase your valued employees.

Product Blog (External)

Having either an internal or external blog for a specific project or product enables you to showcase exciting developments, partnerships, and announcements with the world. Publicly, if the company's privacy policies allow, you can essentially go from documenting the development stage of a product to building buzz about its progress and announcing its launch for your audience on your blog.

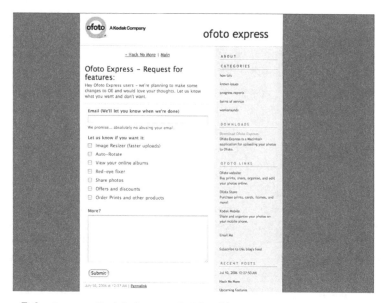

Figure 5.4   *Eastman Kodak Company's Ofoto blog.*

Blog posts for Ofoto include updates, known issues, and upgrade announcements (see Figure 5.4). Users can leave comments to provide feedback, if the information was useful, for example, or to suggest new features they would like to see provided with the service. Because the service is public, it's only natural that the company keep the public informed of upgrades and updates. Ofoto also welcomes suggestions and respond to feedback in the comments section of the blog.

If committing to following and tracking a specific project or product on your blog, be sure to keep the content fresh by updating when new discoveries, updates, or changes are made. Be dedicated to following the entire life cycle.

Public project blogs should also not go dormant after a project is complete. You'll often see campaigns that use campaign-specific slogans as domain names. After the specific promotion runs its course, however, readers and customers do not have a reason to return to that site. To avoid this instant burnout, you can use your blogging platform's tags or category systems to classify all posts pertaining to the project (instead of creating a distinct domain).

When publishing a blog post, you can provide the author several options. You enter a title, content for the post, perhaps add an image, and also select tags or categories. By using these classification systems, the blog platform sorts your content, which makes it easy for readers to search archives and helps it get picked up in search engine results. Tags and categories are created by the author and saved so that later the author can simply check the box next to an existing tag and add the post to that classification.

For example, a blog post about a new vehicle could be tagged using the words *convertible, roadsters, performance*. In the future, whenever another post is written about this vehicle or a similar vehicle, the tags and categories can be checked so that the post is classified within the same searchable directory. Most blog platforms also create specific URLs for tags and categories. This way, you can go to http://yourcompanyblog.com/tag/convertible to see all posts tagged as "convertible."

Tags and categories provide a way of classifying your blog posts. Each tag and category receives its own link (for example, http://yourblog/category/umbrellas). Thus, readers can follow posts about a product that interests them, and they can also see all archived content for this item.

Tags and categories can also be assigned their own RSS feeds so that readers can subscribe to all your content that is specifically tagged with a topic they want to follow. RSS, or Really Simple Syndication, is a way of subscribing to a blog or specific post categories. Readers can obtain this special link by clicking an RSS icon or "subscribe" link. Readers can then input this link into a feed reader, such as Google Reader, through which they can be instantly notified of news on the blogs they are following. The idea is that updates come to your feed reader inbox like unread emails so that you don't have to go out to each site and check whether there is new content.

Case Study: Procter & Gamble's Man of the House

Procter & Gamble's *Man of the House* (http://manofthehouse.com/) is an online magazine for the "real man." It also has a blog component, although many of the magazine articles online can also translate well as blog posts (see Figure 5.5).

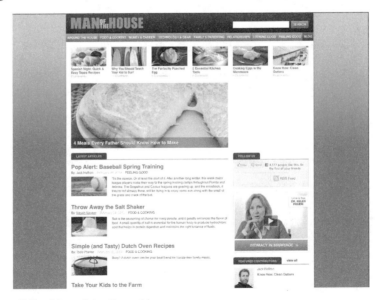

Figure 5.5 *Man of the House blog.*

The About page states that *Man of The House* is not "one of those magazines you have to hide from your wife or boss." It provides information and daily tips on everything from fatherhood to boneless skinless chicken breast preparation.

Various themes flow throughout the site under general category headings such as Around the House, Food & Cooking, Money & Career, Technology & Gear, Family & Parenting, Relationships, Looking Good, and Feeling Good. Under each of these categories lie subcategories of content. Under Food & Cooking alone, you can find Basics, Easy Recipes, Grilling, Eating Better, For the Kids, and Kitchen Gadgets. With so many themes, including "Your Weekly Sandwich," a cast of more than 30 authors (including several women) keeps fresh and lively content flowing through its online pages.

Case Study: CafePress

CafePress is simply described as an online print shop where everyday designers can have their images or brands added to a variety of clothing and accessories; it also serves as an e-store for these products.

Through the blog (blog.cafepress.com), CafePress engages customers by showcasing vendors, designers, and online shops where user-generated designs appear.

For Halloween 2011, the blog launched "A Photo Contest to Quench Your Halloween Thirst!" campaign (see Figure 5.6).

Figure 5.6   *"A Photo Contest to Quench Your Halloween Thirst!" at CafePress blog.*

In this case, the blog asked readers to submit photos of their pets or children in their favorite Halloween costumes. The readers' prize was getting their own photo mug printed up, using the image they submitted. Users were then directed to Facebook to upload their image and for the voting round. Those who didn't participate could still vote on their favorite image and have their say in the contest. CafePress handed out free printed mug prizes to the top 25 photos, as voted on by the public.

With graphics and visuals being the core aspect of the CafePress business, photo contests (and recently Pinterest board contests) have been successful in generating traffic and interest in its services.

Summary

In blogging, content is king. You can have great search terms that draw people in from search engines, but the key is to have content that keeps the readers captivated and motivated to return to your site or subscribe. The way in which you present your content helps engage your audience and encourage them to participate or become a part of your project. In this regard, blogs can be used internally for company use, or they can be public-facing to promote and get exposure for your products, projects, and content.

Now that you have a few ideas when it comes to content and timing for your posts, you can start to think about how that content will be presented. The following chapter will help all of your hard work look as well as it reads.

6

Designing Your Blog

After you have your content in mind, presenting your posts in an easy-to-read format helps the reader navigate through your site. You want to welcome readers to your blog with an eye-pleasing layout, allowing them to spot post titles, tags, or categories; do searches; and get all of the information they came for. The easier your blog is on the eyes, the longer your readers will stay on your page and the more likely they will be to share your posts and recommend your content to their peers.

Understanding the Function of Your Blog

Whether you've decided on a fully customized layout or a theme to match your current website or marketing material, there are actually thousands of options and tools to assist you in getting just the right look for your blog. You can either use professional design resources or do a one-click install of a beautifully laid-out theme. The visuals of a blog are paramount in showcasing your content in a clean and easy-to-read format. The following sections discuss how you can incorporate function into design.

Readability Is Functionality

In the digital age, attention spans are slim, and multimedia captures more eyeballs than blocks of text. When you are composing blog posts, be aware of your word counts and try to break up large chunks of text on the screen with images, logos, icons, or video embeds. Keeping the readers' attention is as simple as writing content that gets straight to the point and leaves them wanting more, whether by coming back to check out the next post or by leaving a comment to continue the discussion with the author.

The Functions of Color and Text

Website design also has a lot to do with content being readable. As noted previously, up-to-date content also attracts readers, so your latest content should be at the top of your blog. If your most recent post is from two months ago, readers may not become engaged with your site, knowing that it is not current. An effective blogger should write a new post at least once a week.

Blog layouts should feature your core content by displaying it in the clearest manner possible. Your content should fit nicely on your blog layout without expanding too far across the page, causing readers to scroll left to right. Content can also be presented alongside an image or thumbnail so that the text is broken up, making it easier on the eyes than a single block of text.

Tiled image backgrounds, faint yellow text on a white background, or colors that are too bright may turn readers off your content before they get a chance to read it.

Choosing colors for your blog that complement its theme, design, or your corporate branding can ensure a consistent design. If you have a black blog background, white is probably your best bet for clarity and readability; the opposite then applies to a blog with a white background. Contrasting colors make the text easier to read (see Figure 6.1). You may also want to choose a typeface that is easy to read, such as a sans-serif font, as opposed to a cursive font such as Comic Sans.

Size is one of the most important factors when it comes to selecting your typeface. According to an article by Smashing Magazine in 2001 (http://www.smashing-magazine.com/2011/10/07/16-pixels-body-copy-anything-less-costly-mistake/) the author presents several reasons why a larger font size is beneficial:

- "The distance at which we can read letters is a common measure of both legibility and reading speed. The greater the distance, the higher the overall legibility and comprehension are considered to be. The biggest factor that determines how far this distance can increase is font size."

- "Most people, when sitting comfortably, are about 20 to 23 inches from their computer screens. In fact, 28 inches is the recommended distance, because this is where vergence is sufficiently low to avoid eye strain. This is much further than the distance at which we read printed text—most people do not hold magazines at arm's length!"

Figure 6.1   *Choose a font and color scheme that is easy to read and easy on the eyes.*

Make sure your hyperlinks are underlined, bold, or a slightly different shade of font color. Your readers will immediately know when text is linked if it is displayed in this manner. You can also configure your design to have hyperlinked text or images change slightly when readers hover their cursor over it.

Read other blogs to help you write yours. You can use any of your favorite blogs as reference points. Determine what designs or layouts are most enjoyable for you to read and go from there on your own site. We discuss this topic later in the chapter, but doing online searches for blogs containing keywords that interest you is a good way to start finding favorites.

Designing for Your Blog Audience

You don't need to be a graphic designer or artist to appreciate a good-looking blog theme. You should make sure things are easy to find, easy to read, and visually engaging in some way.

When it comes to layout—using an analog comparison—you'll want your content to be "above the fold" on a website. When people arrive, no matter what size screen they are using (laptop, mobile, desktop), your content should be right there for them to read. You don't want readers to find your site and then spend the next few seconds scrolling down to find what they actually came to read.

Here are some things that might go through a reader's mind upon arriving at your blog:

- Can I find the story I want to read right away?
- Is it easy to read and easy on the eyes?
- Does it have images and graphics to break up chunks of text?
- Does the site automatically play a loud video or audio track? Is it impossible to find the "off" or "mute" button?

You might have a similar unconscious list of criteria upon landing on a website or blog page. You should make your posts easy to read through a clean and catching layout and by showcasing your content.

Just as thought is put into the content or tone of a blog, or even its authors, it should also be given to the layout and design. You have several options to consider when selecting a design or layout for your blog, including these:

- **Match your main website:** You can design your blog to match your website exactly, regardless of the blogging platform you have decided to use. Color, font, column layout, and so on can seamlessly integrate your blog with your company's main website.

- **Customize your design but make it appear to be part of our company's brand:** You can select a fully customized design unique to the blog using your current collateral, logos, fonts, and colors. It can still appear to be a part of your company's branding but have an original feel to differentiate it from your main website.

- **Create an original design:** You can decide on a completely unique design or theme layout as a departure from anything your company has published before. You need to ensure that logos and branding are present to let the readers know that the blog falls under your company's umbrella. However the layout of the blog, colors, and font could all be different.

With each of these options, it's important to know the audience for whom you are publishing the blog, which would ultimately be your customers.

If it is directed at children, perhaps bright colors are in order. For an international audience, you need to consider translation options such as Google Translation integration or a plug-in that can be added to your blogging software to give the readers language options. Your blog readers are the same people who purchase your product or services so naturally the presentation of the content should have them in mind.

Finding Themes and Templates

All bloggers want their piece of the blogging web to be unique, attract readers, and reflect their content. This can be achieved using some of the tools that come packaged with your blogging software. In some cases, this step—to apply a theme to your blog—is as simple as clicking a button. The following subsections look at blogging software themes and how to use them.

WordPress

WordPress.com has thousands of free themes as well as selected premium themes available for purchase. When setting up your account, you can use the default theme and customize its elements (header image, background, and so on) or select a theme from the online database, as shown in Figure 6.2. You access this directory by logging in to your blog, going to your main Dashboard, and clicking Appearance. The Theme options are displayed. You can then click to preview what your blog would look like with a new theme and apply once you have made a choice.

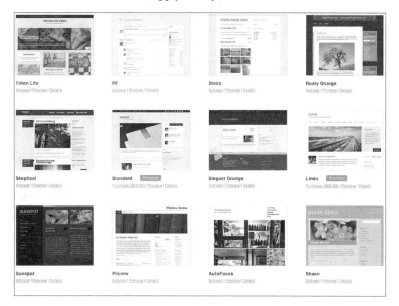

Figure 6.2   *WordPress.com Theme directory.*

You can search the themes by column layout, colors, theme designer, or with key-words such as *photography* or *magazine*. The results display themes that have tags or keywords associated with your search terms.

If you are using WordPress as a self-hosted application—the version of WordPress that is downloaded and hosted on a server (yours or a hosting provider's)—you also have theme options. You can also search the WordPress theme database for free or premium themes by going to Appearances then Themes from your WordPress dashboard.

You can find WordPress themes at http://wordpress.org/extend/themes. As with the WordPress.com theme directory, you can search for a theme for your blog using keywords, layout options, and more. WordPress.com's theme directory within your site's dashboard will present you with a pre-determined set of available themes for your site. However within your custom WordPress application (from WordPress.org) you will be able to search through thousands of submitted themes using criterion such as number of columns, color layer, theme author, and more.

You can also develop a theme in-house or hire a WordPress theme developer to design a custom theme for your blog. With the self-hosted WordPress application you have more theme possibilities because you can build a theme from scratch. For example, instead of purchasing a new motor for your car (the car being your WordPress application) you can have someone assemble a custom motor for you from parts. The benefit to doing this yourself (or most likely hiring a theme devel-oper to do this for you) is that you can create a completely unique-looking blog, tailored perfectly for your brand.

Tumblr

Tumblr's theme options (at http://www.tumblr.com/themes/) are sorted by the date the theme was posted, its popularity, whether they are premium (must be purchased), or whether they are featured. Tumblr also posts the number of users currently using a specific theme, and in some cases that number reaches into the millions.

If you are starting your company blog on Tumblr, you can select a theme from the directory and apply it to your site with the click of the mouse. To get to your theme, log in and click on Preferences and then click Customize. Tumblr then offers an HTML editor view, as shown in Figure 6.3, where you can make edits if you are comfortable using HTML.

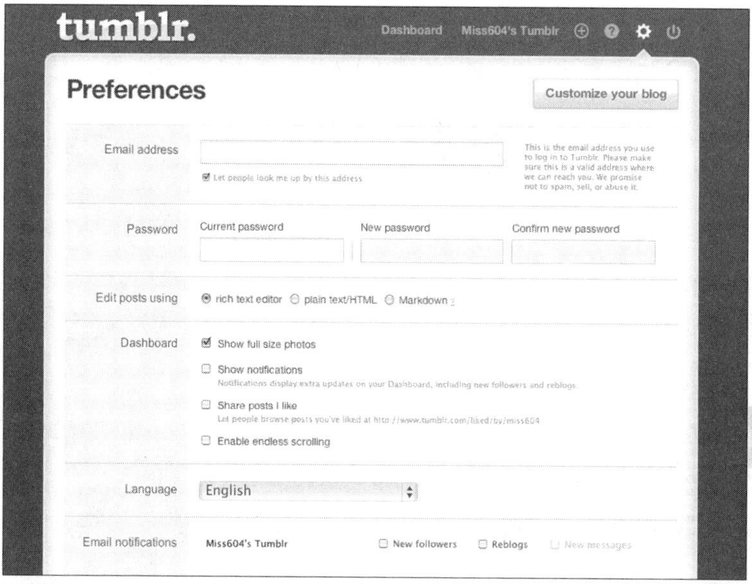

Figure 6.3   *Tumblr's theme customization options.*

Depending on the theme you select, you might be able to edit elements such as the text color, link color, header color, or mobile options.

The customization view does have a What You See Is What You Get (WYSIWYG) editor if you are not comfortable with HTML code. This enables you to select the color "red" and watch it get applied to your blog on the fly. These settings can then be saved or discarded.

Blogger

As with Tumblr and WordPress, Blogger offers an array of preset, free themes that are available in an online directory. There is also an option to edit the HTML code of your theme to apply a custom look to your site.

In your Blogger dashboard or home screen, after you log in, you see a tab labeled Template, as shown in Figure 6.4.

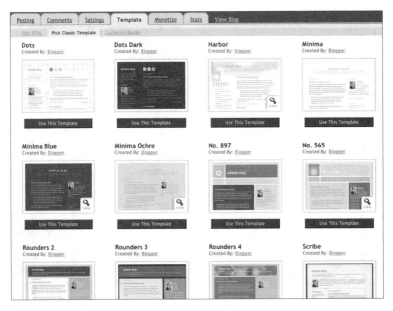

Figure 6.4 *Blogger template options.*

At the top of the Template tab, you can choose options that enable you to edit the HTML code of your current template, apply a new custom template, or pick a classic template. If you select a classic template, you can still edit the HTML code if you want to customize some of the elements.

Other Blog Platforms

A general feature of a blogging platform is its offer of free or premium themes that may be customizable. When selecting a theme for your company's blog, you can choose the layout that 500,000 other users have applied—which could be for good reason because it may be the most clean and crisp design offered—or you can opt for customization. Choosing a suitable base theme, no matter how many other users have applied it, is the best place to start. Customization can follow based on your company's specific needs and vision for the blog. Although many themes are free, getting something custom or more unique and standing out in the crowd may be worth spending a few extra dollars.

Tips for Editing Your Theme to Drive Business

A well-designed theme can be the key to keeping readers on your blog, and maintaining them as an audience—and ultimately as a customer. We shouldn't judge a book by its cover but frankly, most do. Think of how many people purchase a bottle of wine based on its label alone. Does the art speak to you? Is it amusing?

Is is appealing? You have the ability to keep readers on your blog from that ever-important first impression to that 300th return visit from an active member of your commenting community.

When you select a template theme for your site that 20,000 others are using you know it has appeal. You won't want to tinker with its settings and you may not even know how but there are a few things you can do yourself. The following discusses how you can decide what to do yourself and what you may need to hire a professional theme developer to do.

Doing It Yourself

You can do many small updates yourself such as changing the header of your site. The header is the large banner image or logo at the top of the page. Most blogging platforms that provide template themes also allow you to change your header image. The ideal dimensions for the image are usually listed and you can upload an image directly from your computer to have it appear at the top of your site. The process is similar to attaching a photo to an email. Remember, it's your cover image so make sure it looks great and represents your blog and your company.

Other edits that you can do on your own include changing the font size, color, and weight (bold or italic) on a per-post basis and updating sidebars (like in Blogger and WordPress).

Hiring a Professional

You should hire a professional to handle theme updates if you are uncomfortable with doing them yourself, if you have little or no knowledge of HTML or CSS, and if you want something of high quality that is beyond your scope of expertise.

Professional theme developers can help you with a template theme or build one for you if you have decided not to go with a theme that is readily available through your blogging platform's directory.

You can do a Google search for a firm in your area including your specific blog platform, such as "WordPress Theme Developers in Seattle." Look through its websites, at its client showcase (the firm should feature work it has done), and see whether it's a fit for you.

Case Studies

The Webby Awards (http://www.webbyawards.com/), established in 1996 to honor excellence on the web, has two categories for design: Aesthetic and Function. You can obtain both of these elements on your blog whether you create a custom theme or are using one of the thousands that are available for free in various blog platform directories.

Tumblr Staff Blog

The Tumblr Staff Blog (http://staff.tumblr.com/) has a clear message: Celebrate blogging, celebrate staff, and keep users up-to-date on policies and services. That message is not actually written on the blog, but it will become clear to any average reader upon visiting. The main tags (keywords that help sort the content on the site) are "Spotlights," "Features," "Events," and "Community."

More than 100 team members are listed on the sidebar with links to each member's Tumblr blog, and blog posts are published at a rate of about two a week. It would make sense for a blogging platform to use one of its own themes for its blog, and that's what the Tumblr staff have done. The default Tumblr theme is applied to the Tumblr Staff Blog, and theme elements, such as posts that can have a yellow notebook paper background, are used for specific post types. For example, the Tumblr Staff Blog profiles Tumblr blogs around the world. For these profiles, the blog uses the yellow notebook paper background to make them stand out (see Figure 6.5).

Figure 6.5 *Tumblr Staff Blog feature of another Tumblr blog.*

Naturally, a great way to promote your service is to use your service. Tumblr uses its blog to showcase other Tumblr users. Other industries and companies can use this same method. If you provide video services, post videos on your blog. Companies that do not live in the digital realm can use a bit of a different approach to apply the same concept. The layout and theme of your site can reflect this for you. If you have a tree-trimming service, for example, you might want your site to have shades of green, leaves, evergreen silhouettes, and more of a nature theme. The look and feel of your site should reflect your business and the impression you would like to make through the blog. Celebrate your industry and services through the look and feel of your site.

Case Study: Ree Hammond, Pioneer Woman

Ree Hammond is a writer, photographer, author, television host, and mother of four. She started The Pioneer Woman (http://thepioneerwoman.com)—shown in Figure 6.6—in 2006 using a Blogger account to blog about her "long transition from spoiled city girl to domestic country wife." The Pioneer Woman has since earned her Weblog of the Year titles in the 2011, 2010, and 2009 Bloggie Awards.

Figure 6.6 *The Pioneer Woman main page.*

Ree is also the author of the #1 best-selling cookbook *The Pioneer Woman Cooks: Recipes from an Accidental Country Girl* and the 2011 memoir *Black Heels to Tractor Wheels—A Love Story,* which debuted at #2 on The New York Times Bestsellers nonfiction hardcover list. She also received a Bloggie Award in 2011 for Best Design on her blog.

Her commitment to the blog (and the millions of page views that ensued) opened up opportunities such as becoming a Food Network host and published cookbook author. Now, the blog is not only an online resource, it has become a main source for book sales and other profitable opportunities and design elements have played a large role.

In 2011, she told the Huffington Post (http://www.huffingtonpost.com/2011/08/26/ree-drummond-pioneer-woman-food-network_n_937724.html) about how and why she began using more photos in her posts. "I was getting ready to cook my husband a steak, and I thought, 'I've blogged about every other thing I've done, so I'll blog some photos of the steak.... I wound up posting 12 or 13 photos, and the response was really favorable. Even if somebody already knew how to cook a steak, they enjoyed watching it unfold through pictures."

The Pioneer Woman is laid out with categories across the top of the page, with a drop-down menu of sub categories for easy reference. Photography plays a major role in promoting featured content and articles are previewed with an excerpt and thumbnail image on the main page. Ree's unique point of view combined with solid writing and beautiful pictures of food and scenery help her drive her career, which has evolved into television and cookbook publishing.

Summary

The layout and theme of a blog can truly make your content shine, delivering the information in a way that readers can easily read it and share it. Blogging platforms allow you to use free tools and themes or go the extra mile and fully customize your blog, either to stay consistent with brand messaging or truly *Wow!* your audience. You can find more details about attracting readers to your blog in Chapter 8, "Getting Eyeballs to Your Blog."

7

Who Will
Write the Blog?

A business blog requires passion and dedication. After all, you must produce quality content on a regular basis. In companies of any size, finding someone to manage this task can sometimes prove difficult. Some companies assign responsibility for the blog to an existing employee or department, making it everyone's responsibility but moderated by a single individual. Other companies hire someone to specifically handle their social media strategy and profiles.

Writing from Within a Company

A common question asked when companies consider starting a blog for their business is this: Who will author it? Companies have several options for this, but the optimal scenario under any option is to find someone willing to take on authoring responsibility. You need dynamic content that can be updated often, so finding room in existing job descriptions might not be easy.

When looking for a contributing writer, remember that someone who is passionate about a subject will provide the best content about that subject. (And readers can pick up on an author's passion and willingness to share on a blog.) Topics flow smoothly, discussions are created, and the author's enthusiasm for the subject matter becomes contagious.

The job of writing for a blog can be added to the author's job description. That description can note how many posts are required each week and any moderation duties. However, running a blog consists of much more than composing posts. You need to decide whether your author will take on the rest of the responsibilities that come with overseeing a blog. These responsibilities include coming up with content ideas, moderating comments, tracking statistics and metrics, setting up alerts online to monitor feedback, and so on. The author you use might not be the best fit for this entire scope of work. Therefore, having a separate person in charge of your social media plan might be necessary.

If you assign these management tasks to someone else, your authors can then focus on content. You may even want to create a Director of Social Media position so that one team member can manage social media elements and possibly gather material from multiple authors while monitoring the success and reach of the blog. Without a position such as this, management of the blog could inhibit the author's creative output or might put too much on the author's plate if she is an existing employee who has expanded her job description. An entire department can also manage various tasks pertaining to the blog or take turns writing posts from different points of view.

Identifying Authors

An important step when starting out with a blog is to introduce the audience to the author. This can be done in the first blog post, on a page called "About" or in the sidebar of the blog.

Putting a name to a passage and having a subsequent biography page for that name allows readers to see where exactly the information is coming from within the company. This information provides context and a more personalized look at the content that is presented.

Blog posts should convey the voice of their author, who should have a specific username assigned. When you sign up for a blogging service, Admin is usually the default username. However, you can assign your own chosen username to a blog account. After setting up the blog, just change Admin to a writer's name. Doing so not only adds security (because Admin is the most common username on blogs) but also adds a level of personalization. Nothing makes a blog post seem more insincere than when it is signed Admin (and not by a "real" person in the company).

After you have your main administrator account set up, add more authors or begin blogging under the personalized author profile. Figure 7.1 shows more authors being added with WordPress.

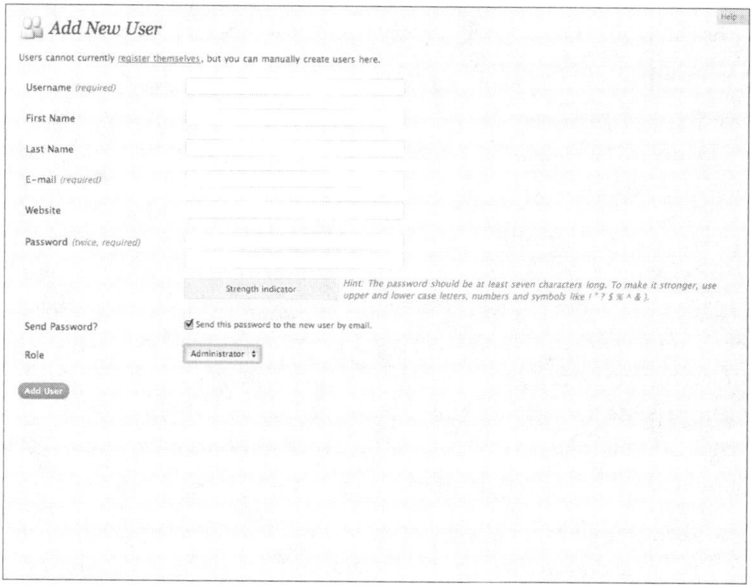

Figure 7.1   *Adding a new user on WordPress.org.*

Your blog's About page (or Biography or Author page) should contain the names of the contributors and a few lines about their involvement with the company. This page can include their name, title, location (if the company has multiple offices), and sometimes a personalized icon called an avatar. This avatar can be set up to appear next to blog posts that are written by the blog's authors, helping the readers easily identify the writer of the post.

Multiple Authors

Having multiple authors is a great way to give depth to your blog's content while also saving some time with more than one contributor. By assigning multiple authors, you not only give many voices to the blog but also get a more personal delivery of the specific content the specialized authors supply.

If more than one person from a department contributes to the blog, be sure to have appropriate author names and profiles in place for each. You do want to let your readers know who is "speaking" to them. In addition, crediting authors may lend credibility to blog posts, too. For example, a blog post by the CEO of the company will carry more weight than one written by an intern. In the same vein, a blog post written by "Bob in I.T." about a system status update will also be more applicable and personal to the reader than a system status update from "Tina in Sales."

A real-world example would be Southwest Airlines' "Nuts About Southwest" blog (www.blogsouthwest.com/) that boasts more than 30 contributing bloggers. The authors range from Multimedia Manager Rich Matthews, who contributes video posts through embedded YouTube videos; Joe Gautille, who has been a pilot with Southwest since 1994; and Lead Planner Bill Owen, who shares posts about the air-line's schedules, equipment types, and more.

Because Southwest has been blogging since 2006, the company even has retired bloggers who are labeled as "Original Bloggers" on its "Meet the Team" page (www.blogsouthwest.com/team).

If you have multiple contributors, you can profile the entire team on the site. Doing so may draw attention to the diversity of the content and the multiple voices from the company that are represented on the blog. Readers may also become fans of certain authors on the blog, so having RSS feeds set up for each author can help readers customize their interaction with the blog and its authors. Most blogging platforms provide RSS feed capability based on author, category, or tags. You can also syndicate your blog or use feed services such as FeedBurner, which helps you create and track statistics on multiple feeds for your website.

RSS feeds are created by blogging platforms so that readers can subscribe to the content. Subscribers can then receive instant notification by using a feed-reading service such as Google Reader whenever a new post is published. Blogging plat-forms such as WordPress automatically supply an entire site feed as well as a feed for each author or category.

> ✉ **Note**
>
> If frequently posting content is a concern, consider having a higher number of contributors. Although this adds many voices to your blog, it can divvy up the workload so that six team members could each have a light schedule by post-ing once a week, but that would equal at least six posts on your blog.

The Marketing Department

As mentioned previously, the best person to write the blog is someone who is passionate about the subject matter. Starting out with someone in the marketing department would be a good fit. Marketing and communications professionals know how to address clients (and potential customers) while keeping the best interests of the company in mind, so this department is a good fit for managing the blog. In addition, blog writing should be consistent, personable, thought provoking, and interesting to the readers.

Composing a blog post isn't entirely different from preparing a press release. The biggest difference is in the messaging and the personality of the writing. For example, to complement a press release about a new product launch, you might hear the thoughts of "Jennifer from Marketing" on the matter. Her thoughts about this latest release or its specific campaign can be expressed in the blog, perhaps using her enthusiasm to pass along the company's excitement to the consumer.

Key elements of a press release include the headline; the subject line; the release body; the who, what, when, where, and why; company information; and contact information. Releases are tailored at news agencies to get picked up and are "to the point" in the hopes that larger stories will grow from these resources. Blog posts should also have keyword-rich headlines. However, the content should be used to inform and generate a discussion. Blog messaging can work in tandem with news releases to capture the attention of the online audience, while the release heads out to the rest of the world through various dissemination channels. Blog posts are usually published immediately, but several blog publishing platforms also enable you to configure them for publication at a future date (much like embargoed press releases). They can also be edited at any time, which makes them more flexible than press releases. For example, if there is a typo on the release or perhaps the wrong contact information was given, the company needs to contact the newswire and issue a correction. With a blog post, you instantly have access to your published content and can edit it as necessary on the spot, providing the most up-to-date information for your business as needed.

Blog responsibilities can be shared among an entire group of people (from any department) or be assigned to a single person. Knowledge of the marketplace, the consumers, and the industry help build a blog's presence online, and so the marketing team is a great place to start.

The marketing department can be vital to a blog's existence, especially in the early days after a blog's creation. Logos, messaging, header images, and branding need to be considered; these are the marketing department's specialty. These branding elements might differ from existing company standards because they can be made to look more social media friendly. So, a customized Twitter logo with the company's username might be used, for example, along with a custom Facebook page icon. You may find that those who are already tasked with getting the business message out, such as those in the marketing department, will be willing to work on a blog. The blog will complement and evolve their existing messaging and tailor it to an online-specific audience. There, again, your marketing department is the first place to look!

Client Services and Tech Support

Search engines such as Google are becoming the "go-to" source when people need information about something. Therefore, a blog that's searchable (and findable) will lead those seeking information about your industry or products directly to your site. Remember, too, that you can leverage client services skills on your blog; the folks in this department already know how to converse with customers. These professionals will quickly understand how to moderate comments and publish concise and comprehensible posts. Client services can answer frequently asked questions or perhaps contribute content about product care and maintenance.

You might not want to burden existing staff with additional tasks (such as writing a blog post), but you do want their valuable input. If you have a Director of Social Media in place or a team of authors, these people should reach out to the existing staff to help target messaging.

When creating content for a site, the blog's manager can contact client services to find out common customer queries. Each of these questions is fuel for a blog post. Such blog posts then provide answers to readers before they even ask the questions (at least in this forum).

If your company provides forms or documents online, you might want to post details about how to fill them out properly. If you have an accounting firm, you can post tax tips for individuals or ways to contact the IRS. If your business cleans gutters, you can post ways to keep leaves from clogging drains.

Such customer assistance provided in blog posts doesn't take business away from your company. Instead, it shows that your business cares about educating its customers and making sure they have all the pertinent information necessary to troubleshoot problems before having to escalate the issues.

This subject matter can be collected from the client services department and then composed in a blog post either by the designated author or someone in the department. Remember that you want to convey credibility via the writer's profile. So, for example, a post about how to install a program on your computer written by someone in the supplier's client services department will have more credibility than an anonymous or Admin-signed post.

Tech support is also a good department to turn to for blog input. When an issue arises, this department can post updates, thus allowing the blog to become a support resource (without interminable wait times on the phone or at a "genius" bar). As with client services, posts published by writers from tech support will be credible within their domain of expertise. Online updates about services will empower your client base and serve as a selling point for potential customers.

If your company offers a service that requires status updates and support, you can task tech support with updating its own section of the blog. When services go offline, systems go down, or an outage occurs, customers and clients will go online to try to find information about the problem. Your blog can be the home for such critical updates, informing people fast. Many website hosting services provide these status update blogs and services (for example, the microblogging platform Twitter). In August 2009, Twitter was hit with a direct denial-of-service attack that caused the system to stop functioning for millions of users. Fortunately, Twitter had http://status.twitter.com up and running and so could provide updates for users who could not reach the service.

Authentic Content

Business blogs may also feature employees or officers of a company writing about their professional experiences. An example is John Heald, Senior Cruise Director with Carnival Cruise Lines. Whereas Heald notes on his blog that it is a personal account, he openly discloses his position with Carnival Cruise Lines and discusses all aspects of his life as a cruise director (see Figure 7.2). Heald's blog is promoted and linked from Carnival.com and is also syndicated on Carnival's official "Blogs" page as a resource under the heading "Fun Online."

Figure 7.2   *JohnHealdsBlog.com—Carnival's Senior Cruise Director.*

If each department does not have time to compose posts, a single coordinator can collect articles written by contributors throughout the company and publish those on the blog. In either case, it is important to remain transparent, noting the original authors and sources of the piece. Ghost writers are not recommended; you don't want readers to feel misled or betrayed. Because audiences online value authenticity, such feelings may lead to social media backlash that can include negative blog posts about the content, negative comments on Twitter, or grassroots online campaigns to dissuade others from reading disingenuous content.

Consider the case of a person reading a blog post by the president of a company. That reader then communicates with the president, but only later finds out that the president of the company had nothing to do with the post. That reader feels betrayed. This sense of betrayal exists because blogs make writers seem personal and approachable, which might not otherwise be the case. Consider Oprah, for example. Within the first week of signing up for Twitter, she had more than one million followers. Perhaps people wanted to show her they were fans, or maybe people wanted to see and read updates directly from the talk show host herself. Her name attached to even the most mundane update creates a thrill for those looking to connect with her. In some cases, a team of people post updates on behalf of a single person or product. In any case where a team is involved, a system should be in place so that the reader still knows who is posting on behalf of the account. For example, United States President Barack Obama's Twitter (https://twitter.com/BarackObama/) account has a team that assists with updates. Posts directly from the President himself are made known within the account's biography section: "This account is run by #Obama2012 campaign staff. Tweets from the President are signed—bo."

Individual messages can be a great way to reach out to audiences from within a company, but you must handle them with care. Note the true author, and be sure to respond in the comments to keep the genuine conversations flowing.

Hiring a Blogger

Blogging has been around for more than 10 years now, and many individuals across the globe blog professionally. These bloggers are either experts in their field, journalist-like in nature, passionate about their subject matter, or resourceful researchers who can put together interesting posts on any topic. Not everyone is a great writer—or wants to be—so there is value is finding a writer to make your content shine.

A hired blogger can instantly get your company up-to-speed with all the elements involved in managing a blog while allowing you time to consider the content you want to use.

When hiring a blogger, you need to become familiar with the blogger's current body of work. Make sure the content he is passionate about and has covered in the past is a good fit. Also make sure that he has not published anything questionable that you wouldn't want linked or brought to your company's blog.

You can ask the blogger about his statistics, such as how many unique visitors a month he has coming to his sites or how he would moderate comments. You can get a feel for an existing online presence by asking what social networks he currently uses and whether he has used these tools in a business capacity before.

A notable social media presence is a bonus, but the author should know how to separate his career and paid work from personal profiles and account. For example, a company blogger might have a personal Twitter profile using his first and last name. He could then sign up for a profile based on his work with the company's blog. If you are the ABC Company Blog, your blogger could sign up on Twitter as ABCJohn while also keeping open his John Smith profile.

Another option is for John Smith to add ABC Company to his personal Twitter profile biography, such as "John Smith, blogger for @ABCCompany." In this case he should also add "Tweets are my own and not that of my employer." Finding that balance with your team showcases them in a professional capacity on behalf of your company.

Tinhorn Creek Winery in British Columbia's Okanagan Valley is owned by Sandra Oldfield and her family. While the winery has its own Twitter account, @TinhornCreek, Sandra also maintains a personal Twitter account (@SandraOldfield) for her own interactions. This separation allows her to have a voice outside of the winery while @TinhornCreek can focus on wine, events, and local news.

Tips for Hiring a Blogger

You can also hire a blogger who does not currently write about your topic, as long as she is willing to immerse herself in your company's industry. You always want someone who is passionate about the subject matter. If you've found a fabulous blogger who can bring in an audience, spread your message, and get you ranked highly in search engines, you want to also make sure that she can write compelling and interesting content about your company and industry. If she is completely new to your business, you could even disclose that on your blog and have the blogger learn along with the audience.

For example, a personal blogger was hired to provide new media services to a payment gateway company that handled secure financial transactions online. The company wanted to include a blog in its new media strategy and knew that this blogger could get it on track because the blogger knew the blogging industry. The blogger created the blog, filled in a biography for herself and the company, and began writing her first blog post about the Payment Card Industry Data Security Standard (PCI DSS). This was something that the blogger had never heard of, so in her first blog post she said exactly that, and "let's learn about PCI DSS together."

Over the next few weeks, she featured YouTube videos, quotes, and links from other financial blogs with information about the process and the regulation, all while "learning together" with the audience. Within a month, if you searched "PCI Blog" on Google, you would get the blog she had built. The audience knew that she was just learning, but it was able to pick up tips, information, links to useful sites, and also learn about the company she was helping.

Bloggers can be hired to write or to manage your company's social media strategies as a whole, including the blog. But you should always make it clear who wrote the blog posts and who is managing the blog. Such transparency not only builds up trust with readers but also helps them identify the voice of the blog.

To post a listing for a blogger, you can publish a job listing through regular channels (classifieds, Monster.com, Workopolis.com, and your regular employee search avenues) or find a blogger-specific directory such as the one Darren Rowse curates on Problogger.com, shown in Figure 7.3.

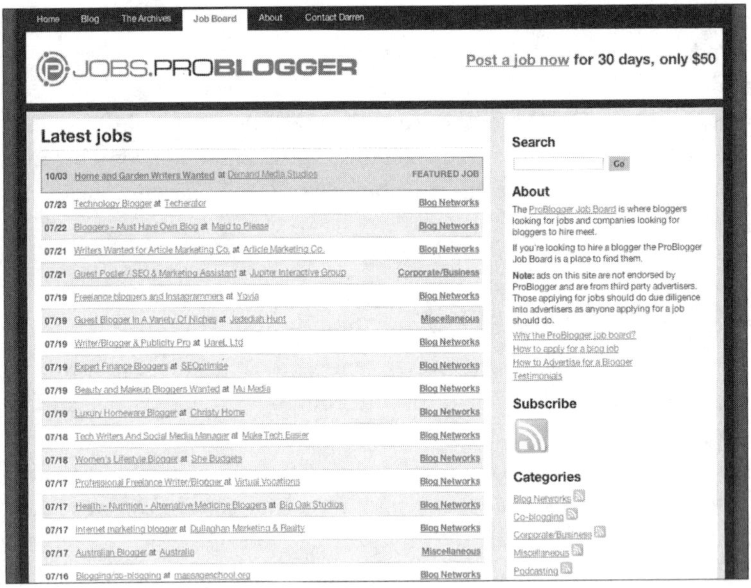

Figure 7.3 *The blogger job board at http://jobs.problogger.net/.*

Hiring a Blogger from Your Industry

A search for someone who knows the ins and outs of trackbacks, statistics, link tracking, blog terminology, and overall etiquette online combined with personal writing skills may very well lead to hiring a professional blogger. Finding one who already knows the ins and outs of your industry's online audience is a bonus.

If you are in the fruit business, it might be beneficial to approach the top peach blogger to see whether he would like to contribute to your site. If your business is hockey equipment, hire a hockey blogger to talk about what the professionals use or how to keep skates sharp.

These individuals have dealt with commentary in their respective industries, so they should have an idea about site traffic, and most of all, they are already passionate about the topic. They also know what kind of content gets a response, how to write for an audience, how to use social media tools to expand an audience, and how to track and measure successes. An individual might know all there is to know about computer keyboards, but that doesn't necessarily mean that person knows how to write about them to engage an audience. Much more is involved than just laying out the text of a blog. For example, you'll want to use images and video and reply to comments. An existing industry blogger may be well aware of all of this and would simply need your company's guidance in order to contribute online, on your behalf.

Create a Blogging Position

Director of Social Media positions and such are becoming more common as companies realize that managing all aspects of a corporate blog (and all that comes with it) is often worthy of its own position.

In July 2009, CNN's CareerBuilder.com writer released "Five Jobs for Facebook Addicts," which included a Director of Social Media position. (You can read the other listings at www.cnn.com/2009/LIVING/worklife/07/28/cb.best.job.facbook.addict/index.html.)

Social Media Director Requisites and Responsibilities

Companies need someone to manage all aspects of a social media strategy, of which the company blog is one component. The Directory of Social Media oversees the company's entire online presence, tracks statistics, creates partnerships with other bloggers to publicize campaigns, and manages blog content by moderating comments and coming up with the general road map for the company's use of social media.

A person hired for a social media position should know the following:

- How to set up the company with a YouTube account, including what should be posted there
- How to use Twitter and Facebook and engage with the different audiences on those platforms
- How to reach out to existing customers through the current website and introduce them to the blog
- How to get more blog readers, comments, and feedback flowing
- How the company wants to measure success with each one of these strategies

The person in charge of social media for your company should ensure the company is represented online through open, interactive, and personal communications while remaining professional at all times.

The search for your Director of Social Media (or similar role) could be internal if someone in the company already knows the ins and outs of social media. Otherwise, taking to the networks where you would like to see your company have a presence is a great way to find your champion of social media. Publish job postings online, or if you already have a blog, feature the job posting there.

Fitting In with the Company Dynamic

When supporting a blogger who is writing for your company, you can supply key messaging. However, authors can also do research for their posts, to provide the most informed content for your audience. You can give the author free rein with regard to her writing, as long as it pertains to your industry. For example, if you have an Indian restaurant, you could ask the blogger to cover Indian cuisine in general. The blogger could write a post about specific dishes, how they are prepared, where to get the best ingredients and spices in town, and so on.

You can also provide the content on which the blogger will expand. If the company is issuing a press release, information should be given to the blogger so that he can create a post or story pertaining to the news.

Suppose, for example, that you issue a press release about an employee's promotion. In this case, the blogger may want to interview the employee or post a photo (something more personal than the press release but that also complements the same news).

You get to set the rules for your blog. You may allow the blogger to write about specific topics, an industry, or within other specific parameters. To add structure to a site, you might want to impose word counts on posts and consider daily or weekly themes. Such guidelines help ensure that posts stay on topic and that the blog's author stays within the company's key messaging. You also want to make sure that your bloggers do not overstep boundaries by perhaps sharing personal information about employees or private information about upcoming projects.

Supplying More Than Content

Creating blog posts, managing the online presence (for example, checking out Google Alerts or using Twitter search), moderating comments, analyzing traffic and search terms, posting responses to comments, and researching content are just a few of the tasks that an internal blogger or social media professional can handle.

Professional bloggers should be able to do most of their work after a blog post is written. When that content is out there, they need to follow up and see just how far of a reach the content had. They can do this using statistics applications and by checking a few of the basics:

- Have there been any comments on the post?
- Has anyone linked or tracked back to the post from their own website?
- Is the post searchable in Google? If so, under which terms does it appear in search results?
- Has it been retweeted (that is, your link reposted on Twitter)?
- Has the post appeared yet in your RSS feed? How often do you get new subscribers?

Bloggers also know their audiences by looking at comments and tracking statistics. Should you determine that your blog's traffic is highest midweek during the nine-to-five hours, you thus understand that your audience is at work and reading during the day. This audience might not be around on the weekends (and hence the drop in traffic). In this scenario, you don't need to worry about publishing content on the weekend; your audience won't be back until Monday anyway. This is an example of what a good Director of Social Media (with blogging experience) can assess for you.

Advantages of Hiring a Blogger

By having a blogging position, you welcome the blog's author into your company, and by so doing get the best content published. This person will have the knowledge required to cover your business and will also be personally invested in doing the best job possible. Representing a company online is much easier when you feel at home within the company. The passionate content can then flow much more easily.

Managing a blog and its social media elements can be a full-time job and may be impossible for existing employees to work into their current workload. The blogger will need input from the rest of the departments, however; after all, they are creating and nurturing this online space for the company. The company blogger should clear the way for more involvement, including the possibility of having multiple authors.

The key to finding a professional blogger that is the right fit for your company is to read the writer's blog and get to know his online writing style and behavior. Ideally, you want to find someone who is responsible with online content, who is courteous to readers, and who hasn't posted material that could embarrass you should that blogger become associated with your company.

One advantage of hiring an experienced blogger is that he should already know the ins and outs of the online realm. This means he should know how to compose a blog post, arrange RSS feeds, moderate comments, and publish your links to Twitter or other social networks.

Even those who have only been blogging a short time can still figure out statistics, commenting, and Google searches. Experienced bloggers know how to collect this data and use it to their advantage, tailoring posts and adding keywords to make sure their message gets spread.

Experienced bloggers may already have a presence on multiple online networks or directories and could boost your company's presence there, too. For example, someone who has created Facebook fan pages followed by thousands will know how to boost your presence on that network. That person could also apply those skills to blogging.

There are thousands of professional bloggers in North America, and millions of bloggers worldwide write consistent content online. You can find one for your company by doing blog searches for key terms, checking in on industry blog-gers, and listening to what people are already saying about your company online. Sometimes those who are already fans of your company (and who may already have fan-based blogs about your business) can be your biggest asset.

For example, Mike Pegg was a fan of Google Maps and so ran the Google Maps Mania Blog (http://googlemapsmania.blogspot.com). He collected stories and images from all over the world and published them online. He ended up on Google's radar, and the company then recruited him to work for Google Maps & Earth. (See his bio online at www.google.com/profiles/113532747879926407110.) Pegg is now the Product Marketing Manager, Google Maps API, at Google Inc.

Case Studies
Linda Bustos: An Elastic Blog from Elastic Path

Linda Bustos is the E-commerce Analyst for professional e-commerce solutions provider Elastic Path. She began her career with the company as a guest blogger for the Get Elastic blog (see Figure 7.4). Elastic Path currently serves more than 200 clients worldwide, including Samsonite and Aeroplan, and it also powered the Vancouver 2010 Olympic store.

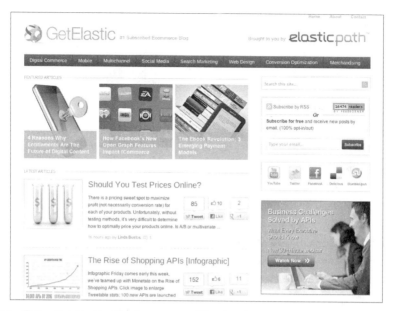

Figure 7.4   *Get Elastic, The E-commerce Blog, by Elastic Path.*

In 2006, Bustos began her own blog about social media and search engine optimization (SEO) after attending local news media events in Vancouver, British Columbia. Around the same time, Elastic Path was looking for ways to expand its communications presence online, and so it started a company blog. Linda soon met Elastic Path's cofounder, Jason Billingsley, at one of these networking events and began checking out Get Elastic (because its subject matter was right up her alley).

She often commented and engaged the authors in conversations and was eventually invited to write a guest post. "It wasn't a full-time position in the beginning but just contributing as a guest. After that, there was opportunity to continue full time, as they really wanted to go ahead with the blog."

As the company expanded its blog to provide an industry service, sharing tips and insights about the e-commerce realm, Linda's role began to grow. She was welcomed into the company officially and was included in conversations such as the sales and marketing meetings. These more personal interactions benefited her writing almost immediately. "It really, really helped me to come in and actually learn about the product, and learn about the company," said Bustos. "I think I can help them more with blogging when I keep in mind what their goals are and what they're working on."

Linda's passion for social media, writing, and online marketing truly helped her apply what she knew about the online world and combine it with Elastic Path's endeavors. "They gave me complete flexibility, complete autonomy in what I wanted to write about," noted Bustos, who was able to write passionately about a topic she knew very well. "I try to use the blog as much as possible to build a community around us."

In just over two years, Bustos went from being a guest blogger to being the author of the number one blog in the industry. She offered some advice on how to choose a blogger who will work for your company, recommending that businesses find someone who can be committed, either full or part time, to writing and managing the blog.

"If they can't be a full-time employee, at least be a permanent contractor," Bustos noted. "Because on the blog, you definitely don't want to build up trust with one person both internally and the readership and then swap them out for someone else." Finding the right blogger for the job and nurturing that person's messaging is paramount. "It's important that you do your diligence and find somebody who is going to be committed and that can kind of prove themselves as a right fit for the content you want to go with before you have them publishing."

In terms of hiring an external individual to manage your company's blog versus having someone on the inside commit to contributing, Bustos says a "hybrid of both" can work.

"If I had to choose I would like somebody who was full-on a part of the team because that's also the trust that you're communicating in a business blog," said Bustos. Having someone on board who can spread your message effectively in the online realm and build up a community of trust with readers and clients is key. When you find this balance, your company's blog can position you as a thought leader in your industry.

Having a game plan in mind when starting up a company blog is always a great idea because it will serve as a road map and help you plot out goals and strategies. "Be clear about what the game plan is for the blog in terms of keeping a consistent posting schedule," recommended Bustos. With a plan in place, your company will have a road map to plot out goals and milestones for your online communications strategy.

When your company designates a blogger, it is also important to make sure that person is supported. Bustos noted that setting up processes and support for the blog is a great help when it comes to upgrades and technical issues on the back end. This can be internal support or through a contracted partner.

Bustos was passionate about a subject, and because of this, she was able to commit to writing and blogging while building an audience. She has helped her company build its readership by being someone who knows the blogging and e-commerce industry. At the same time, she has learned how to share Elastic Path's messaging, and as a result, Get Elastic has been recognized by TopRank as a top search marketing blog (www.toprankblog.com/search-marketing-blogs/), by the *Wall Street Journal* as one of 15 entrepreneur blogs worth reading (http://blogs.wsj.com/independentstreet/2008/06/13/15-entrepreneur-blogs-worth-reading), and is on the AdAge Power 150 (http://adage.com/power150/).

Rob Jones: BuildDirect Blog

In 1999, Vancouver-based BuildDirect began as an online marketplace for high-quality building materials in volume quantities for less than retail. In 2007, BuildDirect's marketing department set out to start a blog, with company founders Jeff Booth and Robert Banks backing the project (http://blog.builddirect.com/). Rob Jones, who has been with the company since 2005, is now the Content and Social Media Manager and oversees the BuildDirect blog (shown in Figure 7.5), which has three regular contributors (employed by BuildDirect), a CEO blog, a Green blog, and a handful of guest authors.

Figure 7.5   *BuildDirect blog.*

"When it originally started, the blog was purely product-oriented. The original authors were actual sales people, so we wanted to have as many of those guys blogging as possible to get all of their perspectives on the various products that we had," Jones says. "Later on, the blog evolved and moved in a different direction, talking to our customers in a more holistic kind of way."

The shift took the blog from being about sales and products to attracting authors who could write content about home design, home décor, and related industry themes. BuildDirect began accepting posts from bloggers who were interested in writing about related topics, and for the bloggers, it was an opportunity to share their own expertise, expand their portfolio, and get additional online visibility.

"We're building blog posts that are useful to an audience but are also a way of building links," Jones adds. By this, he means that the contributing bloggers are not only getting links out to their sites, but also are linking into the Build Direct Blog and sharing their work. The new content such as urban home renovations, wood floor finishing options, or pop culture in interior design are garnering interest from other websites, search engine results, and more. All these efforts lead to more incoming links to the blog and, in turn, the Build Direct website.

Jones adds that some of the blog content doesn't even have to do with the product the company is selling. "The general idea is that people buy building materials from BuildDirect because they want to do some kind of transformation in their lives and that's not the whole picture, so we need people who are experts in their field to write about those other areas."

BuildDirect also offers the chance for readers to submit a guest post, and Jones looks for specific types of contributions when sifting through the pitches from potential bloggers.

"Basically, I'm looking for something that is a bit granular. I get a lot of pitches that are general or broad, and what I look for is something that's like 'how to you use mirrors effectively,' 'what are recent trends in wood flooring.' Things that you as an expert or you as an enthusiast are seeing—detailed stuff." Having this wide range of specified topics also helps the BuildDirect blog get picked up in search engine results. When people search something very specific on Google or Bing, they just might come across the BuildDirect blog post about that very topic.

Jones adds that having a variety of voices also adds a level of interest for blog readers. "Our primary focus for the blog is to be as useful and as interesting as possible to our audience." With more perspectives and focused content, it appeals to the current audience who will also return to check out new niche posts, tips, and ideas that might be published.

The shift from being sales and product specific to expanding its author pool and in turn providing more specific types of content has helped the BuildDirect blog double its traffic over the past 12 months.

Jones concludes: "Once you begin to build content this way and begin to be known for being useful and being a trusted voice, the referral traffic back to the main site and into the sale funnel is often more highly qualified than it would be if [readers] just found your site without the blog."

Summary

Companies can become overwhelmed with managing a blog, finding where it will fit in, and writing it. As demonstrated in this chapter, plenty of resources are available out there to help you get your blog started, whether it's hiring an experienced blogger or rounding up departmental teams to share the work.

After the blog has an author or authors, the focus should be on content and how to share that content in a way that it attracts readers. The following chapter details ways to boost your online presence so that when your blog goes live on your end, it will also hit the radar of the online audience you hope to bring in as your reader base.

8

Getting Eyeballs to Your Blog

You may not instantly find readers for your blog within the first few minutes of publishing a post, but there are ways to boost your audience and bring awareness to your writing.

You can add your blog to directory listings or use search engine optimization (SEO) tips so that it is searchable, but when it comes purely to content, you also need to attract readers who will want to return with each post. Great content that serves to educate, inform, or entertain is the driving force behind building an audience with your blog. This chapter shows you how to get your audience to return to your blog.

Writing Effectively

After you get an audience to your site, it's key to provide content that will capture audience members' interest and encourage them to return again with each new post. Effective writing includes the following characteristics:

- **Appropriate length of writing:** You need to learn how to edit your content for appropriate length.

- **A voice or tone that is human:** Your writing needs to be personal, written with tone, emphasis, emotion, and other "human" elements.

- **Readable language:** The words you choose are important in that they need to be clear and readable.

Editing for Word Count and Brevity

Effective writing on a blog should not sound like a text message in short code or chat room speak, nor should it sound like an extended press release. It can contain the same key elements of information of both because when you need to get your message across with a limited word count, you make sure to say what you need to say in that space. Learning how to self-edit is key.

When putting blog posts together, you aren't necessarily limited to word counts; however, having a milestone in mind can help you weed out the best information you want to present. Blog posts of about 250 to a maximum of 700 words allow enough room for the content to flow without sounding too choppy or brief while not extending the post so it stretches beyond the readers' attention span.

Write the post, save it, preview it, edit it, and then repeat the process. Editing down your content so that you can publish the most clear and concise information will make your posts easier to read.

Most blog platforms enable you to preview your post before it is published, and you should preview your article before making the post public. You can preview your post and also read through it several times to make sure you can get the most pertinent information included before losing readers to a long word count. Setting a word count goal often helps authors keep their posts as clear and concise as possible.

Representing your company, the blog should also be reviewed for spelling and grammatical errors. Most browsers and text editors have a built-in spell-check function that can be run either on the fly or with the click of a button.

With the growing popularity of microblogging sites such as Twitter, people are finding more ways to cram as much information as they can into a strict and often very short character limit. It's amazing to see what you can produce when given guidelines like these.

One of Technorati's Top 100 blogs, Boing Boing, is a hub of information, photos, videos, and links to cool sites across the Internet. Blog posts about the world's smallest robots show an image, a quick blurb, and a link to the website where the content is posted. When this blog's authors are excited about a new film that is about to launch, they post an embedded YouTube video, some text about the film, and a link to the film's website for more information.

These short yet helpful posts provide multiple forms of content while also leading to discussion in the comments. When your post is brief, you can easily expand on its content through reader feedback. Even though your entry may be but 200 words, your interaction with readers in the comments helps continue your thoughts while at the same time showing readers you would like to hear their thoughts, too.

In April 2008, the popular photo-sharing site Flickr also began allowing its pro users to upload and share videos. The site decided to put restrictions on those videos, allowing clips that were no longer than 90 seconds or no larger than 150MB in size. The 90-second limit never ended up being an issue for users because most video clips on the Web these days are 90 seconds or shorter. Anything more and you risk losing the audience's attention or becoming a full web series or episode rather than a video clip.

The same applies for blog posts. There should be an element of brevity, but at the same time you should still be able to fit all necessary information in the post. Also, if blog authors look at their website's statistics, they should see a Bounce Rate section. This section tells you how long readers are staying on your blog before heading to another website. Typical bounce rates are anywhere between 60 and 90 seconds, which means you have only a short time to grab your readers' attention and keep it locked on your blog.

ProBlogger answered the question "How Long Should a Blog Post Be?" in 2006 by looking at the following issues:

- **Reader attention span:** Once again, pay attention to the "bounce rate," or how long you can keep readers captivated by your content.

- **SEO:** Search engine optimization refers to making sure that your blog and its contents are going to be picked up by search engines through keywords and other elements. According to ProBlogger, extremely short posts and those that are extremely long have a hard time being picked up by search engines. The suggested blog post length is between 250 and 1,000 words.

- **Number of posts:** Having shorter posts allows you to write more often, because it shouldn't take as long to write a 300-word post compared to one that is 1,200 words. When you write shorter posts, your search engine ranking can improve (based on the preceding item), and you'll pull readers back to your blog more often with fresh content.

Read the full post on ProBlogger at www.problogger.net/archives/2006/02/18/post-length-how-long-should-a-blog-post-be.

A great resource for checking the reading level of your site is http://readability.info. You can use this website to determine how "readable" your content is. According to Readability.info, a typical *New York Times* article has a fifth-grade reading level, whereas a *PC World* article is at an eighth-grade level. A professional blog that is between these levels will be quick and easy to read while still providing knowledge and insight.

Blog posts don't need to always include text. Posts can take on many forms and may be as quick and simple as an embedded video with a caption or an entire gallery of photos from an event or product launch. Choose multimedia that is relevant (for example, using images to illustrate an object or place). Visual aids help readers get a better idea of what you're talking about in a post, and they also break up chunks of text. If the images or video are not your own, because you can source these from networks such as Flickr or YouTube, be sure to always give credit by linking to your original sources online and making sure the image is free to use. This means that you have permission to use the image and/or the license assigned to the image allows you to share it and it is not copyrighted.

Sound Human

The corporate and company blog connects with readers, clients, and your audience on a personal level, so writing in that exact manner is paramount. When you're writing for a blog, losing sentence structure and grammar is not an option; however, you'll want to make sure your posts have a voice and can connect with readers on a familiar and friendly level.

An individual or group of individuals should write company blogs. You can set your blog's preferences to display author names, which can help create that voice, or set a more personal tone. Reading a post from Administrator is not as personal as one from Jennifer in Marketing, especially when it pertains to a specific aspect of the company.

A good example is the Disney Parks Blog, which does not speak down to readers although most of its audience worldwide consists of children. The blog provides an inside look at the Disney parks, including individual items of note that readers might not already know. These insights include blog posts about how you can burn 350 calories an hour by walking briskly from *land* to *land*, a feature about dishes you should try at the Epcot International Food & Wine Festival, or an announcement about handheld audio devices that now play descriptions of the attractions.

Other authors on the blog include Thomas Smith, the Social Media Director of Disney Parks; however, having a blog post about "Cinderella's Coach for Disney

Weddings" written by the company's wedding specialist gives it context and more of a human element. Each post is also professional and informative while still using the author's own voice.

Another example is the official Google Blog (http://googleblog.blogspot.com), which also has many authors who all contribute to the same site. At the end of each post that is written, each author clearly states who wrote the post, and each one's job title is displayed. For example, you can read a post about Google's translation services, written by Jeff Chin, a Product Manager.

Adding these personal touches boosts the credibility of your posts. Who better to inform you about Google's open source initiatives in a blog post than Leslie Hawthorn, Program Manager of the Open Source Team? The author can have a biography on the side of your blog, at the bottom of each post, or on a separate About This Blog page. This feature helps readers connect with a specific person at the company and the blog as a whole, enabling the audience to connect with a human.

The blog is not the place for a press release or similar verbiage either. Should your company disseminate a release, feel free to link that information or include it in a post; however, its entire contents should not be included. The blog should be conversational and encourage discussions. It's also a great place to include photos or accompanying multimedia that helps assignment editors, readers, and journalists get even more information from the company.

Through accompanying images or videos supplied on the blog, you can share more content, and your message can reach a wider audience through photo- or video-sharing networks. Readers might not be interested in an image of a new product, but a fun video posted to YouTube might catch their attention.

Reading Blogs Helps You Write Blogs

When you decide to write a blog, the best way to find out what to write and how to write it is to seek out blogs that you like to read. What keeps your attention? What content styles are the most appealing to you? By reading successful sites, you can collect valuable publishing ideas that can be easily applied to your own blog venture.

Commenting—More than Leaving a Calling Card

According to Technorati's State of the Blogosphere 2011 (http://technorati.com/social-media/article/state-of-the-blogosphere-2011-part1/page-2/#mediahabits), bloggers are most influenced—and inspired to write on their own blogs—by topics presented on other blogs.

If you read an interesting blog post on another website, it's perfectly acceptable to join the conversation in the comment thread. Leaving comments on another blog shows other readers that you are active in the industry's blogging community; you have ideas and thoughts to share; and, you hope, your comments will lead readers back to your site to see your expanded insights.

However, when you comment on other sites, remain tactful in your message. Leave a comment only when you genuinely have an interest in the post and can contribute something productive. Simply leaving a link to your site and saying you also wrote about a certain topic can easily get your comment flagged as spam. When you share information and encourage others to do the same on your blog with your own posts, you help create a respectful blogging community for your industry within which you'll be a key player.

You can also see how others respond to posts and comments, what works for other blogs, and what doesn't in terms of connecting with an audience. If you notice that you start getting more comments on posts about a particular topic, continue writing about that topic in more entries.

Blogger Outreach

Approaching other bloggers, whether they are in your industry or a fan of products and services pertaining to your industry, can also be mutually beneficial. Going beyond a simple link back to a preferred blog, you can even approach these writers when you have a campaign to promote, an event, or perhaps a guest blog post.

Professional bloggers live all across the Internet, and chances are, some cover your industry on a daily basis. Feel free to add these bloggers to mailing lists or visit their sites to touch base. Once again, the importance of "being human" and personable is key in these communications. Emailing full press releases to other bloggers might be an instant turn-off. However, if you read their sites, get a feel for their coverage and writing style, you can send them a personalized note if you think they would be genuinely interested in your news. Getting picked up on their sites could drive some valuable traffic your way, and in exchange, they get to cover your interesting news.

Product launch parties and even press trips are organized for bloggers in the hopes that companies will get applicable coverage online. For example, in the summer of 2009, Coast Hotels & Resorts invited six bloggers from the Vancouver area to Victoria, the capital of British Columbia, on Vancouver Island. The idea was to highlight the quick trip from Vancouver to the island and feature restaurants, businesses, and activities in the greater Victoria region. The blogger guest list consisted of travel bloggers, food bloggers, and photographers. Coast Hotels sponsored the bloggers' stay in Victoria and hooked them up with Tourism Victoria so that they could explore the city. In no way were any of the bloggers obliged to write about Coast Hotels or even any of their experiences. However, Coast did provide the bloggers with multimedia (images from the Royal BC Museum, a menu from featured restaurants where they ate, and so on) and even created a hashtag on Twitter, #newvictoria.

> ✉ *Note*
>
> *Hashtags* allow readers of a specific following to track topics on Twitter. Placing a hashtag, or pound sign, next to a word allows others to click through and follow all instances of that word or topic using http://search. twitter.com. A great example is a conference called AB Conference. All attendees could include #ABConference in their tweets about the event so that everyone (in attendance and at home) can follow the flow of information online.

Throughout their stay, bloggers could tweet, blog, and post content about their experiences while Coast tracked their messages using the tags that had been set up. By the end of the weekend, almost 1,000 photos were uploaded to Flickr, which were all tagged "new Victoria" and the bloggers also used "Coast Hotels."

Providing bloggers with links to a Flickr group, where they could submit their own images to a community pool of photos, and a hashtag enabled Coast to track the content that was created.

The same applies to hosting an event or a product launch party. You can provide the Twitter hashtag, a link to your blog post about the event, and a place for bloggers to find images (or upload their own), and then facilitate content creation by not demanding it.

If you're open to inviting mainstream media, also consider bloggers who cover your industry. Their audiences are even more specific and may be those you most want to reach. You can offer them access and any other event benefits, and in turn they might write about it on their site (and perhaps even include photos).

The opportunity to write a guest blog post for your blog may also appeal to bloggers who cover your industry, or even to your readers within the same industry. Bloggers get added exposure and the prestige of writing professionally for your site, and in exchange, they will link and promote their article on their own outlet. Each option provides links, promotion, and visibility to both blogs and businesses.

LinkedIn, one of the world's top professional social networking sites, runs the LinkedIn Blog (http://blog.linkedin.com). Multiple authors post about everything from small business to networking tips. The site runs a blog series called Success Stories for which it welcomes guest posts from LinkedIn users. The series is searchable through a category tag (http://blog.linkedin.com/category/success-stories), and guest authors are given a biography at the top of each post that includes a link to their own websites. The Success Stories series not only gives users a chance to provide feedback, but also encourages readers to use the LinkedIn service based on the positive outcomes that are highlighted.

Linking Out to Get Incoming Links

Getting an idea of what your industry is currently doing in the online space is a great way to put together your own blogging plan. One of the best ways to become a part of the blogging community in your industry is to become active on other sites and perhaps even link them from your blog. Linking out to your competition might seem like a silly idea, but it's just another step in becoming a total resource for your clients and audience.

When you read an interesting post or article online, you can copy and paste the link into your own blog post, attaching it to reference text. For example, "I read an interesting post about the new MP3 players over on ABC Company's blog [link]." You can even include some of the post's text as long as you are sure to reference it and include a link back to the original source.

Finding the link is as easy as looking in your browser's address bar and copying the blog post's address. After you copy that code, you can highlight your text, and in most blogging platforms, you can click the Link button to paste in the code you just copied.

After you include a link in your post, the original site's author is able to see this incoming link using her own statistics applications.

Because most blogs have systems in place to track statistics, incoming links are a closely watched metric. It's always fun to get quoted or linked in someone else's blog post, so providing links and credit on your site to others can help this chain continue.

Search Engine Optimization

Search engines have their own specific algorithms for which content they pick up and place in their results. By having good search engine optimization, or SEO, your blog can get readers with little effort.

Search engines look for keywords and key content when scouring your blog posts for content they can index and call up in their search results. Keywords in the title of a blog post, the title of a blog page, and the link structure can help boost your SEO.

For example, if your blog post is about a new brand of jeans, it would be useful to include those keywords in your post's title (for example, "New Bootcut Jeans Released This Winter"). Titles should be keyword-rich but still make sense and pertain to the post's content. Search engines can also penalize a site (refusing to include it in results) if it is clearly milking keywords that are irrelevant. It may seem poetic to name a blog post after a song lyric, but if you're looking to drive traffic to the content, using keywords in the title is much more effective.

Blogrolls

If you want to become a one-stop resource for your company's online presence and your industry, providing the most information and media for your audience should include adding a blogroll to your site. A blogroll is a list of links to websites that you would like to share with your readers. They can be other blogs from your company, blogs from your industry, or simply links to blogs that you find interesting.

As with linking out in a blog post, other blogs can see links coming from blogrolls using their statistics tracking applications. These applications provide data on traffic sources to your blog; sources can be blog posts, search engines, or other blogrolls.

For other blog authors, being linked off a reputable company blog in a blogroll may be considered a compliment or sign of prestige. If you have a favorite blog or find other blogs you think your readers would enjoy, you can show your appreciation to those blogs' authors by linking to them.

The professional NHL team the Vancouver Canucks have a section on their official website just for blogs. They host fan blogs and link out externally to blogs that have been submitted by fans, as shown in Figure 8.1.

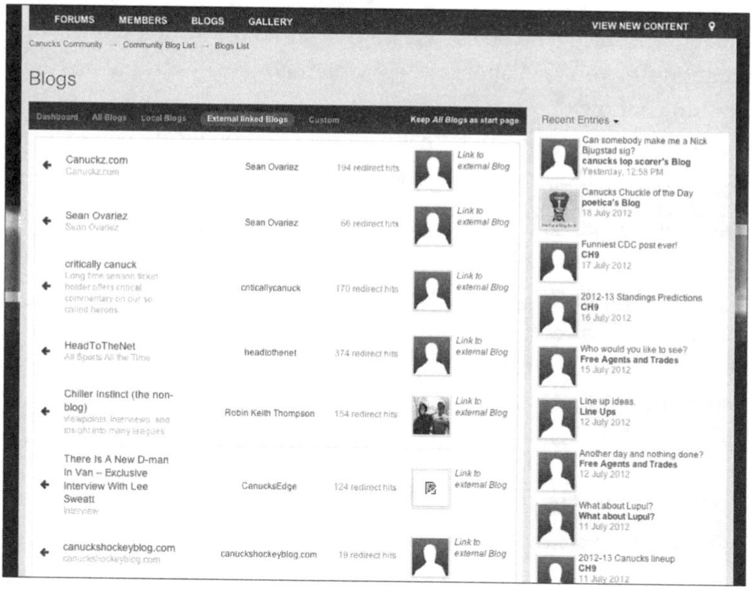

Figure 8.1 *Featured blogs linked from the Canucks blog section of their website (http://forum.canucks.com/blogs/)*

By visiting the Canucks blog section, readers can find other resources and points of view from a variety of bloggers who are not necessarily associated with the team, but are fans like them. It's not a guarantee, but if your site can provide useful information, including links to other sites with comprehensive data and reviews, you could find reader loyalty there, which can translate to customer loyalty.

Linking to Other Blog Posts

Reading other blog posts to get ideas for articles of your own is a great way to build content on your site, as mentioned earlier in the section "Linking Out to Get Incoming Links." If you see a post elsewhere that is worth quoting or expanding upon on your own site, be sure to copy only a portion of the post and provide a link back to the source, crediting the author. This courtesy goes a long way when it comes to blogging etiquette. The original author will see your link and may come over to your site to see your additional thoughts.

You will at least get the original author to view your post. If he has a trackback system in place, where your link shows up as a comment on his blog post, your post will be linked from the original post automatically. With your link now on his post, you'll attract readers from the original source's site because they may want to see how you have continued the conversation or why you have linked that post.

If your thoughts on a particular blog post expand beyond just leaving a comment for another blogger, you can create your own post inspired by the original. Mention that you read about the topic on the source's site and expand your thoughts on your own post. If you set up the link correctly, you will get the trackback on your post showing up on that post. This allows the discussion to continue on your site, alongside your own thoughts and productive/relative notes.

When linking out, do so for good reason and be sure to link appropriately. Your post should expand on the other post or have something to do with the content to which you are linking. If there is no relevance, your attempt at linking out to draw links back in could be seen as spam. By being courteous, adding to a conversation, or simply highlighting something great that you read, you'll attract positive attention and, hopefully, new readers.

Write Interesting Content

You can include keywords, add links, and write as many readable blog posts as you like, but if your content isn't interesting, you won't have people to read what you are publishing.

Highlight Industry Players

Profiling some of your favorite blogs is a great way to showcase your involvement in blogging and maintain your blog's profile as an industry resource. Should your company be in the restaurant business, an interview with an executive chef could attract readers. If your business is selling bicycles, an interview with a rider or manufacturer could be of great interest to your readers.

Interviews are always a good way to change up the flow of content on your site, and depending on your subject, the rich keywords and tags associated with the names of those you interview can boost your blog's SEO significantly. You can interview someone who writes a blog, talk to an individual who has expertise in your industry or field, or even do a customer or client profile. As a result, fans of your interview subject will come to your site, ultimately expanding your own audience.

You can also highlight other bloggers in your industry. Michaels stores has a sidebar on its Community page featuring "Blogs We Love" (see Figure 8.3) These include blogs like (http://www.livinglocurto.com/) Living Locurto, a blog about "Printables, Recipes, Parties, and Crafts," and Tatertots & Jello (http://tatertot-sandjello.com/) a blog about "DIY Decorating and Crafts."

Mushrooms Canada, an association for mushroom producers, writes a blog about all things mushroom – from recipes to health and wellness tips. They have a section on their blog dedicated to "Food Bloggers We Love" where they have invited food bloggers to contribute posts to their blog. An example is a guest post from blogger Renee Kohlman of SweetSugarBean (http://www.sweetsugarbean.com/), who wrote a post called "Wild Mushroom & Asiago Risotto Cakes" and provided a recipe (see Figure 8.2). Mushrooms Canada gets informative information to provide its readers and customers while blogger SweetSugarBean gets exposure and can direct its audience to the post it has made for the Mushroom site.

Figure 8.2   *Mushrooms Canada Guest Blog Post by SweetSugarBean (http://blog. mushrooms.ca/2012/05/guest-post-wild-mushroom-asiago-risotto.html).*

Company Profiles

Businesses should be proud of their employees, from the management team down to part-timers and interns. Showcasing your team members in blog posts is a fun way to introduce your audience to your company in a more personal manner, and it shows that you truly value your team. Highlighting employees or departments proves that you care not only about your customers and clients, but also those who help make your company work from the inside-out. This can be a nice morale booster and a chance for your company to truly shine in your industry.

The outdoor clothing company Patagonia hosts a blog called The Cleanest Line (www.thecleanestline.com). It describes the blog as a "Weblog for the employees, friends, and customers of the outdoor clothing company Patagonia. Visit Patagonia.com to see what we do."

Because the company is all about the outdoors, Patagonia occasionally asks employees to share their experiences from their own hikes and adventures in the open air. In the summer of 2009, the managers of the blog caught wind that one of Patagonia's customer service representatives, Adam Bradley, would be doing the Pacific Crest Trail. It then asked him to share thoughts and photos from his journey on the group blog (see Figure 8.3).

Figure 8.3 *The Cleanest Line: Weblog for the employees, friends, and customers of the outdoor clothing company Patagonia.*

A feature like this not only engages employees and gives advice to those who would also like to venture across the Pacific Crest Trail, but also shows that employees of this outdoor clothing company actually do spend time out in the open air.

Being Searchable

As previously mentioned, search engine optimization, or SEO, is a hot topic and much sought-after resource for bloggers and website managers alike. A website that comes up in search results for your targeted industry keywords is extremely valuable. This allows those who are not already aware of your company and blog to discover your resources.

With some blogging platforms, most of your SEO is already taken care of in the way that the system publishes your content and pushes its keywords out to search engines. However, it's beneficial to make sure your blog is optimally set up for these search engines.

To ensure that your blog will get picked up by sites such as Google and Bing Search, you can proactively submit your blog to those directories. With Google, you can visit the directory listings site to request to be added (https://www.google.com/submityourcontent), and with Google, you can also submit your link for consideration (see Figure 8.4).

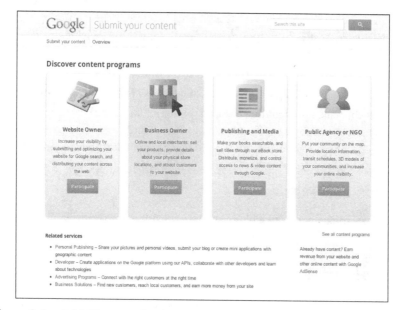

Figure 8.4 *AddURL service from Google.com/SubmitYourContent.*

Check Your Current Rank

A great first step to working on your SEO is doing a current search for your company name, a post title, or a product or service your business offers.

You can check out your current ranking by going to Grader.com (www.grader.com). This analytical tool lets you know your current search engine ranking, Google page rank, and a few other helpful details. From there, you can take steps to improve your results.

You can also give your blog results a push by using Google's Webmaster tools (https://www.google.com/webmasters/tools/home?hl=en). Google allows you to submit your blog, and it generates a list of top search queries that led users to your site, along with incoming links and other useful information.

Clean URLs

A URL is your blog's unique website address or link. A clean URL contains actual words that apply to the content. Because website addresses are one of the first things crawled by search engines when including your site in their rankings and results, clean URLs can be beneficial. For example, a blog with the address http://yourcompany.com/?1234 is less likely to come up in a result as http://yourcompany.com/blog. For individual posts, say one about high heel shoes, the URL should come out as any variation of http://yourcompany.com/blog/latest-high-heel-styles instead of http://yourcompany.com/?1234. Having the keywords directly in the link means you have clean URLs set up on your blog, which means search engines are able to scan your site with ease.

This feature does not come standard with all blogger platforms. Using it may be as simple as choosing a setting in your blog's configuration if you are using a popular blogging platform. However, if it is not already standard, you might have to take a few more technical steps behind the scenes to get clean URLs in place on your blog.

Keywords and Tags

A distinguishing element of a blog versus a regular website is the ability to add tags or categories to posts. Using tags or categories is similar to sorting files into folders. Should you apply a tag called *events* to a blog post, you then are able to search your blog for all posts you have tagged with *events*. Posts with similar tags are grouped so that you can sort and find them later. Your blogging platform is able to present all tagged items on a page and can also provide you with an RSS feed for each. Categories and tags should be keywords that are associated with the content in the blog post. If the blog post is about a fundraising event in Seattle, you could apply the category or tag *event*, *fundraiser*, and *Seattle*. In the future, you will be able to search for a post based on any of those keywords.

If your blogging platform provides both the option for categories and tags (they serve a similar purpose), you can treat them differently. Categories can be used at a higher level or more general form of sorting. You could have a category that pertains to an overall topic while tagging can be used for specific keywords, to get more granular in the description of the content. For example, A blog post in the category Food could have a subcategory of Vegetarian and a tag of Gluten-Free. Categories and tags are also assigned their own URLs or website addresses. This allows you to further sort your content or provide links to an entire range of posts rather than a single item.

These keywords serve a dual purpose in that they sort your content and also make it more searchable. Once again, using the high heel shoe example, http://your-company.com/blog/tags/shoes is much more likely to get picked by search engines because the tag name is listed directly in the website address. You can also include coded HTML tags when you embed links, photos, and video. This bit of code lets the search engine crawler know exactly what type of content is supplied.

Including a keyword in the title of the multimedia is a quick way to get picked up, too. For example, an uploaded photo called DSC1234.jpg will not get picked up as easily as Stilettos.jpg. An alt tag is also attached to an image and you can customize its text in the same manner as the title. Your photo can be Stilettos.jpg, with a title of Stilettos, and alt text of shoes, high heels, and perhaps a brand name.

Search engines also look for title information in blog posts. So, when you are naming your articles, include the keywords directly in the title field. However, remember to keep your site readable and "human" sounding by avoiding keyword overload. The title "Shoes High Heels" might get you some great rankings, but it tells your readers nothing specific about the post. A title such as this may not lead them to your site from the search results to read more. However, including key-words and keeping the theme of the post within the title should accomplish the clickthrough (for example, "The Season's Hottest High Heel Shoes").

Promotion

Launching a blog is a newsworthy and notable event for any business. Some com-panies include such information in a press release, and others host launch parties to celebrate the addition to their online presence. Whatever way you plan to launch and promote your blog, the most important thing to do is let people know it exists in the first place. Linking to your blog from your main website is the natural place to start, but you can also use your current publicity resources to drive traffic to your blog.

Social Media Networks

Blog promotion can be achieved through other social media networks. If you already have a Facebook page, posting an announcement there is an obvious decision. The same applies for Twitter or any other social networking service you use. These sites most likely contain the audience you will be looking to nurture on your blog, moving conversations from external sites to your very own.

Announcing Your Blog Launch to Other Communities

You can also reach out to your local or industry blogging communities. In doing so, ask for feedback and be open to suggestions and comments. Be sure to be personal and get a real sense of the blog that you are approaching. If the blog is focused on food and is located in Florida, the author might not be the best person to contact about Rocky Mountain hiking gear.

When approaching bloggers by email, be sure to know the authors' names and address them appropriately. You can also reference recent posts they have written or even a favorite of yours if you have been following a particular site. Look around on the blogs to see whether you think other bloggers will in fact be open to sharing your story. (For example, have they written reviews or news articles before?) You also need to make sure the blogs you are considering aren't questionable in terms of content and that they're not the sorts of sites your company would not like to be associated with online.

Target Your Newsletter Members

Sending email blasts to your newsletter distribution lists can also bring traffic in to discover your blog. A great way to add more to a newsletter is to link to your blog and expand on topics back over on your blog. This is one way to convert your current audience from an email blast to a more permanent home on your blog. Services such as MailChimp and FeedBurner can even convert your blog posts into digest-type emails that can be sent to your distribution lists.

By reaching out to an already-established and dedicated email audience, you can bring them in as readers of your website with these links. If your blog is the best source for your company news, or if you sell advertising on your site, you'll want to pull in the largest audience possible. In an age when emails fill up inboxes fast and furiously, you could easily convert email subscribers into RSS subscribers or daily blog readers.

Your newsletter or email blast subscribers would still be receiving your content; now they'll just have more options for how they go about reading it.

Press Releases

Launching a blog is a big deal for any business. It's a progressive step toward expanding an online presence and offering rich, informative, and useful content to clients and potential customers. You should treat the blog as an important advertising and communications tool, and a press release is a great way to initially drive traffic in. Not only will recipients see the link, but if the release is picked up on any online news outlet, the link there may boost your blog's search engine ranking.

Online newswire services such as PRWeb, PRNewswire, and traditional newswire services such as Marketwire currently offer social media press release formatting. With this format, you can include links in your press release, add online photos, and even embed YouTube videos to enhance your news. Linking to your blog is always a great idea so that those who enjoy your news through this method will now know they can get daily updates from your company through your blog.

Case Study: Vancouver Opera

The Vancouver Opera began blogging in 2008 because the staff knew they wanted to get into the social media space. The opera company approached Ling Chan, who at the time was Assistant to the Managing Director, to set up, write, and manage the blog. Chan, now the Social Media Coordinator, was already a personal blogger and was the immediate choice for the organization. She set up the blog using Google's Blogspot blogging platform, and it is currently linked from the main page of the Vancouver Opera website (see http://vancouveropera.ca and http://vancouveropera.blogspot.com). Chan said that she approached the opera's blog with great enthusiasm.

During the 2008–2009 season, the Vancouver Opera saw increased interest due to its wide social media presence. "I love opera, and I love the pop culture tie-ins, so it's very easy for me to find things to write about." Chan noted that each blog post starts off with a simple idea and then is researched with care.

"The blog then grew to a place where we could have a new theme each day. Mondays feature opera videos, Tuesdays are trivia, etc." Research for their themes or weekly series includes seeking out the top 10 haunted opera houses in North America or even the top 10 science fiction movies that could be made into operas. The weekly Operamania blog posts appear each Wednesday (see Figure 8.5).

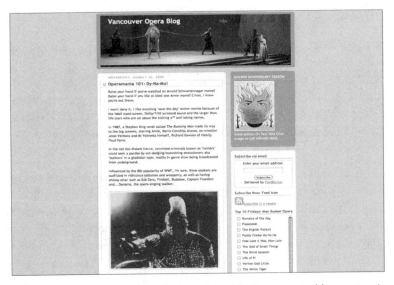

Figure 8.5   *The Vancouver Opera's themed weekly Operamania blog post series.*

However, the traditional opera audience is not necessarily composed of those who are also into social media or blogging. "We promoted it through our website, word of mouth, and Facebook. It just grew from there." Chan also said that the new generation of opera goers is finding them online, "just as often as the hardcore opera lovers."

Along with setting up a blog, finding a passionate writer, and promoting the blog, the Vancouver Opera also created Blogger Night at the Opera. For the first time, it opened up the opera to established bloggers from Vancouver who had never experienced the opera before to live blog their experiences from the theater. "We approached them because we wanted first-time opera goers for the blog. We wanted the readers to relate to the live bloggers." For the 2008–2009 opera season, Chan set the bloggers up in the lobby along with signage displaying their blog URLs, supplying them with wireless Internet. Before the opera and between acts, the bloggers could then come out to their table and record their experiences. The Vancouver Opera has continued Blogger Night every year since.

Chan also started a photo series on Flickr and Facebook that she called Fashion at the Opera. She takes photos of willing participants before the opera and during intermission, and then posts their images online. The public can comment, add tags, or add their own photos to the Vancouver Opera Flickr group. The bloggers could also use these images in their live blog posts. The Blogger Night at the Opera events were so successful that Chan had other opera companies from around North America calling to ask how to organize their own and also how to set up their own blogs.

To complement the blog, the Vancouver Opera also set up a Twitter account and offered specials during the season. Through Twitter, it ran BOGO (Buy One Get One free) campaigns and noticed an increase in sales, directly from the updates.

Going forward, Chan already has comments from those wanting to attend a show during an upcoming opera season. She plans to continue blogging, offering weekly themed posts and online specials, as well as continue the Blogger Night at the Opera events. She has her own word of advice for opera blogging in particular: "Write about things that are interesting to both you and the community. Make sure to have fun with it and be creative."

For the 2012–2013 season the Vancouver Opera blog has changed its theme and layout, focusing on visuals and providing links to music from the season's shows through the Opera Live portal (http://www.vancouveropera.ca/oper-alive/2012-2013/la-boheme-operalive.html). Photos are also posted directly on the blog including the VO's Manga series, which depicts their operas in a Japanese comic style. Bloggers at Blogger Night also use a hashtag for Twitter when posting their updates.

Case Study: Translink's Buzzer Blog

Translink, the Metro Vancouver BC transportation authority, has published its in-bus and in-train flyer *The Buzzer* for the past 95 years, and in 2008 it started up The Buzzer Blog (http://buzzer.translink.ca/); see Figure 8.6.

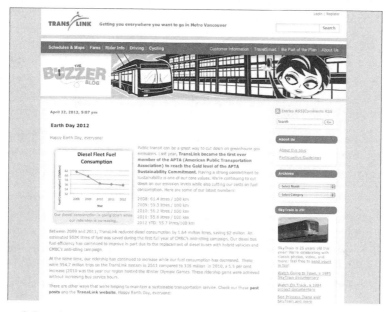

Figure 8.6   *The Buzzer Blog, Translink.*

The blog is the official web companion to the newsletter, something that took time to promote in order to shift the audience from the paper bulletin to the online presence.

Jhenifer Pabillano, who has a background in journalism, signed on with Translink in early 2008 as the Online Communication Advisor. Her job was to write *The Buzzer* and eventually transition it over to a blog.

Translink wanted to connect more with customers through new technologies, providing more information, and the blog was a part of that plan, along with initiatives such as Next Bus (a real-time mobile map of bus locations along Translink routes).

Leading up to this initiative, *The Buzzer*—which has always had a community connection—had gotten a bit "stale," according to Jhenifer, who said it was no longer living up to its full potential. "Initially, there was talk about turning it into a blog full scale—just getting rid of the newsletter entirely." However, the company wanted to maintain *The Buzzer's* physical paper presence to cater to all audiences—and all transit users. But its content, printed every two weeks—then only once a month—would be thinned out in exchange for more frequent updates posted on *The Buzzer* Blog. This is when promoting the blog became a priority.

"When I first started, the articles I put on the blog were more things that would be more useful to read online, as opposed to in *The Buzzer*. For example, the first issue when we launched the blog was actually about hearing the sounds of the SkyTrain and SeaBus." Jhenifer recorded podcast-style interviews of the transit stop announcers and posted the audio on the blog—something she wouldn't have been able to do in the print edition. "Then you could read the newsletter and be intrigued enough about the story of the audio to go over to the blog to actually hear it."

Jhenifer said that the intent was to have the two outlets complement each other, driving those who pick up *The Buzzer* over to the blog and vice versa. She and fellow Online Communication Advisor Robert Willis wanted to cross-promote the platforms while still offering up unique content. She wanted to avoid having regular blog readers pick up *The Buzzer* and see the same content that they had already read.

Without an advertising budget for *The Buzzer* (or the blog), the newsletter was the key source of traffic for the blog, along with Translink's main website. Jhenifer also considered "Who would possibly come to the blog, and how do we find those people?"

The next step was outreach. "We talked to blogs that had similar outlooks and had the possibility to let people know that something like The Buzzer Blog existed." Jhenifer said the key from the start was to write good content. Her goals were to (a) write good content, (b) connect with the customers, (c) have them feel that they've been listened to, and (d) share exclusive content that only Translink could provide (such as new SkyTrain station mockups or photos).

Posts range from bus route features to transit history in the region, and because these posts connect with customers directly and provide a variety of interesting transit information, a transit community also has emerged through the blog. After two years, The Buzzer Blog won the American Public Transit Association's "2010 Best Blog Award."

All these posts are also promoted through the @TheBuzzer and @Translink Twitter accounts, which have a combined 23,800+ followers as of July 2012.

Summary

Although a great deal of work is involved in bringing readers to your blog, just as much effort needs to go into keeping them there. Returning readers become the foundation of your blog's community. You can achieve your goal of bringing readers to your blog by having easy-to-read content that is informative, educational, or purely entertaining. On top of supplying great content, you need to work at getting the word out through various mediums so that you can continue to grow your readership. You can use a variety of tips, tools, and tricks to promote your efforts and really get your company blog noticed, and they all involve a dedication to two-way online communications. Blogging can be moved beyond the written word to amplify your message that much more. In the next chapter, you can learn how to create interesting and visually stimulating content through video and audio to build your audience and customer base.

9

Getting Interactive with Multimedia Blogging

Blogging doesn't always have to be purely about text. With the use of images, audio, and video, you can enhance any blog post. Images help break up text and provide visuals for a story or news item. Some blog posts could consist of images only or an image gallery about a particular place or product. With photo-sharing services such as Flickr, you can also pull user-generated images in your blog posts. On Flickr, you can search for photos based on tags. So, if you want to include photos from Washington on your blog post, you can search for applicable, public images to include.

The use of audio in a blog post is more complicated because it involves more than copying and pasting or uploading a photo. However, audio clips can add context to an interview, for example, enabling readers to read and listen to the original conversations.

Videos are a fun way to enhance your posts. And as with images, you can create a blog post that consists of an embedded video only. Should your company have a new commercial or informative video, blog text can introduce the piece that can be embedded in the post.

All these methods help give your readers more ways to interact with you on your site. They can click through and comment on photos or video and also be introduced to your other online presences, should you have a video or photo network account. In this chapter, you find even more ways to connect and interact with your audience using all these multimedia tools.

Content for All

Content on your blog should always be available to everyone, either on your blog posts, through subscribing, or through a social network that you are tying into your blog. This can include Twitter updates, Flickr photos, audio interviews, podcasts, or videos on a video-sharing network.

As previously mentioned, these forms of content can complement your work, but it is also important to allow others to use them in their works (with attribution or a credit link back to your source). The benefit of having content that others can share is that your readers or audience can take your information and share it across their networks. For example, Flickr has licenses, and podcasts are available on iTunes via subscription.

Your blog is also a gateway to all your company's other online presences, such as a Facebook page or Twitter account. You might have some readers who do not look at blogs often, but they are active on YouTube. By having a YouTube channel, you can reach out to those readers. By promoting your YouTube channel on your blog or including embedded videos, you can let readers know they can also follow you on that network.

If you make your videos available and embeddable to the public, your content can get blogged on someone else's site, and your audience may then increase exponentially. The value of this public content on your blog and on multimedia networks is that what you create becomes shareable by others.

Images

Flickr is an online photo-sharing network that enables users to upload photos (or short video clips), use tags to sort them, share them through embeddable links, or group them with other users' photos. You can sign up for a free Flickr account, which has a monthly limit on the number of photos you can upload, or you can go with a Flickr Pro option. Flickr Pro accounts have an affordable annual fee ($24.95 USD as of June 2012) that gives you unlimited access and resources.

On Flickr, you can sort your photos into sets, which are like online albums. A set can include images from a specific event, about a specific product, or about a particular aspect of a company. By sorting and tagging your images, you enable other users on the network, and even public users, to find your photos when doing a search on Flickr or on the Web. All Flickr images marked as public also get picked up by search engines, provided the titles include appropriate keywords.

Businesses can also set up groups on Flickr and thus enable other Flickr users to add or submit images. Lululemon Athletica Inc., an athletic apparel company, has its own Flickr account. The company posts photos that are filed away in sets. Their sets include photos featuring their latest garments (see Figure 9.1) and events such as a warehouse sale in Hamilton, Ontario, or group yoga in Bryant Park.

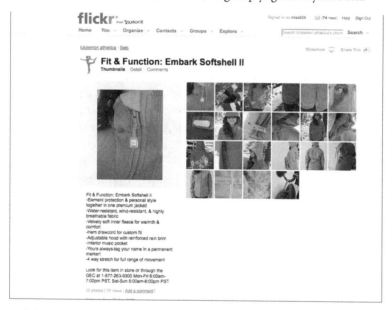

Figure 9.1   *Lululemon on Flickr: Fit & Function: Embark Softshell II photo set.*

Lululemon also created a public group on Flickr (www.flickr.com/groups/883166@N20/) that encourages "Lululemon Lovers" to submit their own yoga-wear photos. Any Flickr users who join the group can submit their photos, which will then appear in the group's image pool. This group image pool can then be embedded into a blog post using the slideshow feature on Flickr.

Keywords and Titles

You also should make sure your images benefit your blog posts by not only looking great but also providing extra content behind the scenes. This means that in the code that makes up your blog post you can include special text that will help with your search engine optimization. For example, when you add an image to a blog post, you should always include an alt tag, and you can choose to include an alt tag. These are extra bits of code that search engines look for when adding your site to their directory listings. Most blogging platforms ask you for the image's title when you are uploading; you can also add titles using HTML code. Although the platform often does not require the title tag, web standards do require it as an alternate description if the image is not shown and also for people who, for one reason or another, cannot see the image. For this reason, you should always add an alt tag.

If you are using an HTML composer, add alt="descriptive text" within the image code so that the image code will appear as follows:

```
<img src=http://yoursite.com/image.jpg alt=" Sunny day ice cream"
title="Eating ice cream in the park">.
```

The result of the preceding code is an embedded view of image.jpg. Thanks to the title tag, when you hover your cursor over the image, you are able to read "Eating ice cream in the park" in a ToolTip by your mouse cursor. The alt tag is useful for the visually impaired who are browsing the Web. Audio reading tools can provide them with the text of the post, but when an image is included, that doesn't translate well into audio. Alt tags included with your image allow them to *hear* the image in your post as "A child eating ice cream in the park" rather than "image123.jpg."

Having the alt or title text allows search engines to pick up on your extra content through the text code. When they scour your site for content, the code for these images also gets noticed.

Tagging Public Images

Tagging your photos, along with appropriate titles, makes your images searchable and helps them get picked up by search engines. This can be for your own reference or for public searches. If you upload a photo of a mop in a kitchen, the tags on the image should be *mop* and *kitchen,* along with any other items of note that you can see in the image. Then Flickr users who want to find a photo that corresponds to what you've posted to view or use in their own blog post can easily locate your image.

Private Images

If you want to upload images that are to be shared only within a select group, you can do so with Flickr. The reason for posting these images to the online service (and then marking them as private) would be perhaps to share them only with a select group of users or employees. You can determine the levels of privacy on each image and those users who might have access to view them, such as those you have added as "Friends," "Family," or "Contacts" on the service. The privacy feature can be applied to an entire set or applied on a per-photo basis.

Protecting Public Content: Creative Commons Licensing

When making your content public, you do not have to give up all rights to your images, video, or even your text. Online content can be protected using a Creative Commons license (http://creativecommons.org), as shown in Figure 9.2.

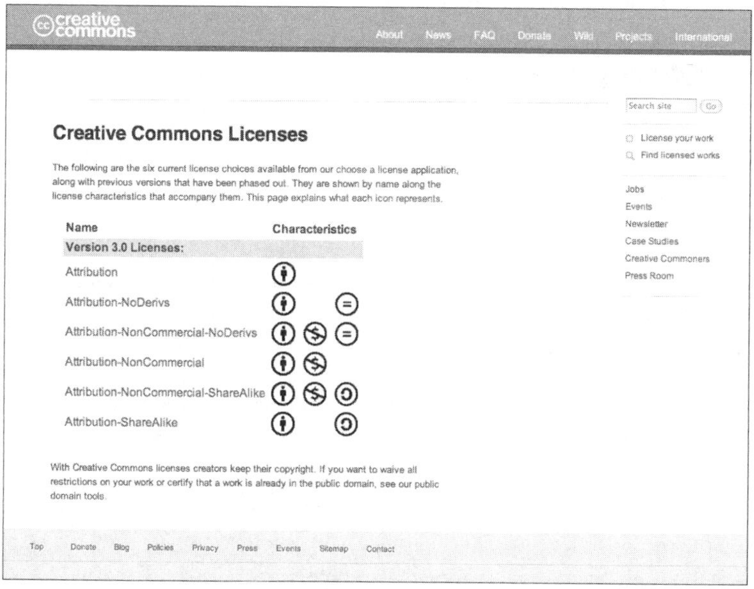

Figure 9.2   *The Creative Commons licenses.*

Creative Commons offers several levels of licenses, which have the following names:

- Attribution

  This means that your images may be used (embedded) by others in their blog posts as long as they link to your blog, state your company's name (or photographer's name), or link back to your Flickr account. You can publicly state what "attribution" levels you would like for your company within the text of your profile page on Flickr. For example, after you have described your company, add a quick note: "Please feel free to share our photos but we ask that you link back to our blog and credit XYZ Company in the photo caption."

- Attribution—No Derivative Works

  With the No Derivative Works license, you are giving the public free-
  dom to use your images (with Attribution as outlined in the preceding
  description), but you are also limiting them by requesting the images
  not be altered or used to create other works (such as a collage or
  another image).

- Attribution—Noncommercial, No Derivative Works

  Adding the Noncommercial license to the mix means that users may
  use your works but not in a commercial capacity where they stand to
  profit from using your images—in advertising, for example.

- Attribution—Noncommercial, Share Alike

  Noncommercial, outlined previously, can also be paired with Share
  Alike. With Share Alike added to your license, you are giving users the
  permission to create derivative works but only if they in turn use the
  same Creative Commons License on that work as you have placed on
  the original.

- Attribution—Share Alike

Creative Commons outlines each level of license by explaining whether you
are allowing users to share, remix, or reuse your content and to what extent
commercially.

Flickr, for example, offers several levels of Creative Commons licenses that can be
preset for your entire account or modified on a per-photo basis. These licenses tell
other users that your content is unavailable for sharing or republishing or that it
is free to be shared but under certain conditions. These conditions allow readers
to use or repurpose the image if it's for noncommercial use, or they may be free
to share it simply by giving attribution to the original source. Creative Commons
licenses exist for audio, video, images, and text content online.

Videos

YouTube is currently the king of online video. Uploading company videos, presentations, or interviews can help you reach out to this vast audience that has passed
more than two billion views. If the goal of your blog is to find readers and build
an audience, making your content publicly available on other networks such as
YouTube is a great way to achieve that.

Using appropriate tags and titles is key with YouTube; according to recent studies,
it is now the second-largest search engine in the world. Using tags and keywords
when providing details of your video on the network is also important to having it
come up in applicable search results among all the others. Although it has a huge
audience, YouTube is not the only video player or video-sharing network on the

block. There are also services such as Viddler.com that enable you to watermark your logo on your videos (as shown in Figure 9.3).

Figure 9.3   *Videos from Powermat on the Viddler video-sharing network.*

Vimeo.com is another video service that caters to top-quality, high-definition videos. All these services enable you to title, tag, sort, subscribe, and embed your videos elsewhere. You can also add clips up to 90 seconds in length to Flickr, which can also handle HD videos.

Audio

Adding audio to a blog post can bring life to an interview or event, or it can enable you to publish weekly podcast updates. As when writing blog posts, you should take the length of the audio clip or podcast into consideration. Podcast episodes should be about 10 to 20 minutes in length, and the same applies for an interview. Bear in mind your listeners will be spending that length of time on your site as the audio plays, or if they have downloaded the audio podcast, they may be listening during their commute. Keeping their attention while not making them commit to an extremely long sound bite is key.

> ✉ *Note*
>
> According to Jeffrey Powers of How To Record Podcasts (http://howtore-cordpodcasts.com/long-podcast-be/), a podcast's "sweet spot" is from 15–20 minutes. Powers also points out that you can capture an audience and get your message out within seven minutes for easy listening.

Attaching audio to a blog post can add a lot to the content if you can find the appropriate service to help you get set up. When putting audio in your blog post or when uploading it to a service, be sure to always add tags and keyword descriptions so that it can get picked up by search engines looking for text.

The following are two online services to which you can upload audio files or record and share audio:

- SoundCloud (soundcloud.com) is an online audio distribution platform that allows you to record or upload audio to your profile and share the audio file through an embeddable player. Uploaded audio files get a distinct URL allowing artists, individuals, and companies to share the link to their audio with ease on social networks, in emails, and so on. SoundCloud is a free service with a pay model for expanded services and features.

- PodBean.com is one online service that allows you to upload or record and share audio clips of any length (see Figure 9.4). When your audio is recording or if you upload an audio file you recorded on your computer, you can then copy and paste the provided embed code into your blog post. This then launches an audio player to play your audio.

Figure 9.4 *PodBean.com audio and podcasting service.*

With PodBean, you can also convert your audio files or playlists into a podcast. *Podcasts* are audio files or shows to which users can subscribe. By subscribing using RSS feeds, users can be notified of new uploads or episodes through iTunes. iTunes lets you know if new episodes from a podcast are available and asks whether you want to download them. This way, your readers or listeners automatically get notified when you have produced new content. Promoting your blog or including your blog's web address on these services and in the details of each audio clip will help drive that audience to your site, where they can get more information from your company.

Slideshows

Another unique tool for sharing content online is Slideshare (http://slideshare.net). It enables you to upload your slideshow presentations online, where they can be tagged, commented on, and put into an embeddable player (see Figure 9.5).

Figure 9.5   *Slideshare.net online slide-sharing social network.*

After a conference or meeting, audience members might want to reference your slides or gather information they couldn't catch the first time around. If you make your slides available online, members of the audience have a reason to reach out to you after the conference has ended.

Slideshare works with PowerPoint or other slideshow application files, and you can also add audio notes or text to explain the slides on the site. Slideshows can be embedded in your blog, just like a regular video, so you can direct people to your blog as a follow-up. Slides can be viewed individually, as a show, or in full-screen mode.

Private or Members-Only Content

Including public content in a blog is ideal, but there is something to be said for rewarding your loyal fans or readers with special members-only deals or exclusive access to your content. Businesses offer loyalty or points cards with special offers, and sports fans or fans of radio or TV shows can sign up to receive exclusive content online. You can offer the same type of exclusive content to registered members or perhaps those who have signed up for your email newsletters.

Locking down your entire site or all your images is not recommended. After all, you goal is to drive traffic to your blog. However, creating a special hidden page that is publicized to only a select group is one way to offer unique content to loyal followers. You can also make this exclusive content available for a limited time, which may help you run campaigns and track statistics. For example, if you have a special new logo or image that others might want to see, you could send the private web link to your fanbase or email subscribers. Let them know the content is up for only a limited time, and then you can pull the content after a week or two and collect data for that period of time, such as number of clickthroughs from the email, the number of visitors to the private site link, and so on.

Keep in mind that whatever content you supply to this special section should also be content you wouldn't mind having in the public realm. *Always* assume that anything uploaded or posted online (if even behind a password) will show up in the public space at some point.

Another example is a recording artist who is releasing a new album. He can preview a new song on a blog by streaming the audio. The artist could send out an email or simply publish a blog post about the exclusive sneak peak that will take place for a certain amount of time. When fans receive the email or notice the blog post, they can come check it out. Those who miss out on the offer will pay close attention next time, and those who were lucky enough to catch it will be that much more faithful to the site.

Podcasting

As noted previously, podcasts are audio files that are made available by subscription. Just as a reader would subscribe to a blog, the reader can also subscribe to a podcast by RSS feed. The podcaster sets up the feed so that when it uploads and publishes a new episode, subscribers are alerted through services such as iTunes. Listeners can then download the episode on their computers or put it directly on their portable audio players.

Contrary to what the name of the medium suggests, you do not need an *iPod* specifically to listen to a podcast. Some argue the word *pod* could stand for "portable on demand," which is exactly how listeners access the audio.

As mentioned in the "Audio" section earlier in this chapter, you can use online services such as PodBean to record, upload, and manage your audio files, but you can also do this through blog posts. Embedding this audio in your blog posts still allows your main blog readers to see this content on your site and to get it automatically if they are subscribed to your main blog RSS feed.

Creating and Promoting Podcasts

When you are deciding to publish a podcast or a series of audio clips/episodes, determining the subject matter of the audio is just as important as it is when you are thinking about content for your blog posts.

If you can record audio onto your computer, you can create a podcast. Popular programs include Audacity for Windows users (http://audacity.sourceforge.net) or Übercaster (www.ubercaster.com) for those using a Mac (see Figure 9.6). Apple's Garage Band (www.apple.com/ilife/garageband/) can also be used for podcast production on Mac computers.

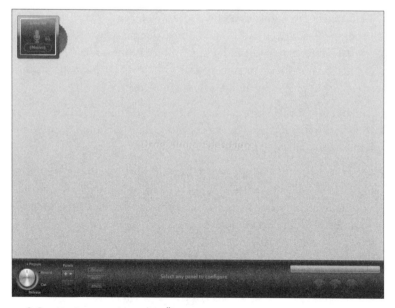

Figure 9.6   *Audio recording with Übercaster.*

Show Notes

If you decide to turn your audio clips into episodes or a series, you can create show notes to help you stay on track. Show notes are items of information in the order in which you will be talking about them on your audio file. For example, if your goal is to talk about a new product and then interview its creator, you can use the following show notes for guidance:

- Introduction
- Product overview
- Introduce guest/interviewee
- Summary

After you record your audio and upload it to a service such as PodBean or through your blog platform, you can then embed the audio in a blog post, much like the way you would embed a YouTube video. In the blog post, you can include your show notes and also put in links, such as a web link to the product or to the interviewee.

Music

If you want to add more to your audio podcast, you can enhance your clips with music. Adding full songs or background music that plays while you speak can spruce up the audio, making it sound more robust to the audience. These pieces of audio or introduction music in your podcast can break up and enhance the speaking portion, just as images break up text on a screen.

Commercial music contains strict usage licenses, but you can look to "pod-safe" music to include in your episodes. Music with this distinction is licensed to specifically permit use in podcast production.

MusicAlley (formerly the Podsafe Music Network) is a great resource that provides a list of artists and songs that can be safely used in podcasting (www.musicalley. com). You can search by artist or genre, and you can see what others have been listening to in the Most Listens section.

Editing and Publishing

You can add music to your audio using the podcasting programs and services previously listed. With programs such as Übercaster, you can control the volume levels on each audio track. Your voice would be track one; and the music, track two. For background music, simply fade down the volume level on track two so that your voice in track one stands out.

After your audio is recorded and background music is added in as you see fit, use the features in your audio recording program to add album art, titles, and tags. You can then export your audio MP3 file, or with a program such as Übercaster, you can upload it directly to a server online.

From there, you can go to Podblaze (www.podblaze.com) to create your RSS feed. However, if you will be using your blog to publish the audio, you might only need to add the audio to a blog post and then submit your blog feed as a podcast feed. With WordPress, for example, a plug-in called PodPress enables you to upload and add your audio to blog posts. The audio is then displayed in custom players in your posts.

You can do the same with FeedBurner (www.feedburner.com), by Google, to create your podcast feed (see Figure 9.7). It has a specific button for you to check that reads "I Am a Podcaster!" after you enter your blog URL or existing feed.

Figure 9.7 *Creating your podcast feed with FeedBurner.*

After everything has been verified, you should be able to publish a blog post that includes your audio file, and your feed will then display the audio button.

Be sure to promote your podcast feed on your blog so that users can subscribe to it separately or alongside the blog feed.

To build your audience outside your blog, you can bring in more readers through podcasting networks. You can add your podcast to a wide variety of directories, including the most popular, iTunes. Through a simple step-by-step process, you can submit your podcast feed to be listed in the global iTunes directory, as shown in Figure 9.8.

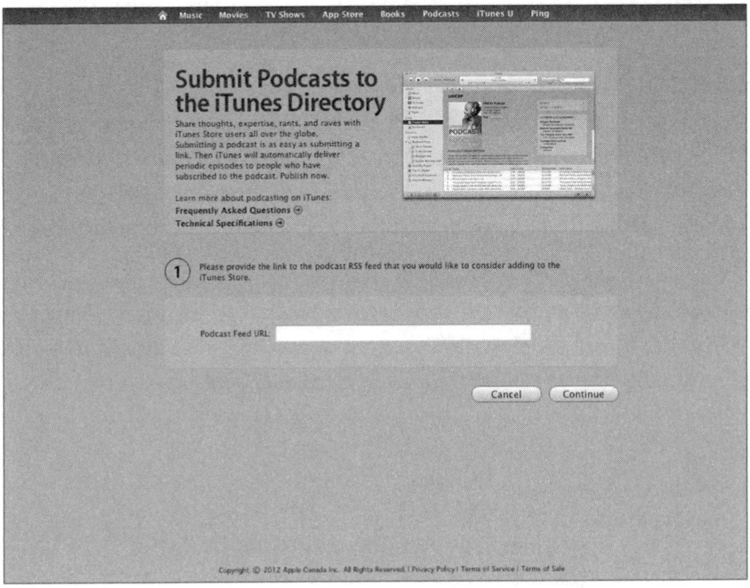

Figure 9.8 *Submitting your podcast feed to the iTunes directory.*

By submitting your podcast feed to iTunes, you not only make it easier for listeners to get your audio (and in turn come back to your blog for more information) but also open up your blog to the entire iTunes audience. Podcasts are sorted into directories on iTunes, so you can gain a new blog reader if someone comes across your podcast and wants to find out more about your company online. By putting more content out to more services, sites, and directories, you can expect to see a bigger audience come back to your blog.

Screencasts

Screencasts are videos that capture what's happening on your computer's screen. These are ideal for product demos and tutorials because screencast-capturing programs enable you to use microphone audio to walk your audience through the workflow on your screen. After you record your screen and save the video file, you can then upload it to YouTube or other sharing services as a fully embeddable video.

On a Mac, you can use an application such as ScreenFlow to record video of whatever you have on your computer screen. For Windows computers, you can use Camtasia, which also enables you to highlight and zoom in on certain parts of your screen. Providing these guided tours in video format can lead to an entire blog series of "how to" video screencasts or demos that your customers may find useful.

Create and Promote Screencasts

To create a screencast demo, you can write up a formal script or just do a walk-through of what you would like to capture. Programs for recording on your screen include Camtasia (www.techsmith.com/camtasia.asp) for Windows users, and ScreenFlow, which comes with Macs that are running Leopard (or later). Snapz Prox (www.ambrosiasw.com/utilities/snapzprox) is also available for Mac users.

These programs enable you to record your computer screen and the actions you make, such as browsing websites or using other applications. They can record your computer's audio or audio from a microphone. You can also include your cursor movements in the screencast, which may prove handy for demos, or you can remove the cursor.

Applications such as OmniDazzle (www.omnigroup.com/applications/omnidazzle) can add graphic elements to your screencasts by attaching animations, such as a spotlight or color-coding, to your cursor onscreen.

After you record your screencast, you can treat it like any other video. You can upload it through your blogging platform or publish it on video-sharing websites. Be sure to include appropriate titles and tags for your screencast, including the tag *screencast*.

Uploading your screencast to a video-sharing network is just as valuable as sharing other forms of multimedia or video because there is an audience for that type of content online. Since July 2012, for example, 31,600 videos have been tagged a *screencast* on YouTube, and 2,680 have been tagged as *screencasting*. If a user wants more information, a demo, or a tutorial video, he will most likely head to YouTube and find your screencast demo show up in the search listings that direct users to your content.

When you are recording your screencast, be sure to begin and end the video with your company's name and how people can find out more, including a visual of your blog or blog URL. Putting content out on other networks reaches broader audiences, but you still want to let them know how to come back to your official home base—your blog.

Contests on Blogs

Running a contest through a blog is a great way to instantly attract readers; however, there are many factors to consider when playing with the idea of hosting a contest, such as what type of prize to furnish, how to select the winner, eligibility, and promotion. You also need a clear objective in mind, which could be to increase your reader-base, engage more readers in comments, or have more shared links on social networks.

Prizing

Blog contests can offer prizes ranging from a $10 value to priceless; that is entirely up to you and your business. Be sure to outline the prize details in full (including estimated value and expiration or use-by dates) and be sure to note how the readers will be able to redeem their prize (will you be mailing it out, will they need to pick it up, and so on).

For a photography contest, you should add more information about the winning photo. Will you use it in any promotions or campaigns? Will the winner need to license the photo? Will the winner be paid or compensated for the image? The same could be applied to a design contest or any other contest in which the company might use a resulting product. Be sure to work through these details before launching the promotion.

Blog Contest Services

Blog contest posts should contain the basics: why you are hosting the contest, what the prize is, who can enter to win, and when the winner is announced. You can set up these parameters yourself and offer entries through your blog's comment form or a form set up through Google Documents, or you can use a professional contest service such as Contest Machine (see Figure 9.9), Strutta, or Rafflecopter.

Figure 9.9 *The Contest Machine online contest platform.*

Contest Machine (http://contestmachine.com) has a basic (paid) service that allows you to embed a contest entry box on your blog. The step-by-step contest creation process guides you through the basics (adding a title, adding the prizes and values) as well as the contest's policy, rules, and regulations.

Strutta (http://strutta.com) offers clients a range of contest options starting with a free contest builder on its website and moving up to a fully customized a la carte hosted solution. The platform can accept images or video (for photo or video contests), allows the contest to be judged by a panel or determined based on a random draw, and can integrate with Google Analytics. It can be used for sweepstakes, coupons, and Facebook application-based contests.

Rafflecopter (www.rafflecopter.com/) creates an embeddable contest box that you can copy and paste on your website after you complete the online setup (much like Contest Machine). It also has integrated Twitter entries into its contest post so that readers can either leave a text entry or click a single button to publish and share their entry on Twitter as well. The Rafflecopter box lets readers know how much time is left in the contest and how many entries they have earned. For example, if the contest states that you can enter using two different methods, and you complete just the comment portion, it lets you know that you can also enter through Twitter for an additional entry.

Legal Items for Consideration

When deciding to run a contest on a blog, your company should take the same precautions to ensure all legal matters are squared away as you should with any other promotion. Even though you're running something on a seemingly less formal platform than a print publication or in-store promotion, laws in various countries, provinces, and states are still the same.

When you are considering the entry methods for your blog-based contest, Facebook is always a popular option. You can run a contest on your blog and ask readers to share on Twitter or "Like" you on Facebook to gain more entries. However, Facebook has its own policies and guidelines regarding promotions (https://www.facebook.com/page_guidelines.php#promotionsguidelines). As of April 23, 2012, Facebook's guidelines for promotions state that promotions must be administered within Apps on Facebook.com, either on a Canvas Page or a Page App. You must include a complete release of Facebook by each entrant or participant, you must not use Facebook features or functionality as a promotion's registration or entry mechanism, you cannot notify winners through Facebook, and more. Because Facebook frequently updates its policies, you are advised to read the guidelines before proceeding with a Facebook-based promotion.

On your blog you also should make sure that your company has permission to use all likenesses, logos, and brand associations that are represented in a contest post. For example, a usable Creative Commons Flickr photo might seem like a fit, but the photographer may not want her image used in a promotion or campaign, which is different from a general blog post. Be sure to secure all permissions before launching your contest.

Select Winners

When it comes time to award your excited contest winner(s) you have several options:

- You can use the built-in selection features with products such as Contest Machine, Strutta, and Rafflecopter.

- You can put "names in a hat" yourself and pull out a winner.

- If you asked readers to leave a comment to enter the contest, you can then copy and paste all the comments received into a text file. You can paste this file into the Random.org List Randomizer (www.random.org/lists/). Just paste in the names of the entrants, click the Randomize button, and watch a random name float to the top of the list. You can then determine this participant as the winner.

- If you hosted a contest with a skill-testing question, you can certainly determine the winner yourself based on merit. A panel of judges can also be used, or you can have readers decide on the winner by implementing a voting mechanism, such as a WordPress plug-in (that will count votes or offer a star-rating system). Alternatively, you can determine the winner based on the number of social media shares it received.

For Twitter entries, you either should include a trackable link in your contest text from the get-go or use a hashtag—using a link shortening service other than the built-in Twitter service. You can track the link, such as a shortened bit.ly link or ow.ly link, by using Twitter's built-in search function. The benefit of using a shortened link is that you can collect analytics with these services, and they are also able to fit within Twitter's 140-character limit.

Using a hashtag (or pound sign, #) in front of a campaign-specific term also allows you to track your entries on Twitter. You could ask readers to "RT to enter to win X prize from ABC Company #ABCPrizePack." Using Twitter's built-in search function, you can then type **#ABCPrizePack** and see all users who have entered your contest using your specific hashtag.

Twitter shares can also be used to track entries if you include your blog post link within the Twitter entry text: "RT to enter to win X prize from ABC Company #ABCPrizePack http://YourWebsite.com/Blog/Nameofthecontest." You can use Twitter share buttons on your blog that show a "Tweet Count" or number of times the post has been tweeted to track entries. Click on the counter, and you see the same list of entries appear as you would with the hashtag or specified short link.

How to Measure Success

At the end of a contest run, you should revisit your goals. Did you gain valuable customer feedback by asking readers to name their favorite product in a comment? Did you gain Twitter followers from all the retweet contest entries? Did your blog receive more traffic during the contest run? You can use your site's analytics to determine how many unique visitors your campaign post received, and Twitter can track the shares. Even posts that do not have a Facebook entry mechanism can receive shares on that social network and others as word spreads.

Run a Contest with a Blogger

You can also approach an outside blogger to run a contest, with your product or services as a reward. You need to consider these same factors, entry methods, and tools when approaching the blogger. Supply the blogger with logos, photos, and detailed prize information. Some may charge a fee for the promotion, but the majority of bloggers offer contest partnerships for free. The benefit for the blog is exposure and perhaps a boost in readership. The benefit for you is getting your product out to a new audience and incoming links to your blog (be sure to include that in your pitch to the blogger). Reputable blogs are able to provide you the same analytics you would achieve on your own.

Case Study: Blendtec

In 2006, Blendtec, a manufacturer of blenders that has been in operation since 1975, took to the YouTube airwaves with a video demonstrating the powerful blending capabilities of its product.

As the video's host put a bag of 50 marbles into the Blendtec Total Blender and turned it on, the question that was asked on the video was this: Will it blend? The response to the video online was overwhelming, and since that time, the company has created 119 videos, and the original marble video currently has almost 6 million views on YouTube.

At first, the series looked like a prank, tossing items into a blender to see how badly they could get chopped up. But the audience quickly realized that in this safe, controlled environment, Tom Dickson, the company's founder, was simply selling his product in an original way.

Dickson has since been featured in his lab coat in all 119 videos by Blendtec produced over the years. This video series was the first to "blend" an iPhone upon its release in 2007, and the follow-up video showing the blending of an iPad is the most popular, with more than 14 million YouTube views to date (see Figure 9.10).

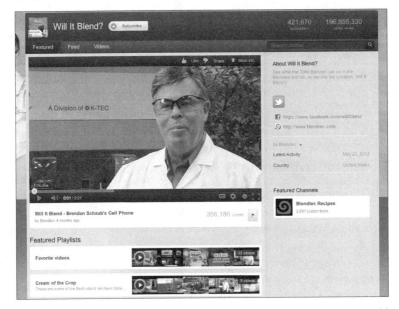

Figure 9.10 *Blendtec's Will it Blend? YouTube channel (www.youtube.com/blendtec).*

Some viewers simply enjoy watching the product being tested, whereas others like to see whether it can truly blend something like Silly Putty, pens, or a crowbar.

Will it Blend? went *viral*, meaning that it was shared and passed along through social networks such as Digg, and the videos have been embedded on countless blogs. The official WillItBlend.com website links to a selection of Blendtec home blenders and Blendtec commercial blenders where you can purchase one for-yourself.

It also sells Will It Blend? merchandise, making it an official Internet pop-culture hit. Tom Dickson has also been asked to make national broadcast appearances to demonstrate the Total Blender's capabilities.

The Blendtec website is focused on the products but links to the company's blog, social media accounts, and Will It Blend website, and YouTube channels in the footer of the page (see Figure 9.11).

Figure 9.11   *Blendtec's website (http://www.blendtec.com/)*

Will It Blend? doesn't stop with video. The company also has a blog (Will It Blog?). This blog features the video series, and it provides general information about company products. On the blog, the Total Blender is opened up and deconstructed to show you how it all works and how it has the power to blend even a set of skis. The blog also features other blenders, ways to clean your product, and company or product updates.

According to Blendtec.com, in 1975 Tom Dickson "revolutionized the way home-makers would forever mill wheat into flour." The Will It Blend? video series reached out to an entire audience it may not have had prior to 2006.

Since then, Blendtec blenders have been used to blend ingredients for baking, smoothies, and now... golf balls. Appealing to the YouTube audience introduced the product to a whole new generation of customers.

Before the video series, most of the younger generation never gave any thought to the brand of blender they would purchase or recommend. But thanks to these clever and entertaining marketing efforts, the company is thriving, most likely in part because of the combined 196,055,330 million views on its Will It Blend? videos.

Summary

By adding multimedia, you can further promote and publicize your blog's great content to audiences of millions around the globe. Your blog might not have many visitors when you first start writing, but by adding photos and video to online networks with millions, if not billions of views, you tap into a whole new audience pool.

Encouraging others to embed your multimedia helps your readers and followers spread your message, and in turn, you can promote their contributions by featuring their Creative Commons licensed photos on your blog or Flickr group.

Each reader and audience member is unique and will come to your blog for the writing, the photos, or for the videos you embed within your posts. Some like to get their information visually, and others audibly. You can cater to these different preferences by using multimedia on your blog and by sharing it on other networks. You goal is to get those viewers, listeners, and readers to return to your blog. That's your priority. By driving them back to your blog, which is your number one online source, you will not only nurture your current audience, but also watch it grow.

10

Taking Advantage of Web 3.0 Blogs

While I was writing this chapter, a news article appeared on the CNN website stating that the one millionth word in the English language is Web 2.0, according to the Global Language Monitor website (www.languagemonitor.com), a site that documents, analyzes, and tracks trends in language. It's really no surprise that Web 2.0 is now part of the lexicon because the term is everywhere.

So what is Web 2.0? It's a set of technologies that took hold in the 2000s and includes collaboration-based services such as blogging and social networking to help people connect on the Web, not just obtain information from static websites. Web 1.0 denoted websites with content that was driven from the top down. In contrast, Web 2.0 describes the decentralization of web content, where it's easy for people to publish content and for readers of that content to interact and respond.

Seeds of the next generation of web technology were planted before that technology blossomed. Blogging started in the late 1990s and became popular in the 2000s. And as we're now in the second decade of the twenty-first century with both feet, we're seeing the seeds of Web 3.0 technologies firmly taking root.

The definition of *Web 3.0* depends on the person defining it. Some think that Web 3.0 is about high bandwidth. For example, Reed Hastings, the founder and CEO of Netflix, described Web 3.0 as being the full-video web that will be made possible by the increasing growth in bandwidth available to customers that will allow transmission of full movies over the Web (http://en.wikipedia.org/wiki/Web_1.0).

Others believe Web 3.0 is "cloud computing," which is the delivery of software and data over the Internet as a service rather than as a product you buy off the shelf. Eric Schmidt, the executive chairman of Google, stated that Web 3.0 will be small, fast applications "in the cloud" that can run on any device (PC or mobile) and are distributed through social networks and other Web 2.0 technologies (www.readwriteweb.com/archives/eric_schmidt_defines_web_30.php).

And yet another definition centers around the convergence of the physical and virtual world, where we'll begin to interact with others in shared 3D online spaces. As futurist John Smart put it, the first indication that we've reached the Web 3.0 plateau is when "the Internet swallows the television"—that is, when video on computers, tablets, and smartphones is so good that the television is no longer necessary (http://en.wikipedia.org/wiki/Web_2.0#Web_3.0).

It's hard to get a handle on Web 3.0 technologies when businesses are already trying to digest what Web 2.0 technologies have to offer. Businesses trying to stay ahead of the curve (and their competition) by investigating Web 3.0 technologies are hampered further because people can't agree on a definition for Web 3.0. This lack of a definition causes businesses to check out a wide variety of potential technologies that might or might not be adopted in the future.

This chapter sorts through the Web 3.0 clutter, tells you what evolutionary trends are emerging, and shows you how to take advantage of "mashing up" different web technologies.

An Overview of Web 3.0 Technologies

If you type **Web 3.0** into the Search box in your favorite search engine, you find several definitions:

- The Web has become much more mobile as smartphones have become mainstream and offer access to the Internet, social networking, and anything else the user wants to do at home or on the go. As of March

1, 2012, 46 percent of Americans are smartphone owners, which is up from 35 percent just 10 months earlier (http://pewresearch.org/pubs/2206/smartphones-cell-phones-blackberry-android-iphone). Apple's iPhone and Android-based smartphones are just two of the latest mobile platforms that offer fast Internet connectivity no matter where you are.

- Tim Berners-Lee, director of the W3C (and inventor of the Internet), described the Semantic Web (Web 3.0) as becoming "capable of analyzing all data on the Web—the content, links, and transactions between people and computers" (http://en.wikipedia.org/wiki/Semantic_Web). Berners-Lee believes that the Semantic Web will take advantage of "intelligent agents" that are autonomous entities that direct their activity toward achieving goals (http://en.wikipedia.org/wiki/Intelligent_agent). In the case of the Semantic Web, intelligent agents will crawl through the Web in response to complex questions. For example, if you want to go to a performance of the San Francisco Opera and then go to a Moroccan restaurant in the city for dinner afterward, you can ask a complex question such as "What is the next performance of the San Francisco Opera and where can I find a good Moroccan restaurant to eat afterward?" The Web takes that information and organizes richer results for you than what is available today.

- The Web will become more personalized to your needs. You're probably used to shopping sites such as Amazon.com learning about your past purchases and offering suggestions based on those purchases the next time you shop on their site. In a Web 3.0 world, online services will learn over time what your preferences are and will tailor your browsing experiences to your preferences. What's more, people's browsing experience will be different even when they all go to the same URL. The Amazon.com website already does this to some degree. When you visit Amazon.com, the site uses browser cookies to determine what you looked at the last time you visited so that it can promote related products that you may like.

So with all this in mind, what technologies are being used right now that are forerunners of Web 3.0 technologies to come? We take a look at Wikipedia, APIs, and widgets.

Wikipedia

You've probably heard of wiki websites. The term *wiki* means "fast" in Hawaiian, but in the Web world it means a website that has a number of interlinking pages that are managed using a relational database system. The pages are Spartan in looks but quick to load, and people can add and edit entries within the wiki system.

Plenty of wiki sites are available on the Web, and you can download and establish your own wiki on your own website. An example of the former is the popular Wikipedia site (www.wikipedia.org), which is a free online encyclopedia maintained by users. You can get a lot of information on Wikipedia that you might not be able to get anyplace else, such as a comparison of wiki software, as shown in Figure 10.1.

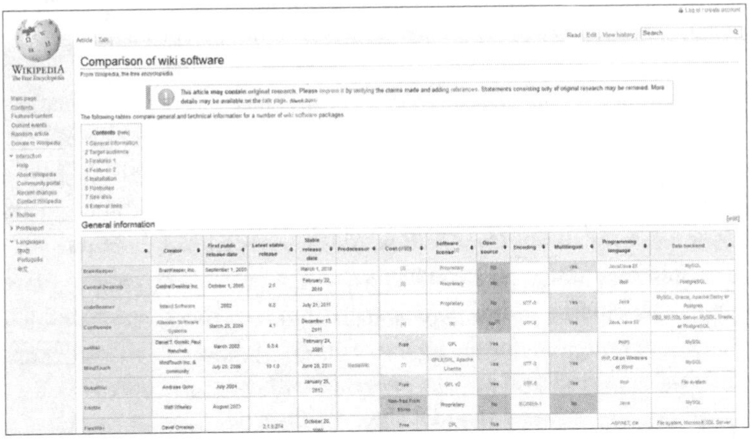

Figure 10.1   *The Wikipedia Web site page that compares wiki software packages.*

Wikis have been around since the mid-1990s, but only recently have companies started to leverage wiki technologies, along with developing Web 3.0 technologies to make data exchange more accessible to businesses. For example, the Swirrl website (www.swirrl.com), shown in Figure 10.2, is staking an early claim on being a Web 3.0 company.

Figure 10.2   *The Swirrl website.*

Swirrl leverages the Semantic Web technology called Linked Data, which is the recommended best practice for exposing and linking data on the Web. (If you want to see an example of how it works and get more information, go to the Linked Data website at http://linkeddata.org/.) Using Linked Data, Swirrl maintains your data online so that people can log in using a modern web browser, add information akin to a wiki, and microblog to other people in the business or project team. Swirrl has positioned itself to businesses as a service using tools that are familiar, easy to use, and easy to access.

APIs and Widgets

Some Web 2.0 platforms currently in use may be the springboard for Web 3.0 technologies. For example, many social networking sites, including LinkedIn and Facebook, offer Application Programming Interfaces (APIs) to developers so that they can create applications using those sites' unique resources. For example, LinkedIn has an application that links to a person's WordPress-powered site.

Modern operating systems such as Mac OS X and Windows 8, as well as mobile computing platforms such as the iPhone and Android, have established small applications called *widgets*. Widgets can also be small applications that link to an object, such as a few lines of HTML code from YouTube that you place in a blog post to show a video presentation you gave recently. A good place to find a comprehensive list of widgets for the desktop, the Web, and your mobile device is the Widgipedia website (www.widgipedia.com), shown in Figure 10.3.

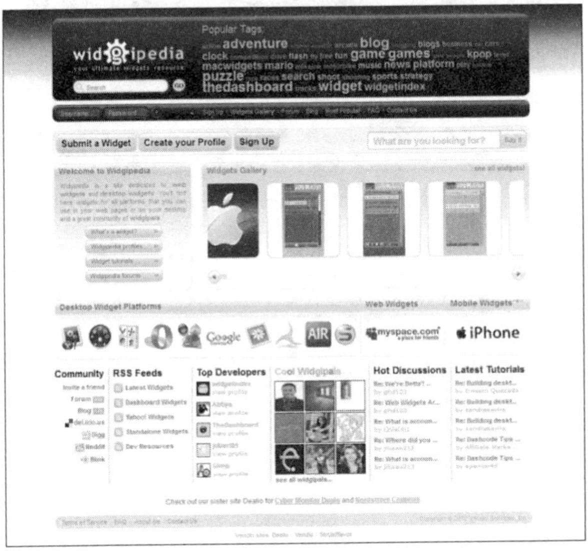

Figure 10.3 *The Widgipedia website.*

So what does this mean for your business if you're trying to reach your customers? First, you might be able to find an application available that you can use to enhance your blog, link to your website, and link to your social networking sites at little or no charge. What's more, developers are working to "mash up" applications to make them more usable and relevant.

Mash It Up!

The term *mash up* (also sometimes styled as *mashup,* but we call it mash up throughout this book for consistency) means to combine one or more applications into a single application. You might have seen an example of this on a business site (or perhaps your own business site) that enables visitors to check Google Maps to see where a company is located, which is a basic example. If you want to see more interesting mash ups, look at the Webmashup.com site, shown in Figure 10.4.

Figure 10.4   *The Webmashup.com website.*

On this site, you can view more than 3,000 examples of how people combine applications into a new one. For example, OggChat (www.oggchat.com) integrates with Google Talk, Gmail, and your smartphone so you can communicate with your customers wherever you are, as shown in Figure 10.5.

Figure 10.5   *The Oggchat.com website.*

▶ *Caution*

If you have developers and you want to create your own mash up applications (such as a blog with another application), make sure it doesn't
interfere, or give the appearance of interfering, with another company's
trademarks. If you don't, you'll probably receive a letter from a lawyer
sooner rather than later.

There is speculation that in the future you may be able to drag and drop different
programs into a web page and have the combined application work flawlessly. For
example, you could drop Google Maps and several local business and newspaper
websites so that you can see where companies are currently building. No one has
figured out how to do this as of this writing, but developers are thinking about it.

Integrate Semantic Technologies

The Semantic Web requires that ontologies, or files that define the relationships
between groups of terms, be detailed and comprehensive so that the Web can find
richer search results for you. The translation of "detailed and comprehensive" is a
lot of work, and there's debate about whether people will be interested in putting
in the work to make their websites as searchable as possible.

On the other hand, blogs, photoblogs, and vlogs all allow you to add categories and
tags so that you can organize your blog posts. For example, in the Halfway There
blog, shown in Figure 10.6, I scrolled down to the end of the post where Blogger
shows that the author has filed the post under the Teaching category. If you click
the Teaching category link, you see all posts that are filed under that category.

Figure 10.6   *The Halfway There blog that shows posts with the Teaching category label.*

If you're interested in integrating semantic technologies into your blog right away, blog software and sites have these taxonomy features so that you can add posts to one or more categories, add a category list to your blog, and make reading a little easier for people who are interested in specific topics.

Make Agents Work for Your Blog

So how do you make your website available to the Semantic Web and get your business ahead of the Web 3.0 curve? A company in Ireland has developed a search engine that will help get your blog and your website noticed, as long as you have a developer on board (or would like to program it yourself).

The Digital Enterprise Research Institute (DERI) of Galway, Ireland, has created the Sindice Semantic Web search engine at www.sindice.com (see Figure 10.7).

Figure 10.7 *The Sindice website.*

This site lets you search websites that not only have the Semantic Web language framework called Resource Description Framework, or RDF, but that also use Sindice APIs and widgets to integrate into your blog and other applications.

The good news is that when your webmaster submits your blog (and even your website) to Sindice, the site will be indexed within an hour. So, people searching for your site will be able to find it even more quickly.

The bad news is that as of this writing, if people want to check you out on the Semantic Web, they need to visit the Sindice website. Even so, if you want your blog and any other web assets to be on the cutting edge, consider making the Sindice agents work for you.

Go Mobile

When the first edition of this book was published, the iPhone ruled the smartphone market, Android phones still hadn't burst onto the scene, and the iPad was a few months away from release. Now the iPhone and Android phones are in a battle for dominance, and the iPad rules the tablet market despite the presence of competing Android tablets from makers including Motorola and Samsung.

Mobile devices are the first wave of Web 3.0 technologies, and if your business isn't using smartphones and tablets, it will soon enough. Blogging services and apps have taken advantage so you and your business colleagues can blog from anywhere and even incorporate pictures from mobile devices. If you aren't sure about what mobile platform is best for your business, we start by explaining the differences between smartphones and tablets and then discuss using moblogs on a smartphone and a tablet.

Understand Smartphone and Tablet Differences

If you have an iPad and iPhone, the differences between the two devices are readily apparent. The physical size of all three iPad models is 9.5 inches high and over 7 inches wide, whereas the iPhone 4S, the latest model, is a little over 4.5 inches high and a little over 2 inches wide. The physical size differences are due to the size of the screens on each device: 9.7 inches diagonally on the iPad and 3.5 inches for the iPhone 4S.

If you have an Android tablet, the sizes vary much more widely. Samsung produces tablets from the Galaxy Note, which has a 5.3-inch diagonal screen, to its Galaxy Tab 2 10.1 with a 10.1-inch screen (hence the name). The Note is considered to be and is marketed as a hybrid tablet and smartphone, so the 5.3-inch screen on the Note is considered to be the largest Android smartphone screen. The smallest Android phone screen so far is 2.55 inches (www.computerpress.org/fun-facts-about-android-phones.htm).

With most mobile applications (better known as *apps*), a smaller screen on a smartphone means that you have to make changes to the interface that won't be there on a desktop or laptop and probably won't be there on a tablet. Then again, what you view on a tablet and a smartphone may be different, with only a couple of minor changes depending on where you are in the app.

As a small example, when you open the WordPress app on your iPhone for the first time, the Welcome screen appears, as shown in Figure 10.8. You can use it to start a new blog on WordPress, add a blog you host on WordPress, or add a WordPress blog that you host yourself.

Figure 10.8   *The WordPress app Welcome screen on the iPhone.*

When you open the WordPress app for the iPad, the Welcome screen shown in Figure 10.9 is much the same, with a couple of exceptions: The text says you can start blogging from your iPad in seconds instead of blogging from your iPhone, and you can also close the Welcome screen to view the main WordPress page.

Figure 10.9   *The WordPress app Welcome screen on the iPad.*

Smartphone Moblogs

You can easily download an app for blogging on a smartphone. (How effective you are at typing any text for your blog, though, depends on your own smartphone typing abilities.) For this example, you install the WordPress app on the iPhone 4S. If you have an Android phone, the process is similar; for example, instead of installing the WordPress app from the App Store, you install the WordPress Android app from the Google Play Store.

Install and Set Up a Blogging App

You can download and install the free WordPress app from the App Store, as shown in Figure 10.10. Tap Install to enter your App Store password and then install the app. After the app icon appears on your screen, tap the icon to open the WordPress app and view the Welcome screen that was shown in Figure 10.8.

Figure 10.10   *The WordPress installation screen in the Apple App Store.*

After you install WordPress, it's time to add a new blog to be hosted on WordPress.com or add a blog that you host either on WordPress.com or your own server. For this example, you add Rebecca's self-hosted WordPress blog, Miss604, that she downloaded from WordPress.org and set up herself. (If you're curious, 604 is the area code for the city of Vancouver, British Columbia, Canada, where Rebecca lives.)

On the Add Blog page, you enter the URL, the username, and the password to log in to the blog and then make changes from the iPhone. If you want to include geo-tagging, which adds your location (such as your current city) when you add a blog post, move the Geotagging slider from Off to On. When you're done, tap Save.

Blog from Your Smartphone

Now that you are logged in, click the blog in the Blogs list. Within the blog page itself, you see a list of your posts. Write a new post by clicking the pencil icon in the upper-right corner of the screen. The Write screen appears, as shown in Figure 10.11, so you can begin writing your post.

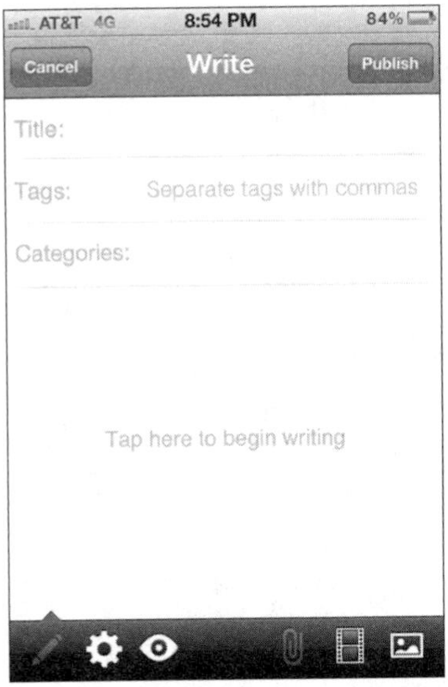

Figure 10.11 *Type a new post in the Write screen.*

Here's how to write your post:

1. Tap the post title in the Title box.

2. If you want to add tags, add one or more tags in the Tags box, and if you have more than one tag, separate each tag with commas.

3. You can select from a list of categories in the blog by tapping Categories and then tapping one or more categories from the list.

4. When you finish selecting categories, tap Write in the upper-left corner of the screen.

5. Tap in the Tap Here to Begin Writing box to start writing the text of your post.

In the black bar at the bottom of the screen, a little triangle above the icon shows you where you are. For example, if a triangle appears above the pencil icon, the app is telling you that you're writing a post. You can also change settings, preview the blog, add an attachment, add a video, and add a photo to your post.

When you finish adding the post, click Publish in the upper-right corner of the screen. The new blog post appears at the top of the blog posts page. Tap a post in the list to review the post within the app as well as within the blog itself.

Tablet Moblogs

Blogging using a tablet app isn't exactly the same as blogging on a smartphone. You download an app for your blog as you do with your smartphone, but because you have a larger screen to work with, you have more functionality as shown earlier with the WordPress app for the iPad.

Next, we use Eric's Samsung Galaxy Tab 2 10.1 to download the Blogger app to the Tab, which makes sense considering that Google produces both Blogger and Android.

Install and Set Up a Blogging App

In the Google Play Store, open the Apps section and then search for Blogger. Tap the Blogger app in the list to open the Blogger download page shown in Figure 10.12. Tap Download to download the app and then tap Accept & Download in the Permissions window.

Figure 10.12   *The Blogger download page in the Google Play Store.*

After you install the app, tap Open. The first page asks you to review the mobile terms of service, but if you don't want to and accept the terms anyway, tap Accept. In the Switch accounts window, select your Google account or add one by tapping the Add/Manage accounts button.

After you select the account, Android asks whether you want to have Blogger access your account—perhaps more than once. Tap Allow to give Blogger access. If Blogger can't find a blog that you've already set up, the app asks you to go to the Blogger site and create one. Tap Go to Blogger to open the Blogger site and sign in using your Google account email address and password.

Because Blogger is a Google product, it makes sense that Blogger is also tied into the Google+ social networking service. That means your Google+ profile is reflected in your blog also, and if you don't have a Google+ account, you need to create one. Here's how:

1. Tap the New Blog button to create the new blog in the window.

2. Type in the title of the blog in the Title box.

3. Type the blog address in the Address box.

4. Select one of the six screen templates for the blog.

5. Tap Create blog.

After Blogger creates a blog, click Done at the lower-left corner of the screen to return to the Blogger screen.

Blog from Your Tablet

In the Blogger screen shown in Figure 10.13, the title of the blog you created appears at the top of the screen. If you have more than one blog in Blogger, the app recognizes this, and you can switch to a different blog within the app by clicking the down arrow to the right of the blog name.

Figure 10.13   *Write a new blog post in the main Blogger screen.*

Add a title and the content of your post by tapping in the Post Title and Post Content boxes, respectively, and type in the text. As you post content, you can select text and then apply bold, italics, or a link by tapping the B, I, or link button. Below that row of buttons, you can add a photo or image by tapping on the photo or image icon.

If you want to add labels to your blog post, such as a subject name so that people can search for posts with that label, tap the Labels box and type in one or more labels. If you have more than one label, separate the label with a comma. You can also add your current location to your blog posts automatically by tapping Location Disabled, Tap to Activate.

When you finish writing your post and you want to share it with your readers, tap Publish and then tap Yes. Your blog post appears in the list of blog posts, as shown in Figure 10.14. You can open the post by tapping on the title in the list. You can also tap the menu icon in the status bar at the bottom of the screen and then tap View Blog to view the blog.

Figure 10.14 *The published blog post and the Blogger menu where you can view the blog by tapping View Blog.*

You can write a new post by tapping the pencil icon in the upper-right corner of the screen. If you want to view the list of posts again, click the posts icon to the right of the pencil icon.

Case Studies

Smartphones and tablets are devices that use Web 3.0 technologies, and in this chapter we look at a website and a product that use these technologies. The first, UrbanSpoon.com, allows you to place a widget on your website or blog and use the site on the iPhone by downloading the UrbanSpoon iPhone app from the App Store. The other case study is the HootSuite tablet app that aggregates your social media messages so you can get your social media website updates in one place.

UrbanSpoon.com

If you're looking for a place to eat in a metropolitan area near you, the UrbanSpoon.com website is a good place to get comprehensive information about restaurants in the area. UrbanSpoon.com, shown in Figure 10.15, is also a good example of using mash ups to create an early-generation Web 3.0 site.

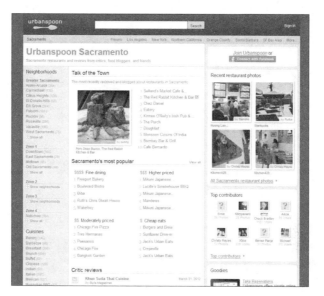

Figure 10.15 *The UrbanSpoon.com website showing Sacramento listings.*

The site in this example is for the Sacramento area; however, you can choose another city at the top of the page or search for a particular term. The site has a number of different category lists, from the top-10 rated restaurants overall, popular restaurants with readers who rate the restaurants, types of food, neighborhoods, features, price, and more.

Part of that "more" includes a widget that lets you select a restaurant at random in the Sacramento area if you don't know where to go, and you can put this widget on your own blog or website. The home page also mashes up information from local newspaper critics and local bloggers.

If you click a restaurant to check it out, you see a number of Web 2.0 and 3.0 features. In Figure 10.16, the Chicago Fire Pizza page on UrbanSpoon enables you to interact with the listing in a number of ways.

Figure 10.16 *The Chicago Fire Pizza listing on UrbanSpoon.com.*

You can write a review; view the menu; and read critic, blogger, and other user reviews. If you want to know the restaurant's location, the Google map tells you where it is. You can also get driving directions, see nearby restaurants, and even see other pizza places if you decide Chicago Fire is not to your liking.

If you scroll down to the bottom of the page, you see a link to another Web 3.0 feature: the UrbanSpoon application for the iPhone. Of course, UrbanSpoon doesn't just use the iPhone; you can also get UrbanSpoon on your Android phone. (However, since Eric uses the iPhone we'll use that app as our example.) After you enter your phone number and choose your carrier, click Send to Phone to send a text message with a link to the app to your phone.

The message contains a link to the UrbanSpoon mobile website. When you open the link you'll be asked to download the UrbanSpoon app from the App Store on your iPhone.

The bottom of the page also has a link to the UrbanSpoon blog, where you can get more information about what's going on with UrbanSpoon and view food blogs by metro region.

Although there is a lot of information on UrbanSpoon.com, the ready availability of that information no matter where you are makes UrbanSpoon a good example of leveraging Web 2.0 and 3.0 technologies to give customers what they need.

HootSuite for the iPad

HootSuite is a social media management service operated by HootSuite Media in Vancouver, British Columbia, Canada. This service is a great example of a mash up application because it combines your social networking accounts and even your WordPress blog into a "dashboard" where you can get information within your social networking site in several columns, as shown in Figure 10.17. What's more, you can also download the app for mobile devices including smartphones, Android Tablets, and the iPad. For this case study, we look at using HootSuite on the iPad.

Figure 10.17   *Eric's Twitter dashboard in HootSuite for the iPad.*

After you install and download the HootSuite app from the App Store and set up your social networks in the app, you see the Twitter page with your home feed, mentions, and direct messages in three separate columns, as in Figure 10.17.

If you tap the Home button at the far left of the blue title bar at the top of the screen, you can scroll down and change the stream to Facebook. When you click one of the streams, you see the two Facebook streams in two columns: the News Feed stream in the left column and the Pending Status Updates stream in the middle column. The right column is blank. If you have more than three columns, such as with your Twitter feed, tap the feed you want to view. You then see that feed in the left or centered column depending on the stream you tap.

Scroll up and down in each column and then tap the message in the appropriate window to view the message in its entirety in a separate window. You can perform other tasks such as replying or retweeting a tweet, as shown in Figure 10.18.

Figure 10.18 *When you tap a tweet, the full tweet appears, so you can reply, retweet, click the link, and perform other tasks.*

HootSuite rounds out the mash up experience by making its functions available from the blue menu bar at the top of the window. You can search for information within your social networking or blog site that you have open in the HootSuite window, write and publish a new entry, find contacts, and get statistics about your usage.

The HootSuite app is free, and you can use basic HootSuite functions for free within the app. If you want more features such as integrating with Google Analytics, you can choose from several plans with different features and monthly charges. If you just want HootSuite to better coordinate your online social life, consider sticking with the free version and let this mash up app on a Web 3.0 platform make your life a bit easier.

Summary

The second decade of the twenty-first century is here, and Web 3.0 technologies are taking root. Several different technologies comprise the Web 3.0 definition, including mobile devices, the Semantic Web that uses intelligent agents to achieve goals, and a Web much more personalized to your needs.

This chapter looked at different technologies and techniques being used that are signs of Web 3.0 technologies to come, including using APIs, widgets, and mash ups and adding tags to your blog. The UrbanSpoon website is a good example of how to use a Web 3.0 site, and HootSuite for the iPad is a good example of a mash up app on a mobile device that incorporates a WordPress blog. As the years go by, it will become more likely that the blog you read is created on a tablet or smartphone.

A great barometer for measuring your blog's effectiveness is to calculate the blog's return on investment, or ROI. Let's continue to Chapter 11 to learn more about how to measure your blog's ROI and track its performance.

11

Maximizing Your Blog's ROI

If you've been in business for any length of time, you know what the acronym ROI means: return on investment. It's what you as a business owner know you need to measure to determine whether your strategy is working. But how do you measure ROI when it comes to your blog, and how do you adjust your strategy to maximize it?

The good news is that there are tools and guidelines you can use to measure the ROI of your blog. The bad news is that there isn't a set formula for doing so. But the information in this chapter shows you how to

- *Use several tools for measuring your blog activity and effectiveness*
- *List a set of guidelines you can use for measuring ROI*
- *Convince the powers that be that your company needs a blog*
- *Update your strategy when you have a sense of your blog ROI*

What's Your Online Influence?

Before you decide where you want to go with your ROI, you should know where you are currently in terms of your blog and overall social networking presence.

One website that attempts to measure your current online social networking status is Klout (www.klout.com), which is a site that tracks all social networking profiles on Google+, LinkedIn, Twitter, Facebook, and Foursquare. Though Klout connects to Tumblr, Blogger, and WordPress blogs, Klout doesn't track blog activity as of this writing.

Your score on Klout is based on the number of people connected to you and who tend to repost your messages on other social networking websites on a regular basis. Klout calculates scores in 400 signals, such as Facebook likes and the number of LinkedIn connections, and gives you an aggregated score of anywhere between 1 and 100, where 100 is best. The score is recalculated daily, and your score appears on your Klout home page. For example, Eric's score as of mid-August 2012 is 46, as shown in Figure 11.1.

Figure 11.1 *Eric's Klout score is 46.*

In August 2012, Klout produced an update to its system that added a number of signals to track, including a Wikipedia page about you and/or your business that Klout says provides a good indication of "real world influence." This new update also introduced a "Moments" feature that tracks the activity of your social network connections and folds in that information into your score. The more active your connections are, the higher your score may be.

Klout is not without controversy. One criticism is that a Klout score is not truly representative of a person's influence, and a recent example at the end of 2011 showed that President Barack Obama's Klout score was actually lower than that of tech pundit Robert Scoble, although you would probably agree that being President of the United States has far more influence (www.businessinsider.com/the-truth-about-your-klout-score-the-math-behind-how-your-phony-number-is-mesasured-2011-12). When the August 2012 update was released, the Klout scores of President Obama and Robert Scoble were recalculated and Obama's score was higher than Scoble's.

 Tip

> There's a good *Wired* magazine article about why Klout does and doesn't matter titled, "What Your Klout Score Really Means" that you can read at www.wired.com/business/2012/04/ff_klout/all/1.

Klout has also been criticized for trying to quantify online interaction, because by promoting social ranking and stratification, Klout is actually promoting social anxiety among its users (http://en.wikipedia.org/wiki/Klout). Even with this controversy, Klout is the de facto social interaction measurement site, and it has enough (ahem) clout to be included in HubSpot's Marketing Grader report, which you learn about later in this chapter.

You should also check the popularity of blogs in your area of interest on the Technorati website (www.technorati.com), a site we mentioned in Chapter 1, "Why Are Blogs So Important?" Technorati contains a blog directory and ranks the blogs according to its popularity and influence in the blogosphere using a formula called Technorati Authority.

When you open a category in the blog directory, as shown in Figure 11.2, Technorati lists the blog sites in the category according to popularity ranking, with the top-ranked site appearing at the top of the list.

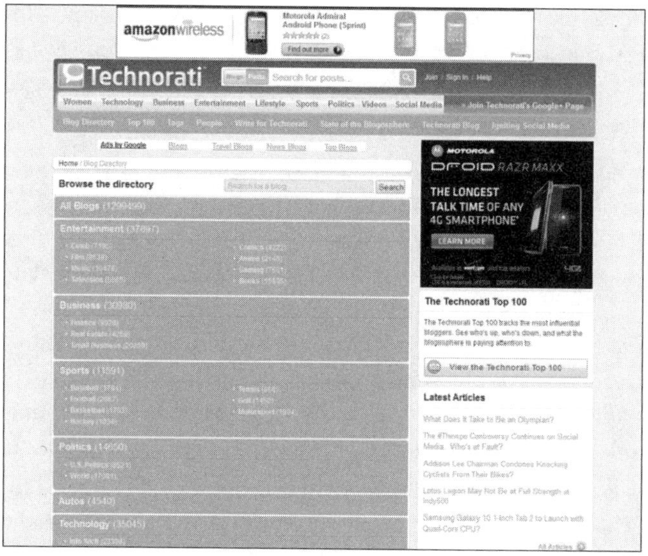

Figure 11.2 *The Technorati blog directory.*

For example, when you click the Info Tech category link, you see the most popular blog; in Figure 11.3, it is Ars Technica, which appears at the top of the list with a score of 953. The number two blog is The Next Web with a score of 926. On the same page, you can also view a list of blogs with rankings that are rising quickly or falling sharply.

Figure 11.3 *The Ars Technica blog is the most popular according to Technorati.*

Put Together Your Strategy

This book describes how you can use different tools and techniques to create the best blog possible, but your blog won't be successful unless you have a strategy behind it. So before you start writing your blog, let's review what we've covered in the book; then you can ask yourself these questions:

- How do you want people to view your blog when they see your website address in their browser address bar? That is, do you want the blog hosted on a site like WordPress.com, or do you want to download a blog platform from a site like WordPress.org and install the platform on your web server? Hosting a blog on your server means that visitors see your website address in the address bar instead of a hosted site like wordpress.com or blogger.com, which gives the impression that you and your company are serious about blogging. However, hosting a blog site on your server takes more time to set up, and time is money.

- Who is going to write the content on the blog post? You need to iden-tify who will be writing and when they will write; you also need to set aside time for them to focus on writing blog posts.

- When will your blog writers post? You should put together a schedule for each person writing the blog so you can ensure that users continue to have a reason to keep reading. Search engines like it when you continually update your blog, too.

- What will you write on the blog? You need to listen to the people who are going to write the blog, listen to your customers, and also research competing blogs to find out what customers and others in your industry are talking about.

- Who will manage the blog? You need to assign a person to make sure that blog posts get done and also respond to negative comments and other potential slip-ups quickly and positively.

- Will you include any multimedia on your blog, such as photos or videos? If so, you need to look at a variety of issues such as how to handle copyrights, where you will take photos, and how you will produce videos.

- What are the policies and procedures on your blog? Management and multimedia issues are two of the key issues that should be covered in written policies and procedures. Be sure to communicate with all stakeholders such as blog writers and management to formulate a guide that you can share with others in the company. Even if you're a one-person company and you'll be doing the blogging, it helps to write down some policies in bullet-point format so you can refer to it if and when the need arises.

- What other marketing tools will you leverage with your blog? For example, your company may hold events and seminars, and you need to promote them not only with your blog but also with other online and offline marketing strategies such as marketing through email and going to chamber of commerce marketing events. You can also use the events and seminars to promote your blog and ask attendees if they want to sign up for your email newsletter.

This list of questions is not exhaustive. Depending on your situation, you might have some other questions you want to ask. For example, you may want to have policies for accepting guest bloggers from one or more of your partner companies.

The Tools You Need

After you answer the questions you need to ask before creating your blog, it's time to start putting together a list of the tools you need to create and support the blog. Some of these tools cost money, but others don't.

- Choose a blog platform, as we discussed in the previous section. We covered a variety of platforms in Chapter 3, "Creating a Blogging Strategy."

- Set up an RSS feed, as discussed in Chapter 2, "Leveraging Your Blog with Marketing Tools," so you can give your readers the opportunity to receive your blog posts in their favorite blog readers.

- Set up social networking profiles and link your blog to them, as discussed in Chapter 2. You should have profiles at least on LinkedIn, Facebook, and Twitter because they are the three largest social networking sites and where your customers are most likely to be. Google+ is growing fast, so consider joining that network also. Finally, research social networking sites that discuss what your business does. For example, if your business involves music, consider joining MySpace because music is that site's primary focus these days.

- Establish an email marketing system, as described in Chapter 2. There are many different systems available with varying degrees of power and price levels.

- Create a marketing automation plan for your various online marketing efforts. Many email marketing systems come with an automation system built in. For example, an automation system sends email messages to recipients at certain times during the month and on their birthday. You can set up a plan for other online marketing systems, as we discuss in the next section. One good source of marketing automation information was produced by HubSpot (www.hubspot.com) in its "10 Commandments of Marketing Automation" report shown in Figure 11.4.

- Implement tracking tools so you can monitor your blog's performance and get the data you need to know how your strategy is working. We get into more detail later in this chapter.

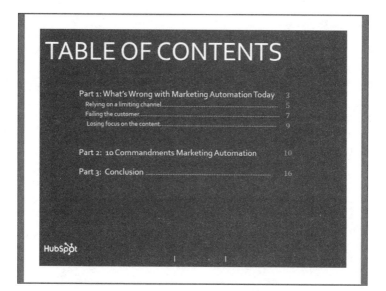

Figure 11.4   *The Table of Contents for the HubSpot "10 Commandments of Marketing Automation" report.*

Tie Your Blog and Other Marketing Strategies Together

In Chapter 2 we described a variety of online and offline marketing strategies that you can use. Now, let's discuss how you can tie those marketing strategies together so your blog can promote your other marketing efforts and vice versa. For example, your email newsletter and social networking site can point to your blog, and the blog can contain an opt-in area so people can sign up for your newsletter.

To tie everything together, you need to map out everything day by day, week by week, and month by month. There are a variety of different tools you can purchase. For example, Microsoft Project is the de facto corporate standard for maintaining projects online, and your company may require its use if you work in a company that uses plenty of Microsoft technologies such as Microsoft Office.

If there isn't a company policy about using a solution from one company or you have the flexibility to try cheaper options, you can try a number of either free solutions or low-cost solutions on a limited basis.

Marketing Calendars

Brandeo has created a free calendar template for Excel (or any spreadsheet that can import Excel files) that anyone can download from its website, as shown in Figure 11.5 (http://brandeo.com/2012_Marketing_Calendar_Template_Free_Download). The template allows you to track both online and offline marketing, and a sample month is included to help you learn how to fill out the template. The template includes each month of the current calendar year. At the beginning of each calendar year, Brandeo creates a new template for the new year.

Figure 11.5 *The Brandeo 2012 Marketing Calendar Template.*

If you use the Salesforce content management system, you can download a free marketing calendar from Cambridge Cloud Partners (shown in Figure 11.6) that integrates with Salesforce. Cambridge Cloud Partners developed this small application in response to repeated requests for it from its customers. Download the calendar application at www.cambridgecloudpartners.com/salesforce-com-marketing-calendar-for-free/.

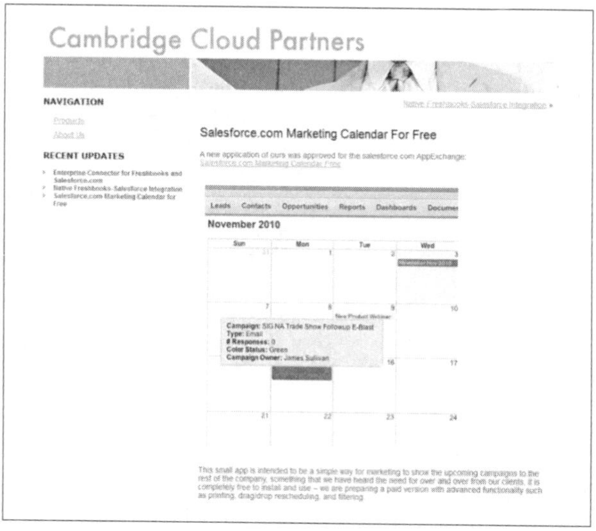

Figure 11.6   *The Cambridge Cloud Partners Salesforce.com Marketing Calendar.*

Project Management

Basecamp is a popular and easy-to-use project management system that's produced by 37signals (see Figure 11.7). Your Basecamp data is stored on 37signals servers, and pricing starts at $20 per month for 3GB of storage and the ability to manage 10 projects at once. You can download a 45-day free trial and get more information at http://www.basecamp.com.

Figure 11.7   *The Basecamp tour opening page.*

If you use or have used Microsoft Project but want a cheaper alternative, consider the free, open source Openproj software package shown in Figure 11.8. Other than being free, other advantages to Openproj are that it can open Microsoft Project files automatically, and it supports Gantt and PERT charts.

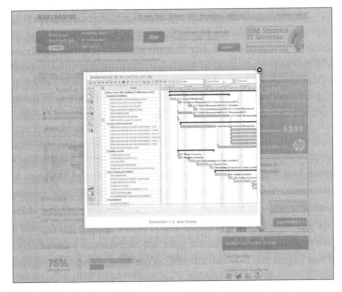

Figure 11.8 *A sample OpenProj screen on the OpenProj download site.*

However, like a lot of free software, Openproj has limitations on what it can do, especially in comparison to Microsoft Project. For example, in Openproj you can't save the changes you make to an imported Microsoft Project file back into Microsoft Project format. Instead, you need to export to an XML file so you can open it or import it into any program that supports XML. You can download OpenProj and try it for yourself at http://sourceforge.net/projects/openproj/.

Present Your Recommendations

If you work in a company with more than one person and you don't have the power to implement a blog and related strategy yourself, you need to put together recommendations in a written report and present it to one or more people in the company. You should consider including the following features in your presentation to make it as persuasive as you can:

- Do you have actual data? You can get data about your competitors' blog sites from the Alexa website. You may also consider running Hubspot's Marketing Grader to check your website against your two biggest competitors to see how they compare. If you don't have a blog, Marketing Grader sees that as a big detriment to your overall score.

- Get input from your stakeholders and include that input, including direct quotes, in your report. Stakeholders include other employees, managers, and definitely customers who are interested in producing and reading a company blog. If you're creating an internal company blog, your customers will likely be employees only. You may even want to invite one or two key stakeholders to your meeting to boost your chances.

- Based on the input from your stakeholders, you can determine who's going to manage the blog and who the writers will be. Be sure to write job descriptions for the manager and the writers so the readers of your proposal and the person listening to your presentation will understand what people involved in blogging will do.

- Your feedback from stakeholders will also determine what sort of content they'd like to read about, what sorts of features they want in the blog, such as video, and whether they want to view the blog on their smartphones and tablets. Then you have to plan ahead to find out how you can meet these demands, such as where you will shoot videos and how you will produce them for integration into blog posts.

- Formulate ideas for blogging policies and procedures including contingency scenarios and tracking blog activity. Research of other blogs, especially blogs from other companies in your industry, is valuable here. You learn more about tracking activity on your blog in the next section.

- Consider creating a couple of mocked-up screens that represent how the blog could look. Images are a great way to get people to wrap their heads around a concept, and blogs are no different.

- Detail a usability plan that includes creating storyboards, going through one or more testing sessions with members of your audience, such as preferred customers, and making changes as needed. If you have a blog for both the Web and for smartphones, you may need to test both platforms.

- Meet with your marketing manager (and others in the marketing department if there is one) about how you can dovetail the marketing of your blog with your company's current marketing efforts. Creating a blog may also prompt your marketing manager and/or department to think of other new marketing opportunities.

- It's important to list the financial costs and potential revenues of the blog, and as part of that you may also need to discuss the opportunity cost for the company. Opportunity cost is an economics term that refers to the value of the next-highest-valued alternative use of the resource you want to use. For example, if the next-best alternative to creating a blog is creating a direct mail campaign, the opportunity cost is the money paid for the blog and potential lost income from the aborted direct mail campaign.

There is no guarantee that all this information will guarantee that the powers that be accept some or all of your recommendations, but they will give you a better chance. You may also want to recommend a trial of the blog for a period of time (such as six months) and track the activity on your blog so you can see how people use and interact with it.

Track Your Blog Performance

As part of your research into creating a blog, you need to know how you are going to track activity on your blog. There are three parts to tracking your blog's performance: getting the right tools, getting the correct data, and translating and reporting that data accurately.

Set Up Tracking Tools

Tools for tracking your blog's activity are plentiful and range from free web-based tools to a suite you can purchase that contains programs built to work together from the ground up.

Free Tools

There are a number of tools you can try that are absolutely free to use.

- Previously in this chapter we discussed HubSpot's Marketing Grader, shown in Figure 11.9, which checks any website URL you specify against criteria that HubSpot identifies as being important to the success of your online marketing efforts. The Marketing Grader assigns different scores to different criteria and gives you an aggregated score of 0 to 100 (100 being best) and any recommendations for improvement. You can also compare your website to one or two other websites. As of this writing, Marketing Grader is still in beta testing, so there may be new features by the time you read this book. Marketing Grader is free, and you can check it out at http://marketing.grader.com/.

Figure 11.9   *The HubSpot Marketing Grader website.*

- Google Analytics (www.google.com/analytics) is a powerful and free analytics tool that shows you a wide variety of information about your blog site, including how many people visited you in a specific period, what keywords people use to search for you, and the location of your visitors.

- Google Webmaster Tools (www.google.com/webmasters) contains a number of methods for checking your blog site to see if you're doing everything you need to make your site as visible as possible to search engines. If you're not doing everything necessary, Google tells you where you need to improve. For example, if you have a link on a web page that goes to another page that doesn't exist, Google will alert you to this problem so you can fix it.

- The Google AdWords Keyword Tool (https://adwords.google.com/o/Targeting/Explorer?__c=1000000000&__u=1000000000&ideaRequestType=KEYWORD_IDEAS) is designed for use with the AdWords paid advertising program, but you can use the Keyword Tool to find out what keywords or keyword phrases are most effective. The more popular a keyword or phrase is, the more likely it is that your site won't appear on the first page of search results. So you might want to add words to a keyword phrase and use this tool to see whether that longer phrase has less competition and may be worth testing.

- Microsoft's Bing is the second most popular search engine after Google according to eBizMBA (see http://www.ebizmba.com/articles/search-engines for the latest list of the top 15 most popular search engines). Bing has become even larger since Yahoo! started using Bing as its

search engine. So you should also visit Bing Webmaster Tools (www.
bing.com/toolbox/webmaster/), check your blog site to ensure that it's
following Bing's recommendations, and make changes if Bing finds
anything that needs improvement.

- Alexa (www.alexa.com/), shown in Figure 11.10, is an excellent site to
get a pulse of your traffic because it compares with other sites around
the world and in your own country. You also can see how many other
sites link to your blog. For example, as of this writing, the Miss604
blog has a global rank of 253,896, which means that 253,895 sites in the
world have more visitors than Miss604. Even better, the blog has more
than 1,000 other websites that link to it. Alexa calculates its rankings by
researching the average number of daily visitors and page views on the
website over the previous three months. The site with the highest combination of visitors and page views is ranked first.

Figure 11.10   *The Miss604 blog activity as monitored by Alexa.*

- Quantcast (www.quantcast.com) is a free service you can use to measure traffic and receive reports about your audience, including user
demographics, lifestyle similarities, and geographic locations. Type a
suggested URL in the Search box, as shown in Figure 11.11, so you can
view a real site profile and see whether Quantcast is worth your while.

Figure 11.11 *The Quantcast website.*

Tools You Can Purchase

If you want to expand your shopping list to tools you can purchase, here are some to consider. Some of these tools allow you to try them before you buy.

- CrazyEgg (www.crazyegg.com) presents visual information about where your visitors click on the web page and how often they click on those points so you can see what features on the site are the most popular. If your page scrolls down, CrazyEgg shows you where people lose interest so you can edit your site and give visitors more encouragement to keep scrolling down. You can try CrazyEgg for 30 days, and if you like it, you can purchase monthly plans ranging from $9 for the Basic plan to $99 for the Pro plan.

- Go Try This (www.gotrythis.com) is a service that allows you to create search engine optimization (SEO) keyword links, Twitter links, and QR print codes and then track all your links in all your websites (such as a website and your blog site) from the Go Try This control panel. As of this writing, Go Try This was developing a new version and had suspended sales until it was finished, so check the website to get the latest updates and prices for the service.

- Market Samurai (www.marketsamurai.com) was described by one of Eric's business colleagues as "Google Analytics for Dummies." Of course, that doesn't mean people who use Market Samurai are dummies; it means Market Samurai is a simple and easy-to-use service for enhancing the SEO of your blog or any other website. You can download a trial version, and if you like Market Samurai, you can buy it for $149 as of this writing. As with all paid applications, visit the Market Samurai website to get the latest prices.

- IBM Enterprise Marketing Management (http://www-142.ibm.com/software/products/us/en/category/SWX00) is a suite of applications built from the ground up to work together. IBM groups the 24 products in the suite into four categories: cross-channel campaign management, digital marketing optimization, marketing resource management, and web analytics. You need to contact an IBM representative so he can tailor a price quote to your specific needs.

- Adobe Digital Marketing Suite (http://www.omniture.com/en/), shown in Figure 11.12, is another suite of applications built by a large company working to expand its web presence beyond just its software. As with Adobe's web technologies such as Dreamweaver and Flash, which the company acquired when it purchased Macromedia, Adobe got into the social networking analytics game when it purchased Omniture. Adobe has worked to improve the suite during the past few years to keep tightening the integration of all its components from social analytics to integration with specific partners such as Salesforce. One feather in Adobe's cap is that the Digital Marketing Suite was the first preferred Facebook marketing developer, meaning it meets Facebook's requirements to manage Facebook pages, applications, ads, and analytics. As with IBM's solution, you need to contact Adobe for a price quote.

Figure 11.12 *The Adobe Digital Marketing Suite website.*

Getting the Right Data

Now that we've discussed some of the tools at your disposal for tracking ROI, how do you get the right data? The Smashing Hub website, shown in Figure 11.13, has a good guide to calculating your blogging ROI in nine steps (http://smashinghub. com/9-steps-to-calculate-your-blogging-roi.htm).

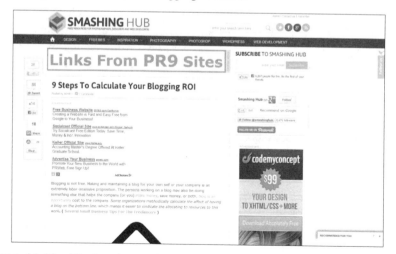

Figure 11.13 *The Smashing Hub 9 Steps to Calculate Your Blogging ROI report.*

For this book we simplify the steps a bit so you can get an idea of how to proceed; you can visit the Smashing Hub website for a more in-depth example. We use the Miss604 blog as our example.

The standard formula for calculating return on investment is

$$\frac{\text{Revenue} - \text{Investment}}{\text{Investment}}$$

The result is expressed as a percentage.

Investment

The first step is to calculate the investment you're making in your blog:

1. Start by calculating how many hours each person in your company spends writing, editing, and managing the blog. (Managing includes tracking blog activity, calculating the ROI, and making changes to your strategy.) For this example, two writers of the Miss604 blog devote six hours per week to writing and managing the blog.

2. Determine how much each person receives in compensation. Rebecca, who's the manager of the blog, works on the blog four hours a week, and her partner Duane works on the blog two hours a week. In a year, Rebecca makes $50,000, and Duane makes $30,000. In 2012, there are 52 work weeks, including paid holidays, so Rebecca will make $961.54 per week, and Duane will make $576.92 per week. Based on those figures, Rebecca makes $24.04 per hour, and Duane makes $14.42 per hour. Calculate the average monthly salary amount by multiplying the hourly amount by the number of hours worked and then multiply by 4.333. Therefore, Rebecca makes $416.66 per month blogging, and Duane makes $124.96. The salary cost of blog labor is $541.62.

3. Figure out how much to add to the monthly salary in overhead and benefits. Overhead includes expenses such as the computer, utilities, and phone, and benefits include such items as health insurance. The company accountant or CFO knows the standard overhead calculation for the business, but for this example we use 50 percent. The overhead and benefits amount per month is $270.81. Add the amount of the salary cost and the overhead and benefits cost to get the total labor cost of the blog per month, which is $812.43.

4. If you had an outside company build your blog, determine the amortization schedule for building the blog (such as three years) and then calculate the monthly cost. You do this by adding the internal and external costs (such as how much you paid the company) and then

dividing that amount by the number of months in the amortization schedule. In this example, the number of months would be 36.
However, if you designed the blog internally, as Rebecca did, you need
to add the labor cost and the overhead and benefits costs not only for
Rebecca but also for anyone else who helped develop and test the blog
before it was published to the Web.

5. If you have any additional blog costs, add them to your investment
    equation. In this example, Rebecca's company pays $10 per month for
    a web hosting company to host the blog and another $9 per month to
    CrazyEgg to augment all the other free SEO tools she uses. So the total
    monthly amount for hosting and maintenance is $19 per month.

Now add it all up to get your overall monthly investment in your blog. The total
monthly investment for the Miss604 blog in this example is $812.43 plus $19.00,
which comes to $831.43 per month or $9,977.16 for the year.

Revenue

Now we need to see how much the blog generates in revenue to justify the investment made in it:

1. First, we need to know what the blog does to prompt revenue-
    generating behaviors. For the Miss604 blog, there are two behaviors.
    One is generating leads for Rebecca's blogging business, sixty4media,
    which produces the Miss604 blog. Another is to generate ad revenue
    from other companies that want to advertise on the blog.

2. Now that we've figured out what the behaviors are, we need to know
    how many revenue-oriented actions are made each month. In this
    example, the Miss604 blog has 20 people sign up each month for the
    Miss604 email newsletter and has 1 new advertiser that signs up each
    month. Of the 20 people who sign up each month, 1 person becomes a
    new customer.

3. Now it's time to assign a value to each customer. Let's say that each
    new customer brings in $100 per month, and each advertiser brings
    in $200 per month. Starting in January, Rebecca gets $300 in income.
    In subsequent months of the year, the total revenue grows by $300 per
    month. So the total revenue before expenses is $23,400. Let's suppose
    that the expenses are 25 percent per year, so the total overall value of
    the behavior is $17,550 per year.

Calculate Blogging ROI

Now that we know what the yearly investment and revenue numbers are, we can plug them into the ROI algorithm to calculate the yearly ROI percentage. In this example, subtract the investment cost ($9,977.16) from the revenue ($17,550) for a total of $7,572.84. Then divide that amount by the investment cost for a yearly ROI of 75.9 percent.

Though there isn't a desired range for an ROI percentage, chances are that your blog ROI percentage won't be as high as in this example. But this should give you the start you need to create an accurate ROI percentage that you can use to justify creation of your blog to yourself or anyone else.

Translate and Report Data

Now that you know how to calculate income, expenses, and the ROI of your blog as well as where to get data, how do you put the information into a format that people can easily understand?

If you've implemented a paid system such as the ones from IBM and Adobe, you can create all the reports you need from those systems. But if you'd rather go the no-cost or low-cost route, you can use those tools with some other software you likely already have on hand to create monthly reports for your own use and to share with others.

Start with your favorite spreadsheet and include the following worksheets:

- A worksheet that aggregates information from the other worksheets so you and others can see trends over a period of months. You should also include the yearly ROI based on the aggregated monthly ROI percentages. You learn more details about spotting trends and how to interpret them in the next section.

- One worksheet for each month you track that includes your current month of investment and revenue data and calculates not only the total investment and revenue but also the ROI for the month.

- One or more worksheets so you can aggregate information from specific tools. For example, you can add scores from HubSpot Marketing Grader and Klout into a worksheet and then average the scores to get a year-to-date average.

- A worksheet of charts generated from the other worksheets if your audience wants to see trend information at a glance, such as costs and revenues from month to month.

You should also include the following information in your report in this order:

1. An executive summary that briefly summarizes what the report contains and what you found at the front of the report. You can create a word processing document or even write it in an email message if that's acceptable.

2. Any examples of issues or screenshots of blogs that you feel that the powers that be should follow up on or to support any recommendations you have in the executive summary. For example, you might want to show a screenshot of a competitor's blog with a feature you think your company's blog should include.

3. Reports from various tools you can use as supporting documents. For example, you can save various Google Analytics reports in PDF format or in CSV format if you want to place the Google Analytics report into your spreadsheet as a separate worksheet.

Trend Watching

You can easily put things together to see how situations or events are going over time. Some trends can be spotted fairly quickly, such as within a month or even sooner—for example, the number of comments to a recent post. Other trends, such as how many people visit your blog, require a long-term view.

Spotting One or More Trends

Spotting trends requires a good eye and a critical mind, so if you're not sure you're the best qualified for that job but someone else in your office is, you might want to approach that person with the job. If you want to do the job yourself, don't be discouraged if you don't pick up on some trends right away. As the trite saying goes, practice makes perfect.

So what kinds of developments on your blog could indicate a trend?

- The amount of traffic on your blog and how much of that traffic is converted into leads.

- See what types of content bring you the most views and comments.

- The locations of your visitors as well as how many people were referred to you by other sites.

- The number of visitors converted into leads, and the number of leads converted into paying customers, advertisers, or both.

- The pages that make readers take action that could result in revenue from the blog. For example, there may be a specific page where visitors are most likely to sign up for your company email newsletter.

- Where people click on your page. You can find this information using tools such as CrazyEgg.

- What pages have the links with the most clicks. You can use tools such as CrazyEgg and Go Try This to find this information.

What Does It Mean?

All the data in the world doesn't help make your blog better unless you know what it means so you can take action (or keep floating on). Here are some basic meanings of trends and what you should do about them:

- Topics with more views and more comments should prompt you and your team to write more often about those topics. The title of the blog posts may also point to a reason why those posts get more attention. For example, if popular posts have titles that contain words such as Tips or Secrets, you might want to write more posts that tell readers how to do more with your company's product and/or service.

- If you find that most of your readers come from a specific area, that could be good or bad, depending on the intended audience for your blog. If you decide that you want to have more people visit your blog from outside that specific area where most of your visitors reside, you need to reach out to those potential visitors. For example, you might want to connect with blogs in other geographic areas.

- When you look at the list of sites from which new visitors have come to your blog, you may find that the site (or the organization that sponsors it) isn't where your company has a presence. For example, an industry-specific social networking site may be feeding visitors to your blog even though you don't have a profile there. In that case, you should consider integrating that social networking site into your online marketing strategy.

- If you have an offer with a call to action on a page that isn't getting the results you want, you need to change the offer, the call to action, or both. Or you might need to move the offer and call to action on a more visible location on the page or to a more popular page so more people will see the offer. You can even make the offer more visible by adding graphics and changing colors to be more attractive. (Attractive, not garish.)

- If you have little traffic to your blog no matter whether or not you have a high number of leads, you need to write more content, improve your blog SEO by adding more of your targeted keywords to your content, and increase promotion of your blog through your other marketing efforts.

- If you don't have a lot of leads even with a high amount of traffic, you need to check your content and see what people are talking about. You should also check the blogs of others in your industry to see how they're getting leads. A more direct way to get answers is to write a blog post and/or approach your best customers and find out what would get them to stay as repeat customers or refer new customers to your business.

- If you find that a healthy number of leads are turning into customers, check that number against other online and offline marketing efforts to see how they compare. You or your marketing department may need to change your marketing strategies in areas outside your blog—and make sure that you stick with your current strategy with your blog. That doesn't mean you shouldn't review your blog strategy regularly, but it does mean you and your blogging team should pat yourselves on the back.

When we looked at companies to feature in our case studies, we gravitated toward companies that have created their own means of tracking their blogs, but we also wanted to see what they learned and how they implemented changes. In addition to these case studies, you should also read posts from online groups such as The Blog Zone on LinkedIn to get real-world stories and suggestions from other bloggers.

Case Studies

For the case studies in this chapter, we look at how two different marketing agencies track their blogs so you can glean some ideas for your own business blog. The first case study looks at the tools and strategies 6S Marketing uses. We follow up with a look at how Yield Software, now owned by Autonomy, created and used its own ROI tracking system.

6S Marketing

6S Marketing is a Canadian digital marketing agency that specializes in promoting through the Internet, optimizing search engine and mobile marketing, determining the right social networking strategy for its clients, and analyzing websites and blogs. (See the company's website at www.6smarketing.com, shown in Figure 11.14.) It was this last part that interested us when we talked to Chris Breikss, the president of 6S.

Figure 11.14   *The 6S Marketing website.*

Use Google Analytics

Chris says that 6S Marketing uses Google Analytics as its primary measurement and tracking tool not only for customers' blogs but for its own blogs as well. He explains that his company's choice of Google Analytics doesn't come down to cost:

> "It's because of features and functionality and the integration onto other Google platforms. While the perception is that Google Analytics is free, to make it most effective requires customization and configuration, which requires skilled people. Our company goes to the Google Headquarters (GooglePlex) every year to get recertified and trained in Google Analytics. We try and send two different people each year so that knowledge is spread across the company."

What's more, Chris says, the company integrates Google Analytics with other Google tools such as Webmaster Tools, AdWords, Google+, Google Places, YouTube, and Google Drive. In sum, Chris says that using Google technologies is a great way to get higher rankings in the Google search engine:

> "You want to use Google products as much as possible so that you can clearly communicate all aspects of your site and business, so that

Google can rank you better. If you were to take two otherwise equal sites with one using all Google products and the other using the competition, which one do you think Google would rank higher?"

With this in mind, Chris says that 6S Marketing measures both its customers' blogs and its own blogs in much the same way:

"We track engagement in the form of opens and click rates and analyze which content is of most interest to the subscriber base and cross-reference that data with Google Analytics if a particular campaign needs to be tracked or if we have abnormal or outstanding results."

An Evolving Strategy

Chris feels that 6S Marketing has stopped looking for new tools because Google Analytics has matured to the point where that tool gives the company the information it needs. For example, analysis of the 6S Marketing blogging site (shown in Figure 11.15) using Google tools brought some interesting insights: "We have found that blog visitors have a poor conversion rate to direct response actions on our site, and most of our traffic comes through Google searches looking for quick access to information."

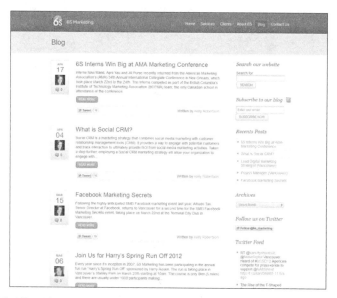

Figure 11.15   *The 6S Marketing blog.*

This information has caused 6S to refine its strategy accordingly. Chris explains, "We are now looking at how long people are watching YouTube videos that are embedded into blog posts and trying to determine exit points, as an example."

Leverage with Other Tools

One tool that Chris is fond of is the MailChimp email marketing system in part, Chris says, because of its RSS to email functionality: "[You] can automatically send an email to your subscriber base with a summary of your three or five most recent blog posts to your subscriber base. There is no need to click set-up and send. You can configure this email to go out on the first day of the month at 10 a.m. and then just focus on producing solid blog content, and MailChimp will take care of the distribution." You can view the MailChimp website, shown in Figure 11.16, at www.mailchimp.com.

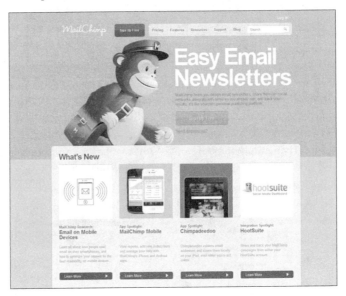

Figure 11.16 *The MailChimp website.*

Recommendations for Improving ROI

Chris has one piece of advice if you want to improve the ROI of your blog: "Make your blog (and your website if you have one) mobile friendly." He says that any blog and/or website owner should "take a detailed look at their website analytics and see what percentage of their website traffic is coming from a mobile device. Don't be surprised if one-third of your visitors are visiting on a mobile device, and that they are not consuming as many page views as through traditional desktops and laptops. Soon that number of visitors will grow to be the majority of all traffic and we will be looking at a whole new set of numbers and conversion rates to base our decisions on in this ever changing world of digital marketing."

That doesn't mean that Chris's customers follow all his advice all the time. "I wish that our clients would listen to all of our recommendations and act faster." But, Chris continues, "I also understand that we need to find a balance between what we think their needs are and their comfort levels. I have been burned many times not sticking up for what I believe and allowing clients to make mistakes in which I ultimately get the blame. I am learning to stand by blogging beliefs more."

What are those blogging beliefs? Chris explains:

> "I believe in business blogging but not in the traditional sense. I believe in producing great new content and not necessarily calling it a blog, and maybe separating it into a news section. I think that too many websites repurpose information and call it a blog post. Too often, we see blog posts that summarize concepts rather than presenting a unique perspective of their own."

Chris recommends, "instead of offering a reinterpretation of the story, I suggest breaking the story" so the blog post offers "an authentic first-person account of what the user wants to see." Chris suggests that such an account can be a mini-case study that tells readers "what you think will happen before, and a basic analysis of what happened after." In sum, Chris asserts, "this type of thinking and planning applies to all industries and blogs and will shape the future with how we develop content."

Autonomy ROI Blog Tracking

In 2010, Yield Software created a nice little checklist of metric areas for tracking your blog ROI that augments what we've talked about in this chapter. We discovered this list in 2011 and planned to write about it before it disappeared with the rest of the Yield Software website. As we searched for this checklist, we found that in the span of a few months Yield Software was purchased by Autonomy, and Autonomy was purchased and became a subsidiary of Hewlett-Packard. (You can visit the Autonomy website, shown in Figure 11.17, at www.autonomy.com.)

Figure 11.17   *The Autonomy website.*

Former Yield Software president Matt Malden is now a vice president at Autonomy and provides his insights into the blog tracking system that Yield Software used for its own blog. Matt explains that even though the company didn't include this list of steps in its service offerings, it shared this list with the world because as "one of the leaders in the [online marketing] space, we wanted to exemplify the best practices in monitoring, measuring and optimizing our online marketing strategy."

The Eight Tracking Metric Areas

You can create the eight blogging metric areas from your web analytics data, and this list suggests how you can place the data into charts so you can see the value and costs associated with the blog. Although this list is at a high level, it does tell you what you need to track and how hard it is to track those metrics.

1. **Traffic:** You can easily track traffic generated by your blog inside Google Analytics and other analytic applications. This chart tracks the traffic numbers from your blog along with the percentage of total traffic that it represents. It's important to compare the cost to attain this traffic to the other methods of pursuing online traffic such as pay per click (PPC) and search engine optimization (SEO). If you know your SEO and blog cost of work, you can pretty easily get to a cost per click.

2. **Traffic Engagement:** This chart compares traffic engagement indicators, including bounce rate, time on site, pages per visit, and contribution to repeat visits across the different online marketing strategies.

3. **Links:** This chart tracks inbound links to your blogs, along with anchor text and the "link juice" each link is contributing. It compares inbound links to your blog with other website links attained through the more traditional SEO. The goal here is to get down to the cost per link level to help compare the tactics.

4. **Keyword Rank and Click Share:** This one can be a bit more challenging depending on the depth of your analytics system. This one also assumes you are targeting keywords in your blog posts (which if you aren't, you should be). This chart compares the rank of your blog posts, web pages and pay-per-click ads for target keywords, along with the percentage of clicks that each brings in. Often the clickthrough rate of blog posts in the natural search results is much higher than other listing types.

5. **Social Buzz:** This chart tracks the social buzz generated by your blog posts, including retweets, social bookmarks, likes, and social mentions. Although this chart is not a direct comparison to other online marketing efforts, it does help to articulate the value of your blog.

6. **Twitter Followers:** This chart measures the number of Twitter followers and quality of those followers achieved from your blogging compared to other social efforts. You can do the same type of analysis for other social media venues in which you participate, such as Facebook, YouTube, and LinkedIn.

7. **RSS Subscriptions and Newsletter Subscriptions:** This chart tracks how many site visitors from your blog signed up for an RSS feed or your newsletter versus sign-ups you receive from other organic and paid traffic.

8. **Conversions:** This chart tracks conversions from visitors who visited a blog post or came to you via a blog post. It includes the number of conversions, the percentage of total conversions, the conversion rate, and the cost per conversion. It's also really important to track conversion assists and not just leave it all to last-click attribution. You'll be pleasantly surprised by how many conversion assists your blog contributes.

The Effectiveness of the Tracking Metrics

That information, Matt explains, determined "where to invest our online advertising budget" and also acted as "a determinant of the content and the editorial direction of our blog." Yield Software didn't make any changes to these metric areas because, Matt says, "we found this methodology to be fairly effective primarily because it establishes a baseline for assessing the effectiveness of our blogging efforts."

Matt believes that "the next generation of marketers is going to leverage data, algorithms, and statistics to deliver superior marketing results." Because "most companies approach marketing using instincts and desires," Matt says, companies should use metrics, including the eight-step blogging ROI tracking list, to drive traffic to your business and beat the competition.

Summary

The success of your blog requires that you create a sound strategy, calculate your ROI regularly, and continually monitor and update your strategy to monitor your ROI. You must also report your findings to the powers that be, even if those powers are entirely vested in you, so you know what's happening with your blog. Your blog and its performance don't exist in a vacuum, either; what you do with your blog also affects other marketing efforts.

We hope you now have enough ideas in your head to create or improve your blog so it will drive business to your company. If you want to chat with us and ask us questions, feel free to visit our website at www.bloggingtodrivebusiness.com.

Important Blogging Sites

In addition to the blogs already discussed in this book, the following sites are important for you to visit. These sites cover various aspects of blogging, from locating blogs online that you might find of interest, to software as a service (SAAS) that provides microblogging services for your business or business groups. You can also visit the Quick Online Tips Giant Blogging Terms Dictionary for more sites and suggestions, at www.quickonlinetips.com/archives/2006/06/the-giant-blogging-terms-glossary/.

Technorati

If you want to know what's going on in the blogosphere, start at Technorati, at www.technorati.com (see Figure A.1).

Figure A.1 *The Technorati website.*

Icerocket

Icerocket (www.icerocket.com), shown in Figure A.2, is a place to search for information within blogs, track blogging trends, add a tracker to your blog, and submit your blog to the Icerocket search engine. You can also search for information within Twitter and Facebook and search for images, too.

Figure A.2   *The Icerocket website.*

Google Blog Search

Google is so large that anything it does is worthy of note, and the same is true of Google Blog Search (www.google.com/blogsearch), shown in Figure A.3. As with the regular Google search engine, when you type a term into Google Search, you get a list of blogs that include those terms. Blogs that have better SEO features are higher up in the results list.

Figure A.3 *The Google Blog Search website.*

News Aggregators

Bloglines (www.bloglines.com), shown in Figure A.4, and Newsgator (www.newsgator.com), shown in Figure A.5, are two of the most popular news aggregators. At these sites, you can read new blog posts online or download them to your desktop.

Figure A.4 *The Bloglines website.*

Figure A.5   *The Newsgator website.*

Podcatchers

If you use podcatchers to download podcasts, two of the more popular ones are Juice (http://juicereceiver.sourceforge.net/), shown in Figure A.6, and Podnova (www.podnova.com), shown in Figure A.7.

Figure A.6   *The Juice website.*

Figure A.7   *The Podnova website.*

Ping Search Engines

If you update your blog regularly, search engines may not pick up on the update right away. You can ping search engines using online services such as Pingomatic (www.pingomatic.com), which is shown in Figure A.8.

Figure A.8   *The Pingomatic website.*

Want to Advertise on Blogs?

If you're looking to advertise your product or service on specific blogs, check out the Blogads site (www.blogads.com), shown in Figure A.9, to help you develop your online blog campaign.

Figure A.9   *The Blogads website.*

You can also make your blog a moneymaking venture by placing ads on the blog. The most popular advertising mechanism for doing that is Google's AdSense, shown in Figure A.10. This site, at https://www.google.com/adsense, connects your blog to Google's large group of advertisers. Note that you must have a separate AdSense account even if you're already signed in with your Google account.

Figure A.10   *The Google AdSense website.*

Getting More Blog Traffic

If you're interested in pushing more people to your blog, some web services prom-ise to do exactly that. Check out Blog Traffic Exchange (www.blogtrafficexchange.com), shown in Figure A.11, and BlogClicker (www.blogclicker.com), shown in Figure A.12. Both sites let you add your blog to a community of blogs where you read other blogs and other bloggers read your blog.

Figure A.11   *The Blog Traffic Exchange website.*

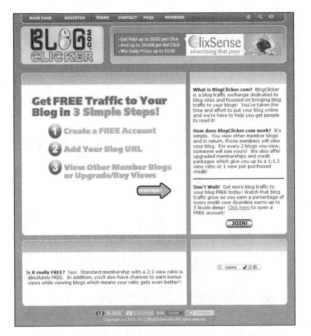

Figure A.12   *The BlogClicker website.*

You should also check out sites that let you post links to your blog. The most popular sites are StumbleUpon, shown in Figure A.13, and Reddit, shown in Figure A.14.

When you sign up for the free StumbleUpon service, you specify your interests and download the StumbleUpon toolbar for your web browser. When you click the StumbleUpon button in the toolbar, then StumbleUpon will send you website links, photos, and videos in your interest areas. This is a great source of blog material.

Reddit promotes itself as the "Internet front page" where people submit various news stories in a variety of categories such as technology, politics, and gaming. Since Reddit is a very popular site, there's always information on the site that you can research and perhaps use on your blog.

Figure A.13   *The StumbleUpon website.*

Figure A.14   *The Reddit website.*

Software as a Service Product

A recent issue of *eWeek* magazine (www.eweek.com) published a comparison of three software as a service (SAAS) products that leverage Web 2.0 technologies, including microblogging and wikis for use in businesses. That is, these SAAS products are access controlled for businesses, and they also compete with established programs such as Lotus Notes and Microsoft SharePoint. The three products are Socialcast, Socialtext, and Huddle.

Figure A.15 shows Socialcast (www.socialcast.com). This site is a Twitter-like service.

Figure A.15   *The Socialcast website.*

Socialtext (www.socialtext.com), shown in Figure A.16, started out as a site that enabled users to create wikis (for example, people in product groups can create wikis about their products) but now includes microblogging and user profiles, much like what Facebook offers.

Figure A.16   *The Socialtext website.*

Huddle (www.huddle.net), shown in Figure A.17, has the most basic social networking features of the three SAAS programs, but you can use Huddle from other social networking systems and plug in to other social networking sites, including Facebook and LinkedIn.

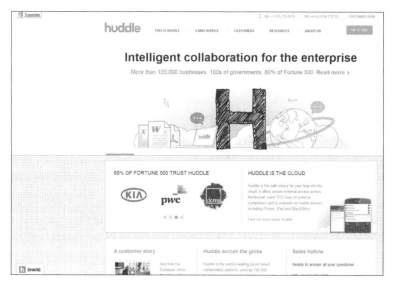

Figure A.17   *The Huddle website.*

Moblogging Apps

Plenty of apps are available on both the iOS and Android platforms for bloggers. We chose iOS and Android to feature moblogging apps for this appendix because they are the two most popular mobile operating systems available as of this writing.

This list is not exhaustive, and some apps may require you to pay a small fee to download them. You can browse for blogging apps in the Apple App Store on your iPhone or iPad, or if you have an Android phone or tablet, you can browse the Google Play Store. From there, you can download, purchase (if necessary), and install the app directly to your smartphone or tablet.

Smartphones

If you have both a smartphone and a tablet, such as an iPhone and iPad, apps available for your iPhone or Android phone may also work on the iPad or Android tablet, respectively.

Apple's App Store does a good job of stating which apps are available for the iPad and which apps are available for the iPhone. When you sign up for the Google Play Store with your phone and/or tablet, the Play Store remembers what devices you have and checks the app for any compatibility issues with the app you want to download.

The figures in this appendix show the app listing in its app store so you can see what to look for as you shop. When you're in the app listing, you can view sample screens, get more information about the app, check user reviews, and more.

iPhone Apps

Here is a list of six iPhone blogging apps that you may want to download and look at:

- **Pinterest:** This is the iPhone app for one of the more popular social networking websites (at least as of this writing), as described in Chapter 3, "Creating a Blogging Strategy." The app is free.

- **Patch:** If you're looking for local information for your blog, consider adding Patch (shown in Figure B.1) to your stable of apps. Patch provides local news and events from a variety of communities in many different states. You can even comment on news stories within the app, which is free.

Figure B.1   *The Patch app.*

- **FileHound:** FileHound, shown in Figure B.2, allows you to access and download all your files from your Windows PC to your iPhone, which is quite useful when you want to add photos or videos to your blog when you're on the go. Unfortunately, as of this writing, the app is available for Windows only, but a Mac version is promised. The app was on sale as of this writing for $4.99, but the regular price is $9.99. Check the FileHound listing in the App Store for the latest price and to see whether the Mac version is available.

Figure B.2 *The FileHound app.*

- **Blogger:** You learned about Google's Blogger platform in Chapter 3, and the Blogger iPhone app is free to download.

- **Tumblr:** You also learned about the Tumblr tumblelog in Chapter 3, and you can download the iPhone app free.

- **Twitvid:** The Twitvid app that's shown in Figure B.3 allows you to capture and share videos and then post them to a post on Twitter or Facebook, or you can send the video via email or instant messaging. If you use Twitter and/or Facebook as your primary means of communicating with your customers, even if you have a blog, this is a handy app to have. And it's free, too.

Figure B.3   *The Twitvid app.*

Android Apps

A number of popular apps are also available for any smartphone running Android Honeycomb (that is, version 3.x) and Ice Cream Sandwich (version 4.0x).

- **Blogger:** The Blogger app is available for Android smartphones, which makes sense because Blogger and Android both come from Google. The app is free.
- **Posterous Spaces:** You learned about the Posterous Spaces blogging service in Chapter 3, and the app shown in Figure B.4 is free.

Figure B.4 *The Posterous Spaces app.*

- **Tumblr:** Tumblr also makes sure that it has an app for the Android platform so you can manage your tumblelog. Like the iPhone app, the Android app is free.

- **Qik Video:** If you primarily create vlogs, then consider the Qik Video app shown in Figure B.5. After you record a video, you can share it with social networking sites, and the video is uploaded to the cloud automatically so you can embed it in your blog. The app is free, but if you want unlimited online video sharing and video storage, you need to purchase the Premium edition for $4.99 per month.

Figure B.5   *The Qik Video app.*

- **WordPress:** We covered WordPress in Chapter 3. It is available not only for the iPhone but also for the Android platform. The WordPress for Android app is free.

- **HootSuite:** HootSuite was one of the featured case studies in Chapter 10, and like the iPhone version, the Android version shown in Figure B.6 is also free.

Figure B.6   *The HootSuite app.*

Tablets

The disclaimer at the beginning of the "Smartphones" section earlier in this appendix also applies to this section: Many tablet apps that are available for the iPad may also have an iPhone equivalent you can download, and the Google Play Store will check the app to make sure that it works with all your Android devices registered with the Play Store.

iPad Apps

Here are six apps to consider when you want to blog on your iPad:

- **Blogsy:** The Blogsy app shown in Figure B.7 is designed specifically for the iPad's touch capabilities. That is, you can drag and drop photos and video from Blogsy into your blog post just by using your finger. When you finish creating your blog post in Blogsy, you can publish it to a variety of blogging platforms including WordPress, Blogger, Posterous, and TypePad. The app costs $4.99.

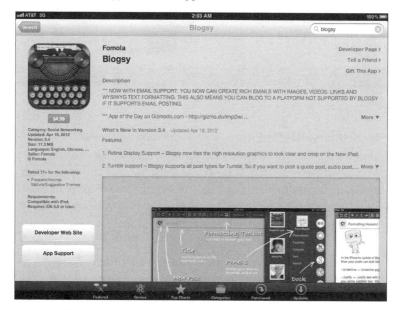

Figure B.7   *The Blogsy website.*

- **iBlogger:** If you want to get a quick tutorial about different aspects of blogging on your iPad, consider downloading the iBlogger app. The app contains six videos and eight e-books, all for only 99 cents. However, as of this writing, the description for iBlogger mentions the 99 cent price is for a limited time, so check the app description for the current price.

- **BlogPress:** This app, shown in Figure B.8, is another blog composition app where you write your blog and add photos and/or videos to your blog using the BlogPress interface. When you finish, you can publish the blog to a variety of platforms including Blogger, WordPress, TypePad, and LiveJournal.

Figure B.8   *The BlogPress website.*

- **Web Albums HD for Picasa:** If you use Picasa and want to manage your photos and videos, you should consider downloading this app. This app lets you view, upload, and manage files not only in Picasa but also your Google+ albums and streams, which is no surprise because Picasa and Google+ both come from Google. Web Albums HD for Picasa also optimizes viewing of photos and videos for the new iPad's Retina display. The app costs $3.99.

- **Quicklytics:** Google doesn't produce an app for viewing Google Analytics on the iPad because that's a competing platform. Fortunately, the Quicklytics app shown in Figure B.9 connects to Google Analytics so you can get the reports you need without going to the Analytics website. The app costs $1.99.

Figure B.9   *The Quicklytics website.*

- **WordPress:** WordPress not only created a free iPhone app but also created a separate free app just for the iPad.

Android Apps

A number of apps available for Android smartphones are also available for Android tablets. In fact, some apps, such as Adobe Photoshop Express, may work better when you use them on a tablet.

- **Google Analytics for Android:** If you use Google Analytics to track what happens on your blog, you can use the Google Analytics for Android app to check your blog performance on the go.

- **Adobe Photoshop Express:** Figure B.10 shows the Adobe Photoshop Express app that allows you to edit your photos and store them on the Photoshop.com website so you can access them later. You can also share your edited photos directly within the app. And this app is free.

Figure B.10   *The Adobe Photoshop Express app.*

- **Pocket Blog:** This app allows you write private blog entries on your phone. If you like keeping a diary or want to take notes, you might want to try out this free app. As of this writing, Pocket Blog had beta status.

- **Blog Success:** This app, shown in Figure B.11, contains blogging information, online marketing tips, and links to the latest blog marketing tips. If you want to augment your knowledge and your blogging prowess, consider downloading this free blog.

Figure B.11   *The Blog Success app.*

- **Stumblr Tablet:** If you use Tumblr and you want to find and follow blogs, find photos from other Tumblr posters, and then view and share photos you find, you might want to give Stumblr Tablet a try. This app was developed specifically for Android tablets and is free to download.

- **BlogPost:** The BlogPost app, shown in Figure B.12, lets you post to different blogging platforms including WordPress, Blogger, and LiveJournal. You can also upload photos and videos to blogs as well as photo and video websites including YouTube. And the app is free.

Figure B.12   *The BlogPost app.*

Index

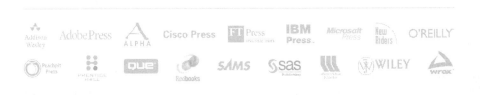

que

Biz-Tech Series

Straightforward Strategies and Tactics for Business Today

The **Que Biz-Tech series** is designed for the legions of executives and marketers out there trying to come to grips with emerging technologies that can make or break their business. These books help the reader know what's important, what isn't, and provide deep inside know-how for entering the brave new world of business technology, covering topics such as mobile marketing, microblogging, and iPhone and iPad app marketing.

- Straightforward strategies and tactics for companies who are either using or will be using a new technology/product or way of thinking/doing business

- Written by well-known industry experts in their respective fields—and designed to be an open platform for the author to teach a topic in the way he or she believes the audience will learn best

- Covers new technologies that companies must embrace to remain competitive in the marketplace and shows them how to maximize those technologies for profit

- Written with the marketing and business user in mind—these books meld solid technical know-how with corporate-savvy advice for improving the bottom line

Visit **quepublishing.com/biztech** to learn more about the **Que Biz-Tech series**

BLOGGING
To Drive
BUSINESS
Second Edition

Create and Maintain Valuable
Customer Connections

Eric Butow & Rebecca Bollwitt

FREE
Online Edition

Safari
Books Online

Your purchase of *Blogging to Drive Business* includes access to a free online edition for 45 days through the **Safari Books Online** subscription service. Nearly every Que book is available online through **Safari Books Online**, along with thousands of books and videos from publishers such as Addison-Wesley Professional, Cisco Press, Exam Cram, IBM Press, O'Reilly Media, Prentice Hall, and Sams.

Safari Books Online is a digital library providing searchable, on-demand access to thousands of technology, digital media, and professional development books and videos from leading publishers. With one monthly or yearly subscription price, you get unlimited access to learning tools and information on topics including mobile app and software development, tips and tricks on using your favorite gadgets, networking, project management, graphic design, and much more.

Addison Wesley · AdobePress · ALPHA · Cisco Press · FT Press · IBM Press · Microsoft Press · New Riders · O'REILLY

Peachpit Press · PRENTICE HALL · QUE · Redbooks · SAMS · SAS Publishing · vmware PRESS · WILEY